"In a world where womanhood is simu[...] despised, Elyse and Eric explain a won[...] Scripture. With chapters filled with compassion and hard questions, they challenge readers to develop a robust view of women in redemptive history."

—Emily Jensen and Laura Wifler, coauthors of *Risen Motherhood: Gospel Hope for Everyday Moments*

"Women along with men are joint-heirs with Jesus Christ of the inheritance of the kingdom. This is good news for all of us, male and female. This book, authored by two respected and wise Christian leaders, can help the church to celebrate the gifting and calling of women within the Body of Christ. As you read this book, pray that God would show you how best to respect and uplift the women and girls in your church and community."

—Russell Moore, president, the Ethics & Religious Liberty Commission of the Southern Baptist Convention

"This is an extremely important discussion for the church right now, and Elyse and Eric are the right voices to provide guidance. This book marks an important milestone of what God is doing in his church."

—J.D. Greear, PhD, pastor, The Summit Church, Raleigh-Durham, NC; 62nd president, the Southern Baptist Convention; author of *Above All*

"This book will provoke many feminists because its authors strive to be rigorously biblical. It will provoke many self-perceived complementarians because . . . the authors strive to be rigorously biblical. This is provocation that we all need, challenging us to look afresh at Scripture, and at our own attitudes and practices."

—Dennis E. Johnson, PhD, professor emeritus of practical theology, Westminster Seminary California

"With candor and wisdom, Elyse and Eric shine a light into the biblical text, showing the ways God has cared for and worked through women to bring about his purposes in the world. Then they shine a light into the church, addressing the significant questions women have about how God cares for and intends to work through them today."

—Nancy Guthrie, author of *Even Better Than Eden: Nine Ways the Bible's Story Changes Everything about Your Story*

"Don't mistake this as a book about gender roles. It is a book about the value of women. I recommend *Worthy* for those of us who are tired of the extremes of the gender debates and want to explore the heart of our convictions. Guided by Scripture, Elyse and Eric come together (in stereo) to challenge our own perceptions of value and how we communicate worth."

—Aimee Byrd, author of *Why Can't We Be Friends?* and *Recovering from Biblical Manhood and Womanhood*

"I like this book a lot. I do not agree with all of it, but I agree with most of it. Too often women fade into the background or disappear altogether in our interpretation and proclamation of God's Word. This is a mistake with harmful and unhelpful repercussions. This book helps us correct this problem. I enthusiastically commend it."

—Daniel L. Akin, president, Southeastern Baptist Theological Seminary

"I have never been more convinced of my worth as a woman made in God's image and redeemed by Christ's blood. I'm eternally grateful to Elyse and Eric for helping me to see God's care and commissioning of women in his Word. Everyone needs to read this book."

—Quina Aragon, author of *Love Made: A Story of God's Overflowing, Creative Heart*

"I became painfully aware of how important *Worthy* by Elyse Fitzpatrick and Eric Schumacher was as I read it, because this biblically insightful book reminded me once again of my own sins and devaluing of women in my own life. I am a Christian man and pastor with a regrettable history of objectifying, demeaning, and devaluing women in my life and in the church. This book is needed because there are others like me who need a loving rebuke from trusted authors who have lived this same struggle in their own life and walked with others who have done the same. Every pastor needs to read this book to help expose the way we often devalue women in the church and don't realize it. Women need to read this book so they can truly know the way God values them, as well as women throughout redemptive history, and how God intends for them to flourish in the local church today. I heartily commend it."

—Brian Croft, senior pastor, Auburndale Baptist Church; founder, Practical Shepherding; senior fellow, Mathena Center for Church Revitalization, SBTS

"An important resource for churches longing to see all their members rise up and fulfill the calling God has for them. I appreciate the honesty and candor both authors bring to this timely discussion of women and the church. Written with empathy and a high respect for Scripture and the image of God gloriously present in all of us, I highly recommend this important read."

—Mary DeMuth, author of *We Too: How the Church Can Respond Redemptively to the Sexual Abuse Crisis*

"This book is so good. It's beautifully written, the theological clarity bursts forth on every page, and it's saturated with the Gospel. False, antiquated ideas concerning women's role in God's kingdom are deconstructed and the Holy Spirit reconstructs a God-glorying perspective for women (and men) in God's redemptive purposes. I *highly* recommend this book!"

—Dr. Derwin L. Gray, lead pastor, Transformation Church; author of *Limitless Life: You Are More Than Your Past When God Holds Your Future*

"Elyse and Eric ask and answer very important questions about the value of women, but it is not just for women. While I hope my wife, daughters, mom, sister, and other women in my life internalize the message of this book, it is also for me and other men. Unfortunately, what is clear and obvious in the Bible is not always clear and obvious in our homes, churches, and culture: Women are valuable and they are integral in God's story of redemption from beginning to end."

—Justin S. Holcomb, seminary professor, Episcopal priest, and coauthor of *Rid of My Disgrace*, *God Made All of Me*, and *Is It My Fault?*

"*Worthy* tackles the difficult and often overlooked questions regarding God's view of women. You'll see how God wove his redemptive message through heroic women throughout Scripture. Be ready to have your preconceived notions challenged and your faith encouraged. Because of that, it's a must-read for all church and ministry leaders."

—S. Michael and MeLissa Houdmann, cofounders, Got Questions Ministries

"Elyse and Eric have written a book deserving of its title. Having been raised Methodist, converted to faith at an Assemblies of God church, and graduated from a Presbyterian seminary, I have heard virtually every angle and teaching on women—especially their role in the church. Opinions abound! What makes *Worthy* stand out is that it starts and ends with Scripture. *Worthy* takes the reader on a journey through the Bible to discover what it says about this crucial topic. Backed by solid exegesis, great wit, and convicting insight, *Worthy* should be your go-to book to inform your theology of women. I enthusiastically recommend this book!"

—Scott Lindsey, executive director, Faithlife, makers of Logos Bible Software

"Many misconceptions about women's place and worth in the church begin with misconceptions about what the Bible actually says. In advocating for the true worth and biblical roles of women, Elyse Fitzpatrick and Eric Schumacher begin—and end—with the Bible. What they show may surprise some readers, affirms all women, and will serve the church well."

—Karen Swallow Prior, PhD, author of *On Reading Well: Finding the Good Life through Great Books* and *Fierce Convictions: The Extraordinary Life of Hannah More—Poet, Reformer, Abolitionist*

"This book is a word in due season. Eric and Elyse give us a powerful, convicting, and honest resource that the church so desperately needs. Beginning with a history of redemption, *Worthy* celebrates the story of women, while unveiling the story of Scripture. I was simultaneously convicted, challenged, and encouraged and believe that you will be too."

—Raleigh Sadler, founder and executive director, Let My People Go; author of *Vulnerable: Rethinking Human Trafficking*

"*Worthy* is a biblically rich, Gospel-centered book that examines and challenges the way the world and the church view the purpose and value of women. Eric and Elyse write in a way that is both life-giving and thought-provoking, showing us that the worth of a woman is not to be defined by the culture we live in or what we've been taught, but by God himself, as written in his Word and displayed through the life of Christ."

—Sarah Walton, coauthor of *Hope When It Hurts*

"From Genesis to Revelation, God's Word proclaims the worth of God's creation. And in a culture that marginalizes or devalues image-bearers in almost every sphere in some way, we need the guidance of Scripture to show us how infinitely worthy God has made his children. In this book, Elyse and Eric illuminate the worth of women in particular from creation to culmination. They correct common tropes and tired church clichés, and they keep the character of God as their guide. I hope women everywhere are encouraged by this book and men everywhere will allow the weight of its truths to bear on their everyday life."

—Lore Ferguson Wilbert, author of *Handle with Care*

"Evangelical Christians were long offered a theology of womanhood that is hierarchical and patriarchal. However, Fitzpatrick and Schumacher desire a biblical womanhood shorn of extra-canonical accretions. Certain interpretations or applications may surprise or delight, but this complementarian theologian hopes *Worthy: Celebrating the Value of Women* will herald a reforming anthropology."

—Malcolm B. Yarnell III, author of *God the Trinity*, *The Formation of Christian Doctrine*, *Royal Priesthood in the English Reformation*, and *Who Is the Holy Spirit?*

"*Worthy: Celebrating the Value of Women* . . . is basically a survey of the import and rich significance of women through both the Old Testament and the New Testament. And it is about women's standing, import, and significance to God the Father and God the Son—in detail! . . . The authors exposit the detailed stories of *women* through the Bible—and they do it well! . . . Page after page pushes male minimizers of women to repent—and to do it because *minimizing women believers in Jesus amounts to minimizing the God who created and redeemed both sexes!* . . . If you're not sure *whether* to read it, begin at the story of the women in the life of Jesus, particularly . . . in the story of his Passion. Contrast who stuck with him (women) and who fled almost immediately (the men)! You'll be hooked!"

—Dr. Rod Rosenbladt, ordained Lutheran pastor (LCMS), professor emeritus of theology, Concordia University, Irvine, California

WORTHY

Books by Elyse Fitzpatrick

FROM BETHANY HOUSE PUBLISHERS

Home

*Answering Your Kids' Toughest Questions**

Finding the Love of Jesus from Genesis to Revelation

*Worthy***

*with Jessica Thompson   •   **with Eric Schumacher

WORTHY

CELEBRATING
THE VALUE OF WOMEN

ELYSE FITZPATRICK AND
ERIC SCHUMACHER

a division of Baker Publishing Group
Minneapolis, Minnesota

© 2020 by Elyse Fitzpatrick and Eric Schumacher

Published by Bethany House Publishers
11400 Hampshire Avenue South
Bloomington, Minnesota 55438
www.bethanyhouse.com

Bethany House Publishers is a division of
Baker Publishing Group, Grand Rapids, Michigan

Printed in the United States of America

ISBN 978-0-7642-3436-1

Library of Congress Control Number: 2019949996

Unless otherwise indicated, Scripture quotations are from The Holy Bible, English Standard Version® (ESV®), copyright © 2001 by Crossway, a publishing ministry of Good News Publishers. Used by permission. All rights reserved. ESV Text Edition: 2016

Scripture quotations identified CSB Scripture are from the Christian Standard Bible®, copyright © 2017 by Holman Bible Publishers. Used by permission. Christian Standard Bible® and CSB® are federally registered trademarks of Holman Bible Publishers.

Scripture quotations identified KJV are from the King James Version of the Bible.

Scripture quotations identified NIV are from the Holy Bible, New International Version®. NIV®. Copyright © 1973, 1978, 1984, 2011 by Biblica, Inc.™ Used by permission of Zondervan. All rights reserved worldwide. www.zondervan.com. The "NIV" and "New International Version" are trademarks registered in the United States Patent and Trademark Office by Biblica, Inc.™

Cover design by Studio Gearbox

21 22 23 24 25 26   8 7 6 5 4

To all my sisters who, like Zelophehad's daughters, say, "The Lord commanded Moses to give us an inheritance along with our brothers" (Joshua 17:4) and who have taken to heart the text of the first sermon preached in Jerusalem, ". . . I will pour out my Spirit on all flesh . . . even on my . . . female servants . . . I will pour out my Spirit" (Acts 2:16–18); to all who want to know the joy of Spirit-empowered disciple-making, you are not insignificant, ancillary, or unloved.

This is your story.

—Elyse

To
my mother, Karen,
my wife, Jenny,
my daughter, Ella.

I love you very much.

Jesus loves you more.

—Eric

Contents

Contents

Worthy: Celebrating the Value of Women in God's Word

Welcome her . . . in a way worthy of the saints.

Romans 16:2

When Paul wrote the letter to the Romans, an epistle so important that Martin Luther called it "the chief part of the New Testament,"[1] he looked for a worthy emissary to deliver it. Whom could he entrust with such a precious document? At a time when travel was very dangerous, and particularly so for a woman who might be alone, it seems strange that Paul would choose Phoebe. Perhaps in her role as deacon from the church in Cenchreae she already had business in Rome and so she was entrusted with this precious cargo. But perhaps not. Perhaps Paul chose her just because he knew she was trustworthy and had sufficient means, wisdom, and courage to complete the 800-mile journey by sea and land. Phoebe had a reputation for her work in the city, using her wealth and influence to assist those in need, including the Apostle Paul himself (Romans 16:2).

Paul's choice of her certainly confronts preconceived notions about proper feminine roles, especially in the ancient Near East. Why would Paul ask such a thing of a woman? Wasn't he concerned that she shouldn't leave her home? Shouldn't he have sent one of the brothers from the church? Didn't he worry that he might be greasing a slippery slope and that women all over the Mediterranean would start looking for ministry opportunities and traveling abroad? We don't know a lot about Phoebe, but we do know this: She was a woman worthy of honor.

Later in this book (chapter 11), we'll look at the life and ministry of Phoebe (and others) in more detail, but for now, let's just think about Paul's instruction to the church about her. They were to "welcome her in the Lord in a way worthy of the saints." When she finally arrived at her destination, undoubtedly a house church, the brothers and sisters were told to welcome her. They were to make sure she knew that the door was wide open to her and that they viewed her as one of them: Not first of all as a woman, but as a saint. They were not to look at her with suspicion or think that she was trying to take away anyone else's position. They were to befriend her as a person chosen and called by God and made holy by his gracious work. They were to treat her properly, acknowledging her worth. In other words, they were to treat her in the same way they would have treated Paul or any other servant of the Gospel.

What Gives Us Worth?

My husband, Phil, and I (Elyse) love *Antiques Roadshow*! Okay, I admit it. I am sure that my adult kids will cringe when they read that confession, but we really do enjoy it. They'll cringe because they think the show is boring and only for old fogies (like us). I think I understand. *Antiques Roadshow* is not a suspenseful mystery or a historical romance, still Phil and I really do find it interesting—and we're not alone. *Antiques Roadshow* is PBS's most-watched ongoing series.[2]

What is it about this show that people find so interesting season after season? I think part of the attraction is watching an appraiser place an astronomical value on an old rolled-up canvas, something that someone just happened to rescue from the trash. When the appraiser notices that all-important signature, what once was viewed as worthless becomes priceless. In an instant, the way it is handled changes. It is cherished. It is valuable. It is celebrated. Why? Because a distinguished artist signed it, and that signature confers worth. Of course, it had great value all along—it's just that now the appraiser has opened our eyes to see it. What changes it from worthless trash into a priceless treasure? The artist's signature. And that signature usually produces great joy to the owners—sometimes they cry, sometimes they just stand there speechless. Still others jump up and down in celebration. But I've never seen anyone yawn in apathy or toss the canvas in the trash.

Whether you're an *Antiques Roadshow* fan or not, I'm sure you understand my point. Value is intrinsically tied to the reputation of the one who created the piece. What is true for paintings and historical artifacts is also true for you and me. All people have intrinsic worth for one basic reason: We are the creation of the living God. We have been made in his image. When the Lord said, "Let us make mankind in our image, after our likeness" (Genesis 1:26),[3] he was applying his signature to the crowning masterpiece of his creation. God's "image" and "likeness" bestow upon humanity an honor and dignity that set it apart from everything else. This is his seal of authenticity and worth. About nothing else did he speak, "in our image, after our likeness." Humanity alone bears this mark, and the implications are vast: *All people, no matter their gender, ethnicity, religion, history, or time, have value.* They have value because they bear his signature, and his seal is invaluable. All people are to be honored and celebrated.

After granting humanity dominion and stewardship over the world he created, we are given even more specific detail:

> So God created mankind in his own image,
> in the image of God he created them;
> male and female he created them.
>
> Genesis 1:27 NIV

By himself, Adam was insufficient to display God's image and likeness. The Lord is so holy, so wondrous and glorious, that one created gender alone was inadequate to bear his image. So he created Eve, a female, a woman. In exactly the same way the male has worth because he is made in God's image, the female also bears God's image and has worth. All women, like all men, have value simply because they bear his image. We image God. And, just as that serendipitous *Antiques Roadshow* appraisal is transformational, this truth should transform us too. The more that women and men believe this truth, the more they will celebrate their creation and learn to honor and love each other as creatures of great worth.

We are created in God's image, and the people we interact with are not worthless, nor insignificant. C. S. Lewis writes,

> It is a serious thing to live in a society of possible gods and goddesses, to remember that the dullest most uninteresting person you can talk to may one day be a creature which, if you saw it now, you would be strongly tempted to worship. . . . There are no *ordinary* people. You have never talked to a mere mortal. . . . It is immortals whom we joke with, work with, marry, snub and exploit—immortal horrors or everlasting splendors.[4]

Understanding that women, as well as men, have been fashioned by God to be immortal creatures eternally imaging his glory must, by necessity, transform the way we think of and interact with one another today.

What We're Up To

As we've said, women as well as men have intrinsic value because they have been created in the image of God. I am saying that because the entirety of God's Word testifies to it. As a woman, I am not declaring my gender's worth to flatter feminist sympathizers. No, Eric and I are declaring a woman's value because that is what the Bible declares. We're simply asserting what the Scripture says: Women have value because they are, just like men, created in the image and likeness of God, and that truth, when grasped and believed, is personally and relationally life-transforming. In addition to this, the Bible is clear that women are not an afterthought, a problem to be solved, nor are they ancillary to the overarching message of Scripture.

On Easter Sunday the Risen Jesus declared the church's one message, "that repentance for the forgiveness of sins should be proclaimed in his name to all" (Luke 24:47). And women were an intrinsic part of this proclamation. In fact, they were the first ones tasked with this mission. Women are every bit as integral to this proclamation of God's sacrificial love for people as men are. As you're about to learn, this is unquestionably and overwhelmingly the biblical record. And we think it is time to challenge and then unleash all believers to fulfill the call of the ages.

Why should we notice and celebrate women in the storyline of Scripture? Where do you look when you're expecting someone important? If you're a child waiting for mom to come home, you look at the front door. If you're at an airport, you look at the returning passenger corridor. If you're at a bus stop, you look up the street. You look toward the place from which you know they will first appear. When God first proclaimed the Gospel, he promised deliverance through the offspring of the woman (Genesis 3:15). The deliverer will come through her. This promise teaches us to "watch the woman" as the storyline unfolds so that we see the Redeemer when he arrives. In looking for, noticing, and celebrating women in the storyline of the Bible, we are not sliding down a slippery slope of liberalism, about to careen off a cliff into all-out goddess worship. Looking for, noticing, and celebrating women in the storyline of the Bible is climbing the ladder of careful Bible interpretation, seeing the rungs that the Author put in place, and stepping accordingly.

Eric and I want to remind you of the honor and prominence of women in redemption's narrative because it is biblical and right to do so. But that's not the only reason we're writing. We both believe that *every* story of misogyny and abuse should be heard and taken to heart. The #MeToo and #ChurchToo movements have demonstrated in spades what many women already knew: Too many of us are not cherished or valued; too many of us wouldn't even know what that means. Instead, many have been disbelieved, denigrated, and dismissed, simply because we are women, and this has happened both historically and in today's churches as well. But merely understanding that the church has been dismissive, abusive, or even misogynistic will not help us. If the heart of our problem is a sinful denigration and distrust of women (who make up more than half of God's image-bearing creation), then responding with care and empathy to negative stories alone is insufficient. Instead, we need to affirm the positive stories and contributions of women—not only as wives, mothers, and daughters, *but primarily as God's image-bearers.* This means we must see, hear, and speak about women just as God does. Once our eyes are opened to the way God values and honors the God-given dignity of women, we each will be able to rejoice in the other, and in what God has accomplished in both his creation and his re-creation. We will welcome one another in a manner worthy of the saints.

What Gives *You* Value

So let's begin by getting a little more personal. Let me ask you, *What gives you value? Have you ever even thought deeply about whether you have value? Do you have significance? Do you matter?* Do you ever even ask yourself these kinds of questions?

It's not uncommon for people to say that they feel worthless, especially if they have been denigrated, molested, or abused in any way. Both Eric and I know women who struggle to believe that they are of value and that this value is central to who they are as humans. They view themselves as insignificant, or unworthy. And they feel ashamed—not merely ashamed of something they've done, but of who they are in their essence. Women who have been systematically disparaged by men (and other women) have trouble believing that God values and honors them. How can we claim that God loves, values, and honors women when it sure seems that historically God's people have seen women as a temptation to be avoided, a house slave to be employed, a voice to be silenced, a rebellious creature to be subdued?

Many women have been brought up in the church and have read the Bible but never seen the way that the Holy Spirit speaks stories of God's cherishing love for women throughout redemption's history. And perhaps they've been taught to see themselves as primarily sinful, fallen, easily deceived, and weak. While it is true that all of mankind has been marred by sin and estranged from God (Romans 3:10ff), our sinfulness is not the most important thing about us. What is most important is that we have been created in God's image and after his likeness. And he said that his creation was "very good" (Genesis 1:31). Again, all of creation— women included—was deemed by him to be "very good." The "not-goodness" of Adam's aloneness was made very good by the joining together of male and female in unified oneness. Adam and Eve together—that was what was very good.

The Bible speaks consistently of God's valuing of women. We see this in the crucial and indispensable role they play throughout redemptive history, from Genesis to Revelation. Consequently, if God so values women that he includes them as a consistent and essential part of his mission, how can we feel and act any differently?

A Few Items of Interest

This book found its genesis on Twitter. At one point in mid-2018, Eric tweeted a list of firsts about women in the Bible, something that coincided with thoughts I was having along those lines, so we connected. Soon afterward, he published the list as an article on The Gospel Coalition's website[5] and made a guest appearance on my family's podcast, *Front Porch with the Fitzes*. During that conversation we discussed the possibility of collaborating on this project . . . and here we are.

Right up front I want to say that Eric has done most of the heavy lifting on this project. We are drawing heavily from work he has already done. I'm so thankful for his desire to honor and value women. Having a pastor's voice join with mine in this endeavor is invaluable. He and I have divvied up the chapters so that each of us will write and the other will edit and augment. When we're writing in the first person (as I did in this introduction), we'll indicate whose voice you're hearing. But even when we do this, you can be assured that everything here is a harmonizing of our thoughts on this topic. Eric will come at this as a husband, a dad, a pastor, a songwriter, and (of course) a man. I'll come at it as a counselor, a writer, a mother and grandmother, a wife, and (of course) a woman. And we'll both come at it as believers who deeply value God's Word and respect and welcome one another.

From beginning to end, the Bible affirms the value of women. In this book, *Worthy*, we will help you see that truth by beginning with the Genesis accounts of creation and the Fall. Yes, even when Eve sinned, and her husband joined her in her folly, the Bible affirmed her value and celebrated her worth. Once we have spent time at the very beginning, we'll work through the rest of the Old Testament (history, law, worship, and wisdom), pointing out the places where the worth of women is revealed and celebrated. Next we'll look at the value of women in the New Testament, especially in the birth, life, death, and resurrection of Jesus. Finally, we'll see how they fit into the church's redemption story and in the new world and in the church today. If one of these chapters is of more interest to you, feel free to jump ahead and read it. Although we believe that the precepts presented in each chapter are significant and build on each other, it's not necessary that you read this book in the order presented. Just jump in where you like and be blessed. Also, if you find one chapter too challenging, feel free to start on a different one. For instance, if the chapter on celebrating women in Israel's law is too difficult or not of interest, just skip ahead to something you may be more familiar with, like the role of women in Jesus' birth. It's your choice!

At the end of every chapter, you'll find questions that will help you crystallize and process the information you've just read. Whether you're going through this book individually or with a group, those questions will facilitate thought and discussion, and we strongly encourage you to make the effort to answer them. There is also a "Digging Deeper" section for you dear overachievers who just can't get enough and want to learn even more. In any case, please take time to work through what we're presenting. You may read some things here that you've never heard before or that strike you as a different way of thinking. Remember that our hope is first of all to transform the ways men and women think about and relate to women in the home, in the church, and in society at large. But we're also hoping to convince women who weep with joy at the thought that God cherishes and values them that perhaps what they've believed about themselves and the Lord is not the truth and that there is welcome and love in him for them.

We hope that, at the end of the book, you will have more than an increased appreciation of the value of women. We pray you'll have an increased delight in the value of the God in whom we find our worth. That is what this book has done for us. The last part to be written was the Epilogue: "Worthy—A Song of Praise," an original worship song by Eric and his collaborator, David Ward. This song walks through the storyline of the Bible, celebrating God in the ways he created and redeems women.

So, no matter who you are or why you're here, whether you're a woman hoping to hear some good news or a man wondering if he's missed something important, you are welcome here. It is our prayer that the Lord who created us in his image will help us all cherish, value, and honor one another, all for his glory.

ONE

The Worth of Women in Creation

Then God said, "Let us make man in our image,
after our likeness. And let them have dominion."
Genesis 1:26

I (Eric) spent countless hours as a child lying on the floor, chin propped in my hands, listening to music on the stereo. At some point, I tired of reading liner notes and staring at album art. I started fiddling with the knobs on the front of the machine. That's when I discovered the meaning of "stereo."

If I twisted the balance knob all the way to R, the music played only from the right speaker, all the way to L and it played only from the left. Listening only to one channel or the other fascinated me. Each channel highlighted a different set of instruments or vocal elements. Both channels played the same song, though they sounded different. They complemented one another, each supplying something the other channel lacked. Eventually, the novelty wore off, and I returned to listening to both channels together. This was "Stereo Sound." To hear it as the artist intended, you had to listen in stereo.

Conversations about the value of women (or men) can unfold like a child playing with the stereo knobs. Some crank the balance knob all the way to *W*. According to them, we understand woman in isolation from man. She is to be known in herself, by herself. She doesn't need him—perhaps, at all!

Others crank the balance knob to *M*. Women are known only in contrast to men. He is primary; she is secondary. We learn what she is by deducing the missing parts of the song. She can remain silent, thank you very much.

The problem with such approaches is that God created humanity in stereo. To understand what it means to be human requires us to hear both channels together. There is a time and place for adjusting the balance knob. Someone before us may have thrown things out of balance. There is a time for focusing on one channel to better understand the song. Even so, the goal is to go back and listen to the song as a whole, both channels playing in balance.

Yet, as any recording artist will tell you, it's not about the speakers, the left channel or the right. It's all about the song, the music as the artist intended it.

In the creation of humanity, God is the artist. He is singing a song about himself, about his glory. His music is the display of his excellence. He plays this composition in stereo. It flows through the corresponding channels of male and female "speakers," if you will.

In this book, we're trying to adjust the balance knob to the Artist's intended setting. We want to see women set free to play the song God is singing through them. We want all to lean in and hear God's music.

This book exists for one simple reason: to glorify God by seeing and celebrating the value of women in God's Word. So we will ask two central questions:

1. Where is the value of women seen in the Bible?
2. Seeing the value of women there, how do we celebrate it?

And in that celebration, her Creator is glorified.

How does seeing and celebrating the value of women glorify God? As we will see in this chapter, women are created in his image and likeness. When the value of women is rightly seen and celebrated, their Creator is honored and glorified.

We must celebrate women—just as we must celebrate the goodness of every created thing. This is not contrary to God-centeredness—it is necessary for God-centeredness. It is not wrong to celebrate a created thing, any more than it is wrong to celebrate an artist's work. When you dine at a famous chef's restaurant, she is not glorified when you say, "I'm unimpressed by every dish you've served, but I glorify you as a marvelous chef." The chef's glory is displayed in the goodness of her meals. To fail to celebrate the meal is to fail to glorify the chef. To fail to celebrate the value of women is to fail to glorify God.

In this first chapter, we'll see how God is speaking of himself through human beings. We'll examine the significant part women play in that symphony. We start in Genesis 1–2, where God created the heavens and the earth. Here we meet the first woman. (We'll be calling her "the woman" in this chapter because she isn't named "Eve" until Genesis 3. Isn't that a great move on God's part? By withholding her name in these chapters, he makes her overtly applicable to every woman on earth!) What God says in the opening chapters of the Bible is foundational for seeing and celebrating the value of every woman—and the value of God himself.

Where Do We See the Value of Women in Creation?

During the Memphis sanitation strike in 1968, black sanitation workers carried placards bearing the slogan "I am a Man." That iconic declaration became a theme of the civil rights movement. It stated the heart of the issue in bold font: Black people are *human*.

We see the value of a woman in her humanity.

That '60s slogan could summarize the first biblical statements about woman. *She is a MAN.* That sounds strange to say, in a world that often equates "manhood" with "maleness." But it is entirely biblical.

The first mention of human beings occurs in Genesis 1:26–28. God says, "Let us make man. . . . And let them have dominion." Man is a *them*—plural, more than one. We soon learn that man exists in two genders. "So God created man . . . male and female he created them." In fact, this is God's name for them both. Moses writes, "Male and female he created them, and he blessed them and named them Man when they were created" (Genesis 5:2). When God made "Man," he made a male man and a female man. This is why the common terms we use for "man" in the sense of all humans is "mankind" or "humanity."

This sounds strange to our modern ears. It may even sound sexist. It is anything but. Instead, the first thing we learn about "male and female" is that they are both "man." They share the same nature. Each is as human as the other. Through these two channels of gender, God is playing the same song.

Genesis 2 zooms in on day six of creation, giving us an up-close look at the creation of the man and the woman. In the search to find a "helper fit for him" (v. 18), the Lord causes the man to fall into a deep sleep. While the man sleeps, the Lord scoops out part of his side—his flesh and bone—and fashions a woman from it.[1] When the Lord brings the woman to the man, he responds with the first recorded human song—a poetic exclamation:

> This at last is bone of my bones
> and flesh of my flesh;

> she shall be called Woman,
> because she was taken out of Man.
>
> v. 23

"Bone of my bones and flesh of my flesh" means "She's made of the same stuff I am! She is what I am!" She is not an animal—she is fully, completely, and entirely *human*. The second half of the statement reinforces this point.

"She shall be called Woman, because she was taken out of Man." The man is not naming the woman here. (God has already named them both man—see Genesis 5:2.) Neither is he exercising authority or sovereignty over her. He is making a play on words. The Hebrew word for a female human, "*ishah*," sounds like the Hebrew word for a male human, "*ish*." The man emphasizes that she shares his essence and nature—she is human, the image and likeness of God.

Consider this wondrous truth:

> *The first recorded song in human history is*
> *a celebration of the fact that the woman is*
> *equal to the man—"She is a MAN."*

Why does this matter? Because we should declare woman to be good! The refrain that echoes through the creation week is "And God saw that it was good" (Genesis 1:4, 10, 12, 18, 21, 25). It is not until after God creates male and female that we read, "God saw everything that he had made, and behold, it was *very good*" (v. 31, emphasis added).

If God has declared the existence of women to be good—indeed, *very good*—our words (and hearts) should say as much. If the first recorded human words celebrate the woman's equality with man, how can we not join him in this celebration?

We should declare her to be *human*, every bit as human as her male counterparts. As we have seen, when the first two chapters of the Bible speak of male and female, they speak to equality in essence. Of course, there are differences between *male* and *female*. (If there were not, we wouldn't be writing this book.) But the Bible does not begin with differences; *it begins with sameness.*

In thinking about women and men, we should imitate God's thoughts. When we speak about women and men, we should imitate God's Word. God begins with what we have in common—a shared name, a shared nature, and a shared mission. Likewise, we should emphasize what we have in common. We share a human nature and a divine mission. *We are more alike than we are different.*

We should defend woman as human. Unfortunately, we must make this point. (This too is an unfortunate reason for writing this book.) We live in a world in which people deny the full humanity of women in word and in deed. The Bible does not allow for such— and Christian men and women should not either. (This point is not aimed at men alone. Women have been guilty of demeaning and devaluing women themselves.)

Women should be treated with the same dignity and respect as men—for both are made of the same flesh! All misogyny (hatred of women) is the hatred of man—for both share the same nature and name. We must refrain from demeaning women with our speech and silence, our actions and inactivity. Expressions such as "You throw like a girl!" or "You're acting like a woman!" reduce women to insults and undesirables. Our silence in the presence of such statements communicates that women are not worth defending.

We see the value of woman in her humanity. But what does it mean to be human?

> *We see the value of woman in her relationship to God— she is created in his image and likeness.*

To be human is to be made in the image and likeness of God. When God defines mankind, he uses these words: "Let us make man in our image, after our likeness." Image and likeness—both those terms are foreign to our modern ears. Yet both terms are essential to understanding the nature of a human being. Thus, they are the first and most important thing about being a woman. Like the channels on a stereo, the terms "image" and "likeness" play the same song. But they play it in different (and complementary) ways. We'll take them one at a time and then bring it back together.

Image of God—To be made in "the image of God" means to rule as God's representative. In ancient Egypt, the king was called the living statue of a specific god, an idea Moses' first readers knew well. As such, the king displayed the "character traits" and "essential notions" of the god he imaged.[2] The title "image of God" was reserved for royalty; it would not be given to a common laborer.[3] Similarly, pagan temples would feature an image of the god who dwelt there. This image would represent and mediate the presence of that deity to the people. The first readers of Genesis understood "the image of God" with the idea of a royal representative who rules on behalf of a god.

God did not carve his image out of stone or wood. He did not select an individual out of the highest class of humans. He fashioned his image from the stuff of earth and breathed into him his own breath. Body and spirit, the man became a perfect representative of God on earth. God did not limit the status of image to a class or gender—he declared all humans his image-bearers. As such, God made humans to be royal representative rulers, exercising dominion over his kingdom (*king's-dominion*).

God's likeness—"In our likeness" refers to humanity's relationship with God as Father. In Genesis 5:1 we read: "When God created man, he made him in the likeness of God." Made in God's likeness, Adam is God's "son" (see Luke 3:38). Then, in verse 3, we read that Adam "fathered a son in his own likeness." "Likeness" connotes sonship. ("Like father, like son," we say.) This sonship means that mankind could relate to God as Father.

Taken together, "image" and "likeness" show us that mankind was made to rule the earth as God's representatives, as God's royal sons. This is why Israel's king was known as the son of God (see Psalm 2:7–9).[4]

How does this show the value of *women*? As the image of God, women were created to be representative rulers, exercising the dominion of her Father-King in his kingdom. As the likeness of God, women were created to be royal children, daughters of God.

Why does this matter? We must include her. God said, "Let us make man in our image, after our likeness. And let *them* have dominion . . ." The woman was not an afterthought. She was there in Genesis 1, in the first recorded declaration of man's nature and purpose. God's plan included her ruling the earth in shared responsibility and privilege with man.

This means that we must include women. We must involve women in ruling the earth—having "dominion over the fish of the sea and over the birds of the heavens and over the livestock and over all the earth and over every creeping thing that creeps on the earth" (Genesis 1:26). When God blessed them—male and female—he said to them, "Be fruitful and multiply and fill the earth and subdue it, and have dominion over the fish of the sea and over the birds of the heavens and over every living thing that moves on the earth" (1:28). There was no realm of dominion from which the woman was excluded. She was to be there with the man as they exercised dominion together.

God said, "And let *them* rule." Man and woman are designed to rule together. Exclusion of women is the opposite of God's design. To exclude women is to exclude half of God's creation means of ruling the earth. This means that we must include and celebrate the influence and presence of women in all realms of life. Women should be sought after and encouraged, educated and equipped, taught, learned with and learned from, celebrated and needed as essential partners in the shared task. In our local church, I (Eric) am making an intentional effort to seek out and invite the feedback of women. This might mean pre-reading this chapter, asking their insights on a passage I'm about to teach, or seeking their wisdom in how to lead a ministry. It also means equipping and tasking women with significant responsibilities—

and then affirming their value and gifts in public and in the presence of male leadership. God has given them strengths and wisdom that are a gift to the church. I don't do this to make them feel good. I do this because I need their help! I do this because I see it as a God-designed and biblical way of life, leadership, and ministry.

Honor her as God's representative. People do not burn the United States flag because they hate red, white, and blue cloth. They burn it because it represents the United States, which they intend to disrespect. How we treat God's representatives (humans, male or female) demonstrates how we value God. The devaluing of a woman is a denial of and hatred of the image of God. *All abuse of women is an act of violence against God himself.*[5]

Honor her as God's child. We should not measure a woman's worth based on her attachment to an earthly husband or father. A woman does not need the voice or presence of a man to validate her. She does not need a particular relationship status, nor should she be valued according to her social proximity to a particular man. She needs only the description given to her by God—"made in our likeness" (Genesis 1:26; 5:1–2). A woman does not need a specific body type or physical features to have value. She is valuable because God is her Father; she is a human, created in the image and likeness of God.

We see the value of a woman in her creation purpose—a priestly-helper.

Why did God make women? On the sixth day, after making the male, God says, "It is not good that the man should be alone" (Genesis 2:18). So, he declares, "I will make him a helper fit for him."

What comes to mind when you think of a helper? Perhaps you have a little helper who tags along in the kitchen or workshop, lending "help" that (though well-intended) only doubles the time it takes to do the job. Kathryn Stockett's novel *The Help* took its title from the derogatory term for African American household workers. "The help" are lower class, forced to do the bidding of another.

Do you think of "helper" as a title of honor? You should. We'll return to the idea of "helper" throughout the book. But there are a few things we should establish about a helper up front. In the Old Testament, the person most often referred to as "helper" is the Lord. He is the helper of Israel.[6] Of the twenty-one times the Hebrew word for helper is used in the Old Testament, twice it references the woman and sixteen times it refers to God, especially in his help in the fight against enemies. "Our soul waits for the LORD; he is our help and our shield," says Psalm 33:20. Obviously, the word *helper* does not indicate a lower status or class, inferiority or subordination. In fact, the word translated "helper" (*ezer*) never means that. On the contrary, the word *helper* implies a deficiency in those being helped! (If they didn't need help, they wouldn't need a *helper*!)

So, what exactly does the woman help the man do? In Genesis 2:15, the LORD God puts the man in the Garden of Eden "to work it and keep it." "Work" means to serve. The word is often used of man's service of God. "Keep" often refers to care for the tabernacle and God's Word. Moses uses these words as a close pair in Numbers 3:7–8 and 8:25–26 regarding priestly service in the tabernacle. This leads us to conclude that God creates the man to serve as a priest in the Garden sanctuary. The core task of mankind is to rule the world as a worshiper.

But even in a sinless state and perfect environment, the man is unable to fulfill his purpose—to be a priest to God. He needs a helper "fit for him." "Fit for him" means one who "matches" or "corresponds." This means the helper must also be created in the "image and likeness of God"—absolutely and entirely human. The only "helper fit for him" is the woman. She alone corresponds to his nature. Far from inferior, she is his equal. As a "helper fit for him," God created women to serve in the priesthood, ministering as worshipers of God.[7]

How do we celebrate the value of women as priestly-helpers?[8]

Mourn her absence. God can declare (of his own creation, *before* it is corrupted by sin) that "it is not good for man to be alone." How can we *not* admit the same? We should mourn the exclusion of women. We should condemn it as "not good."

Confess our need for her help. We (men and women) must confess that the presence of women is a necessity. Our creation purpose—to rule the world as worshipers of God—is impossible to fulfill without the help of women. Women are necessary for more than procreation. We should feel and confess this in every realm of life—church and home, government and education, the arts and skilled labor.

Remedy her absence. When God saw that "it is not good that the man should be alone," he took steps to address it. He created the woman and brought her to the man. Being godly (*God-like*) means following his example, doing what is necessary to secure the presence of a helper. It is not enough to say that women are invaluable and essential. We must work to overcome any unjust exclusion and to invite and encourage their inclusion.

Honor the role of helper. Before the creation of the woman, the Lord paraded the animals before the man. The Lord designed this scene to make a point. "There was not found a helper fit for him" (Genesis 2:20). Animals are *helpful*, but they are not *helpers*. Helper is an exalted status, a place of honor.

The woman is not an animal to be subdued, domesticated, used, or ruled over. To think of woman should bring to mind God and the help he provides. Like God's absence, her absence is "not good." Like God's, her help is crucial. As it is without God, the good life is impossible without her presence.

Depend on her. A helper meets a need in the one helped. We should not honor women with our speech and include women as a token gesture. We should honor and include women *because we cannot live without them*. They are that valuable. Life as God intends it is "not good" without them.

35

Where Are We?

We've only skimmed the surface of the Bible and the value of women. But consider what we've seen in the opening two chapters of the Bible. Women are

- human.
- made to be royal rulers (in the image of God).
- made to be children of God (in the likeness of God).
- made to be helpers in the priestly service of God.

We have this remarkable conclusion: *God created women to be royal rulers and priestly-servants in his kingdom.* "Royalty," "rulers," and "priestly-service." Those probably are not among the first words that come to mind when you think about women. *But they should be.* God is in the business of creating and redeeming "a kingdom of priests" (Exodus 19:6; Revelation 5:9–10). Women are right there in the mix of it. Even Jesus, the King of kings and Lord of lords, will not reign alone. *He will reign with his bride* (Revelation 21:1–5; 22:1–5).

Yet, we need not look far to see that women are not valued the way God values them. Whether in ancient history or current events, local and global, we read of women undervalued, overlooked, silenced, ridiculed, pushed aside, abused, objectified, used, and oppressed. Women are treated as objects for the gratification of men, sometimes traded and sold. The crimes against women are perpetrated by men and women alike.

Humans wrestle with the balance knob. Sometimes it seems like the knob is cranked to W. At other times, it seems perpetually stuck on M. When this happens, we can't hear the glorious song God is singing about himself. His glory is distorted.

This is not how God created things to be. So, what on earth happened? Where did things go wrong? And what, if anything, can we do about it? How can we reset the balance and hear the beauty of God's glory through the corresponding channels of man and woman?

These are important questions. We'll consider them in chapter 2.

──────── **DISCOVERING A WOMAN'S WORTH** ────────

1. Describe your experience of the relationship between man and woman. How were men and women treated as equal or unequal, celebrated or disparaged in

   a. the home you were raised in?
   b. the religious institution you were raised in?
   c. your workplace?
   d. the church you attend now?
   e. your marriage?
   f. your friendships?

   Make suggestions for how each could better reflect God's intentions.

2. Have you ever thought about your creation in God's image and likeness before? Why might it be important for you to think about it now?

3. Say this aloud: "I am created in the image of God. How I act shows the world what God is like. How I treat other image-bearers reveals what I think of God."

   a. If you believed that statement, how would it impact your life in the world? At work? Church? Home? In private? In government?
   b. What has your behavior today communicated to others about what God is like?

   c. What have your attitudes about and treatment of
      women communicated to the world about God's
      worth?

4. Summarize what you have learned in this chapter in two or
   three sentences.

──────────────── **DIGGING DEEPER** ────────────────

1. Read Genesis 1:27–28. "Man" in this passage refers to a
   kind of creature. Every "man," both male and female, is
   created in the image of God, with the mandate to subdue
   and exercise dominion over the earth together.

   a. What implications does this have for gender equality?

   b. In what ways might our present culture (in the world,
      church, or home) diminish the image of God in one
      gender and exalt it in the other?

2. Read Genesis 2:18. The refrain "God saw that it was
   good" occurred seven times in Genesis 1. With those
   words fresh in our ears, the declaration here that "it is not
   good" should get our attention.

   a. What does God declare "is not good?"

   b. What aspects of the creation mandate (Genesis 1:26–
      28) are impossible if the man is alone?

   c. Explain in your own words why "it is not good that the
      man should be alone."

   d. Read Revelation 21:1–5 and 22:1–5. Will Jesus, the
      last Adam, reign alone? If not, with whom will he
      reign?

3. God says he will "make a helper fit for him." What terms does Genesis 1–2 use to describe the distinctive quality of man?

   a. How does this inform the meaning of "fit for him"?
   b. Does "helper fit for him" refer to something inferior, equal, or superior in status?

TWO

The Worth of Women in the Fall

*The woman whom you gave to be with me,
she gave me fruit of the tree, and I ate.*

Genesis 3:12

Take a few minutes to do a web search for Elvis Presley's 1958 No. 1 hit "Hard Headed Woman" and listen to the song. (Seriously. Go do it. We'll wait right here.)

Did you hear the message in those lyrics? Since the beginning of the world, the cause of all trouble is a hard-headed woman. The men were doing fine until the women showed up. The woman is a thorn in man's side.

We don't know where the songwriter, Claude Demetrius, learned his theology. We don't know what Elvis thought as he crooned those words. Perhaps they read Tertullian, the Christian writer who lived in the second and third centuries, who wrote regarding women:

Do you not know that you are Eve? The judgment of God upon this sex lives on in this age; therefore, necessarily the guilt should

40

live on also. You are the gateway of the devil; you are the one who unseals the curse on that tree, and you are the first one to turn your back on the divine law; you are the one who persuaded him whom the devil was not capable of corrupting; you easily destroyed the image of God, Adam. Because of what you deserve, that is, death, even the Son of God had to die.[1]

Such misogynistic attitudes were commonplace in first-century Judaism as well.[2] Unfortunately, as "Hard Headed Woman" illustrates, such attitudes did not remain solely in the first three centuries of Christianity.

I (Eric) have heard it taught that women are more prone to deception than men. Thus, we should not permit women to teach Scripture. Women, some Christian subcultures argue, are more emotional and less rational than men. Such beliefs cast them as unintelligent and untrustworthy interpreters of the Word: think "Ditzy Blonde." Attitudes and policies suggest that women are, by nature, dangerous to men, that they are temptresses and seducers, waiting to do to all men what many perceive Eve did to Adam. Other attitudes suggest that women are overbearing shrews, ambitiously striving to domineer men.

Perhaps someone has made you, our female readers, feel more sinful or gullible than men. Someone has made you think that you are a particular danger to men. You believe the fault for a man's sin is yours (for how you dress, speak, or act). You feel that your motives in interacting with men should be suspect and that you should always second-guess yourself, fearing that your desire to help is actually poorly cloaked ambition to be the boss.

Perhaps you, our male readers, have thought, implied, or stated such things about women. You've treated women with suspicion, avoidance, or disdain due to such ideas.

This chapter aims to state that such ideas about women are entirely false. Such treatment of women is nothing short of evil. In this chapter, we intend to see the value of women in the account of the Fall and its aftermath in the early chapters of Genesis. By correcting wrong interpretation and application, we celebrate and defend the woman's worth. In seeing her value, we condemn her abuse.

The aim of this chapter is not to argue that women are not sinful. We are not arguing that women are inherently righteous and sinless. We are not claiming that women are less corrupt than men. They are not. Scripture is clear on this (Romans 3:10–12):

> None is righteous, no, not one;
> > no one understands;
> > no one seeks for God.
> All have turned aside; together they have become
> > worthless;
> > no one does good,
> > not even one.

We are saying that women—as a sex—are not *more* sinful than men. Women are not *more* deceivable than men. Women are not *less* intelligent than men. Women are not *more* prone to error than men. Women are not *more* dangerous than men. Women are not *more* arrogant or domineering than men. Women are not to be viewed with *more* suspicion than men.

All women are born into sin, unrighteous by both nature and choice—as are all men. We have all become "worthless," meaning that we fail to reflect the worth of God in thought, word, and deed. There are deceptive, seductive, domineering, dangerous women that men (and women) ought to avoid. There are deceptive, seductive, domineering, dangerous men that men (and women) ought to avoid. "All have turned aside," and we confess this truth.

But the image of God remains; its worth is upheld after the Fall (see Genesis 9:5–6). The Lord shows concern for upholding the worth of all humans—men, women, and children—throughout the Bible. Sinful humans have shown the remarkable ability to mistreat other humans—men, women, and children—throughout history. No category of human is to be diminished for skin color, sex, or any other feature. So we denounce and reject any view that actively or passively diminishes the value of women. We condemn any view that actively or passively encourages the neglect and abuse of women.[3]

Sinful Perceptions of Women

There are three wrong perceptions about women often supported by a mishandling of Genesis 3.

Misperception One: Women are more prone to mishandle the Bible.

Let me give you an example of how I (Eric) fell into this faulty way of thinking. For years, I preached that the woman mishandled God's Word in Genesis 3 as follows:

1. **The woman diminished God's generosity.** God told Adam, "You may surely eat of every tree of the Garden." But the woman said, "We may eat of the fruit of the trees in the garden." Omitting "surely," she diminished the generosity of God.

2. **The woman forgot God's provision.** God put two trees in the middle of the Garden—the tree of life and the tree of the knowledge of good and evil. But the woman said, "God said, 'You shall not eat of the fruit of the tree that is in the midst of the garden.'" She mentioned only one tree in the midst of the Garden; she forgot about God's provision of the tree of life.

3. **The woman exaggerated God's restriction.** God told Adam, "Of the tree of the knowledge of good and evil you shall not eat." The woman added, "neither shall you touch it." She added to God's prohibition, making it more restrictive.

4. **The woman lessened the certainty of the consequence.** God told Adam, "in the day that you eat of it you shall

surely die." The woman said, "lest you die." Omitting "surely," she made the consequence less certain.

I argued that in these four ways, the woman mishandled God's Word. Her carelessness with the text was what made her susceptible to deception.

There are a few problems with this interpretation. If this is a mishandling of God's Word, why assume the woman mishandled it? God gave the instruction to the man before he created the woman (Genesis 2:16). Presumably, the man passed it along to the woman at some point. How do we know it was not Adam who mishandled it and passed along this version to the woman?[4]

We might also ask how we know that God did not repeat the instruction to both of them with slightly different reading. In fact, the Lord gives a similar command when he drives the humans out of the Garden. "Now, lest he reach out his hand and take also of the tree of life and eat" (Genesis 3:22). Notice the two parts of this command—"reach out his hand and take" (touch) and "eat." These correspond to the two halves of the prohibition the woman cites—"you shall not eat" and "neither shall you touch it." Rather than adding to the Word, perhaps the woman rightly grasps the nature of the command (perhaps as God repeated it). Moses likely includes it in 3:3 as a literary device tying the beginning of the story together with its end. As such, it highlights their loss. They were only forbidden from eating of and touching the tree that brought death. But now they are forbidden from touching and eating of the one tree that brings eternal life. How tragic!

The Bible doesn't say that either human mishandled the Word of God in Genesis 3. It calls Eve a "transgressor" (1 Timothy 2:14); deceived, she went beyond what was allowed. But in no place does the Bible condemn her for being a careless interpreter of God's Word. Nor does it condemn Adam for mishandling the Word. Rather, "Adam was not deceived" (1 Timothy 2:14); he knew what God said. Adam did not get the Word wrong—he chose to disobey it! The Bible doesn't draw attention to either person's handling of the command.

Finally, the woman quotes the Word in the same way the New Testament quotes the Old Testament. Both Jesus and the apostles omit words and phrases, vary wording, and summarize ideas. For example, compare Jesus' quotation of Isaiah in Luke 4:18–19 and the original in Isaiah 61:1–2. Jesus does many of the things the woman is accused of having done. For further examples, do a web search for New Testament quotations of the Old Testament. Then compare the quotation of the original passage. Biblical authors do not hold to modern quotation standards when quoting material, though they never abuse the text or misrepresent what it says. The woman's quotation is an acceptable summary of what the Lord said to the man.[5]

The Bible never faults her for mishandling God's Word. The source of her transgression wasn't in how she quoted (or taught) God's Word; it was her deception. (Let's not mishandle God's Word while accusing someone of mishandling God's Word.)

Adam's sin was not that he listened to the voice of a woman.[6] His sin was that he listened to the voice of his wife and ate from the tree of which the Lord commanded, "You shall not eat of it." That is, his sin was not in hearing her but in listening as she invited him to sin—and then choosing to disobey. The emphasis does not fall on listening to an *embodied female* but in believing and following a creature in opposition to the Word of the Creator.

Genesis 3 does not teach or illustrate that women are inherently less skilled in the Word of God. We should not think of them as such. In fact, as we will see in later chapters, God works through women who speak, teach, and equip with the Scripture.

Misperception Two: The woman tempted and seduced the man. Therefore, women are chiefly to blame for the sin of men.

Did the woman maliciously tempt the man to sin or seduce him? Did she willfully pressure him to sin?

The serpent told the woman that she wouldn't die, but that her eyes would be opened and she would be like God. She was deceived. So "she took of its fruit and ate" (Genesis 3:6). We're not told that anything happened upon her eating. It is possible that being deceived, she continues to believe there is no death to come. So "she also gave some to her husband who was with her, and he ate." This is the act of a deceived woman—possibly inclined by her "helper" nature—sharing with her husband what she (wrongly) believes to be good to eat. And notice that Adam was with her while she ate. We have no record of his trying to stop her or helping her fight Satan's attack. They were both there together. She was deceived and ate first. He ate next in wide-eyed disobedience.

No Scripture presents the woman's action as one of seduction or temptation. (The Scripture is not afraid to call out and name seductresses elsewhere.) Neither Genesis 3 nor the rest of Scripture put heightened blame on the woman. If anything, they land more severely on the man than on the woman.

The effect of sin comes only after the man eats (Genesis 3:6–7); "and he ate. Then the eyes of both were opened." When the Lord appears in the Garden, he questions Adam first. This is a sign of Adam's special responsibility as head of humanity (vv. 9–11). When outlining the consequences for sin, the Lord is more severe with the man than with the woman. The Lord speaks four lines of poetry to the woman (v. 16). He speaks fourteen when addressing the man (vv. 17–19) and ten with the serpent (vv. 14–15). He uses the word *curse* with the serpent and the man, but not with the woman. The Lord begins his address to the serpent and the man with "because." The man and the serpent each have done something deserving a consequence. But to the woman, he does not use "because"; he simply states what will happen to her. This gives the impression that the Lord punishes the serpent and the man for their actions in particular. But the woman is receiving the consequence as part of sin entering the world through Adam.

This is consistent with how the New Testament presents the
Fall. The most said about Eve is that "the woman was deceived
and became a transgressor" (1 Timothy 2:14). Paul makes that
statement in contrast with Adam to emphasize that his wrong was
more severe—"Adam was not deceived." Keeping suit, the New
Testament puts the blame on Adam as humanity's head in covenant with God. Paul writes that "sin came into the world through
one man, and death through sin, and so death spread to all men
because all sinned" (Romans 5:12). The sin of Adam (not of Eve)
brought sin, judgment, and death upon everyone—even those, such
as Eve, "whose sinning was not like the transgression of Adam"
(Romans 5:14). "In Adam all die" (1 Corinthians 15:21–22). In
covenant with God, Adam represented all of humanity; when
he fell into sin, his nature, guilt, and consequences became ours
as well.

The woman did not cause the man to sin. Nor did she act as a
temptress or seductress, the proverbial "evil woman" who "hunts
down a precious life" (see Proverbs 6:24–26). Though she (wrongly)
offers him the fruit, there is no indication of malicious intent; she
is not enticing him in order to destroy him. Neither Moses nor
the rest of Scripture paint her in any stronger term than deceived
"transgressor."

Even so, Eve has become an example and a warning about the
danger women pose to men. We hear this idea in the Elvis song. We
find this in some (not all) policies discouraging men and women
who aren't married to each other from working, traveling, or dining together. We hear this in the suggestion that men and women
who aren't married to each other should not be friends. We see
this in calls to women to dress modestly to keep men from lust-
ing (something the New Testament does not do). We find this in
shaming female sexual assault victims—"She was asking for it,
dressed like that."

In our chapters on women in the life of Jesus, we find a different
mindset. He was not afraid of or distant from women. He sat alone
with a woman at a well and engaged in a meaningful conversation

(John 4:6–27). He let a woman of ill repute intimately touch him (Luke 7:36–50). Jesus has not called us to be any different; Genesis 3 certainly does not.

Misperception three: The woman's desire shall be "contrary to" her husband. Thus, women are by nature out to overcome and oppose men. Men should treat women with particular suspicion and caution.

In considering gender issues, teachers give significant attention to Genesis 3:16 (CSB):

> He said to the woman:
>> I will intensify your labor pains;
>> you will bear children with painful effort.
>> Your desire will be for your husband,
>> yet he will rule over you.

The discussion centers on the phrase "your desire will be for your husband." The Old Testament uses the Hebrew word translated "desire" in only two other places (Genesis 4:7; Song of Solomon 7:10). Two major interpretations exist for "desire . . . for."

The first interpretation understands this "desire" as a sinful urge to overcome and dominate. It appeals to Genesis 4:7. There the words *desire* and *rule* appear in the same construction—"sin is crouching at the door. Its desire is contrary to you, but you must rule over it." Sin "desires" Cain but he must "rule" over it. Likewise, sin will corrupt the woman's willingness to be a "helper." Instead, she will long to usurp his authority and control him. In response, he will have to rule her. (In this interpretation, *rule* may be either a sinful dominion or a proper exercise of authority over rebellion.)

The second interpretation understands *desire* as the God-ordained desire within the marriage relationship. Song of Solomon 7:10 uses *desire* this way, "I am my beloved's, and his desire is for me." In this view, the woman will continue to desire to be a helper to her husband. She desires to fill the earth and exercise dominion with him. But her desire to fulfill the creation mandate will meet with frustration. He will "rule" her—referring to a sinful and harsh rule. (Though the man has a special role as the head of mankind, Genesis 1–2 never presents the man as "ruling" over the woman. Subduing and exercising dominion is a responsibility they exercise together over the earth. They do not subdue and exercise dominion over one another.)

We favor the second interpretation of *desire* because it better fits the immediate context. The focus is on the frustration and futility experienced as they fulfill their responsibilities.

In Genesis 1:28, God charged both Adam and Eve to "be fruitful and multiply and fill the earth and subdue it and have dominion." In Genesis 2, he put the man in the Garden to "work and keep it" (or "serve" and "protect"), which likely included both cultivation of the Garden and the protection of it.[7] The Lord made the woman to be a "helper fit for him." These responsibilities are not removed after their fall into sin. The desires remain—and they remain good. Fulfilling those desires, however, will become frustrating and painful. This is what the Lord addresses in Genesis 3:16–19.

The Lord speaks of their responsibility to subdue the earth, working and keeping the ground. The man will still want to do what God designed them to do. But instead of cooperating in the production of food, the earth will fight back. "In pain you shall eat of it all the days of your life; thorns and thistles it shall bring forth for you. . . . By the sweat of your face you shall eat bread."

Likewise, the woman will still desire to "be fruitful and multiply and fill the earth." But her body (and her children) will not cooperate. The pain of childbearing multiplies. "In pain you shall bring forth children."

Notice in the previous paragraphs that every desire is a good desire met with a frustrating response. In the parallel structures used in Hebrew poetry we should expect the same pattern in "Your desire will be for your husband, yet he will rule over you." Right desire. Frustrating response.

The woman will continue to have a right desire for her husband—to be a helper fit for him. He will not cooperate with this, however: "but he shall rule over you." Instead of ruling with his helper, he will rule his helper. Such mistreatment and abuse of women is plain as Genesis unfolds.

We should not use this passage to suggest that women are especially prone to oppose, usurp, or destroy men. As a young seminarian and pastor, such interpretations produced in me a suspicion of women. Women-diminishing statements and policies from pastors and leaders strengthened it. My theology affirmed the equality and worth of women. Yet I became suspicious of women who taught the Scripture, wrote theology books, or showed friendly affection. Such an attitude is not only wrong, it is evil. Unfortunately, these attitudes toward women are still widespread today, fueling the mistreatment of women so prevalent in the history of the world.

The Sinful Treatment of Women

In October of 1991, I (Eric) was a freshman in high school. Anita Hill was testifying before the United States Senate. Her sexual harassment allegations against Supreme Court nominee Clarence Thomas dominated the news. As a Rush Limbaugh-reading, knee-jerk conservative fifteen-year-old, I doubted Hill. In my mind, she was part of a liberal, pro-choice conspiracy to bring down a Republican nominee.

A local print shop in our small town made a T-shirt referencing the Thomas-Hill scandal. It featured a gavel with the words "I'm not planning to be on the Supreme Court . . . so watch out, baby!" I thought it was hilarious. I got one.

I don't know what happened between Clarence Thomas and Anita Hill. But I do know what that T-shirt was—wrong. WRONG. Even if Hill lied through her teeth and Thomas was squeaky clean, the T-shirt was not a joke; it was wicked. Sexual harassment of women is not a joke. Threatening to sexually harass women is not a joke.

I wore that shirt to school on a regular basis. I shudder to think what impact that shirt had on teachers or students. How did it affect those who had been sexually abused or harassed? Did they bite their tongue, holding back anger? Did it send the message that their suffering was a joke, that it didn't matter? That I would harass or abuse them? I had no intention of sexually harassing a woman. Yet the shirt was sexual harassment; it made the mistreatment of women into a joke.

My sin in wearing that shirt is the fruit of the Fall. I followed in the steps of my first father, Adam, and the sons born to him.

If the first sin was the eating of forbidden fruit, the second sin was the abuse of women. When Adam and Eve hear the sound of the Lord walking in the Garden, they hide from him. The Lord calls to the man (due to his place of leadership and greater responsibility), asking where he is. The man confesses to hiding because of his fear of being seen naked. The Lord asks him if he ate the forbidden fruit. Adam answers, "The woman whom you gave to be with me, she gave me fruit of the tree, and I ate." Instead of owning his sin, the man points to his wife (and the Creator). By boldly shifting the attention to her offer, he subtly shifts the blame from himself to her. The third sentence we hear from Adam is the denigration of his wife. This is not insignificant.

Such blame-shifting is wicked on several accounts. Adam's words betray great pride. He is not to blame for his sinful actions; she is. If she hadn't made the offer, everything would still be okay.

Furthermore, Adam shows a cruel indifference to the consequence Eve may suffer. He is willing to let her experience shame, blame, and punishment if it means he can escape it. This—the second recorded speech by the first man—is entirely different from his first recorded speech. In Genesis 2:23, he erupted in joyful song over the excellent gift of the woman. Now he uses crafty words to throw her under the bus. He is quite the opposite of Jesus, who stands between his bride and the wrath of God on the cross, bearing her shame, her sin, and her punishment.

We see such indifference and pride today in men (and women) who shift the blame from men to women. We hear echoes of Adam's excuse every time a man says, "If she didn't want me to make sexual remarks, she shouldn't have worn that dress." We hear it when the date-rapist says, "After she went this far, how could she expect me to stop?" We hear it when church ladies whisper, "Well if she hadn't gone to such and such a place, that wouldn't have happened!" When we use the presence or actions of women to excuse the immoral actions of men, we follow Adam in the mistreatment of women. In essence we're saying, "If it weren't for women, I would never sin."

Adam abused Eve with his words in a moment of panic. His descendants would become much more flagrant. In Genesis 4, we meet Adam and Eve's sons—Cain and Abel. Cain kills his brother in cold blood, envious that the Lord accepted Abel's offering but rejected Cain's. Cain is unrepentant and unconcerned for how he has treated God's image-bearer. His only concern is how others will treat him as a murderer. The Lord responds with a mark of protection, warning any vengeance seekers not to kill Cain.

The rest of the chapter highlights Cain's descendants. They follow in his wickedness, culminating in the man Lamech, of whom we read in Genesis 4:23–24:

> Lamech said to his wives:
> "Adah and Zillah, hear my voice;
>   you wives of Lamech, listen to what I say:
> I have killed a man for wounding me,
>   a young man for striking me.
> If Cain's revenge is sevenfold,
>   then Lamech's is seventy-sevenfold."

Cain killed his brother and then tried to hide it ("I do not know [where he is]; am I my brother's keeper?"). But Lamech, a polygamist, boasts of it. Cain fears vengeance; Lamech defies anyone to bring him justice. But notice to whom Lamech makes his boast—his wives. He calls these women to him and insists that they, in particular, listen to him. He then brags of how he killed a man for merely wounding him. He wants his wives, specifically, to know that he is a man who deals in violent severity with those who wrong him.

In the first song sung by a man, a husband celebrated his delight in his wife's equality and worth. In the second such poem by a man, a husband threatens his wives with domestic violence—even murder—if they dare cross him.

The Lord told the serpent that he would put "enmity between you and the woman, and between your offspring and her offspring" (Genesis 3:15). Satan would have a particular disgust and hatred for the woman due to her role as the mother of his downfall. It continues today.

Where does this happen today? There are obvious instances such as rape, sexual abuse, and domestic violence. But what are the areas that we (especially men) overlook? I asked a female friend to identify some "respectable" ways in which women are mistreated. Her reply was helpful, so I'm sharing it in full with her permission:

> I think this goes into the omission category. Not always sin—not always villainous or evil-intentioned, but still hurtful. Some examples:
>
> - Failing to acknowledge or greet sisters in a room (avoiding eye contact, looking past them, saying hello to their husbands without acknowledging them).
> - Failing to know and elevate their sisters (interests, areas of ministry, passions, hopes, desires) when they could.
> - Failing to converse about issues that women understand or can speak into (sometimes work or sports talk dominates mixed-gender environments).
> - Failing to intentionally invite women into mixed-gender conversations (meetings, group discussions, strategic decision-making, etc.), making space for their input and ideas.

Overt (but unnoticed) language that's harmful to women—some examples:

- Insulting or poking fun at someone for looking, acting, or performing "like a girl."
- Eye-rolling or using negative female gender stereotypes as a joke.
- Playing into caricatures of women who are strong leaders.
- Comments about a woman's physical appearance when it would be more appropriate to recognize her character* (when she's there and other men are around too, when it's one-on-one, or when she's not there and it's just men).

*Note: I don't think it's hurtful to recognize beauty and style. In this case, the tone of the comment, the context, and the trust/relationship between the male and female involved matters. Where trust and healthy relationship is established, it's just a simple compliment.

After this, I think it jumps into behavior that's more obviously hurtful/sinful (unwanted physical touch/catcalling/verbal advances/assault, etc.).

A female acquaintance once recounted a story to me, one that I've heard—almost word for word—from many women:

I noticed many harmful and insensitive behaviors in older men (over age 50). I'm not sure why, but that generation seems more oblivious to it. Recently, a much older man made me really uncomfortable in a public situation. When he saw me, he just kept commenting to my husband about how beautiful I was and how I didn't look like I'd had several kids. He patted my husband on the back and praised him for how "good" he did. . . . I guess related to the fact that he had a lovely wife? I didn't make a big deal out of it at all, because I really think he was oblivious and meant it as a compliment (and none of his comments were sexual in nature), but it made me feel really weird. What if I wasn't a beautiful wife? What if I did "look" like I had several kids? What does that mean about my value and personhood? And that's not an isolated incident.

Sadly, I can picture all those things happening, with specific examples, even from pastors. My wife and I have been in that story more than once. Yuck.

What is that all about? What are we seeing in misogyny—the hatred of, contempt for, and prejudice against women? In glass ceilings that hold women back? In negative stereotypes of women in the church? In "locker room talk" that boasts of sexual exploits? In demeaning jokes about women? In rape? In sexual harassment? In objectifying the female body and diminishing the female mind? In pornography? In emotional, sexual, and physical abuse of women? In suspicion and avoidance of women?

We are seeing a demonic, Satanic hatred of women manifest itself in the thoughts, words, and deeds of sinful human beings.

It appeared immediately at the Fall. It continues today.

It must end. It demands a cure.

What will it be?

─────── DISCOVERING A WOMAN'S WORTH ───────

1. Describe your response to each of these observations from the chapter. Where have you seen such things in your life?

   a. The first sin was eating the forbidden fruit; the second sin was the abuse of women.

   b. The first recorded sentence spoken by the man is a celebration of his wife; the third is a denigration of this wife.

   c. In an effort to avoid the consequences for his actions, the man shows cruel indifference to the consequence his wife may suffer.

   d. In the first song lyric by a man, a husband celebrated his delight in his wife's equality and worth. In the second such lyric by a man, a husband threatens his wives with domestic violence—even murder—if they dare cross him.

2. Marriage often is used as an analogy for the relationship between God and his people. In the Old Testament, the Lord sometimes refers to Israel as his bride. In the New Testament, Jesus is often described as the "bridegroom" and the church as his "bride."

   a. How is God's treatment of Israel different from the treatment of women we saw in Genesis 3–4?
   b. How is Jesus' treatment of the church different from the treatment of women we saw in Genesis 3–4?
   c. What do men like Adam and Lamech teach us about how *not* to treat women?
   d. What can we learn from Jesus' treatment of his bride about how to love and honor women?
   e. Where do you need to repent and follow Jesus?

3. Discuss the "Watch out baby!" T-shirt story and the list of "respectable" sins at the end of the chapter.

   a. Where do you see yourself prone to such thoughts, words, and deeds?
   b. Where do you see men guilty of these things?
   c. Where do you see women guilty of these things?
   d. What would you add to the list?

4. Eric mentioned asking a female friend for examples of how women are mistreated.

   a. Women: Would you be willing to have that conversation with your pastor or a male friend? Why or why not?

b. Men: Would you be willing to ask a female friend to share her experiences and thoughts? Why or why not?

c. Pastors: Have you ever asked such questions of women in your church? Why or why not? Will you? When a woman in your church answers these questions honestly, is your first response to doubt her perspective or explain away the interaction?

d. All: How can we promote such healthy conversations in our local churches?

e. Summarize what you've learned in this chapter in four or five sentences.

DIGGING DEEPER

1. Read Genesis 3:1–16 and 1 Timothy 2:13–14.

a. Does either passage fault Eve's handling of God's Word?

b. Was Eve deceived?

c. Did Eve transgress God's command?

d. Does either passage say or imply that women in general are:
   - more easily deceived than men?
   - more prone to mishandle God's Word than men?
   - less intelligent than men?

e. What (if any) conclusions should Eve's behavior lead us to about all women in general?

2. Read Genesis 1:28 and 3:16.

a. What general responsibilities were man and woman given when they were created (1:28)?

  b. How do the consequences for sin in Genesis 3:16 relate
     to these responsibilities?

  c. How do the responsibilities remain the same? What
     changes?

3. Read Genesis 4:23. Why do you think Lamech made his
   boast about killing a man specifically to his wives?

THREE

The Worth of Women in the Promise

And Adam knew his wife again, and she bore a son and called his name Seth, for she said, "God has appointed for me another offspring instead of Abel, for Cain killed him." To Seth also a son was born, and he called his name Enosh. At that time people began to call upon the name of the Lord.

Genesis 4:25–26

Audrey Hepburn. What picture comes to mind when you hear that name? Do you immediately see a young fashionable woman with short hair and a slim figure? Do you see an awarded actress of Hollywood's golden era walking the red carpet? Do you see her as one of her famous characters in *Roman Holiday*, *Sabrina*, or *Funny Face*? What about *Breakfast at Tiffany's*? Do you picture her in the famous little black dress and iconic pose?

Did you envision a sixty-two-year-old woman hugging fly-covered, malnourished children? Perhaps you should. In the last years of her life, Hepburn served as a goodwill ambassador for UNICEF. She testified twice before Congress for the welfare of children. She received numerous humanitarian awards. These include the Presidential Medal of Freedom—the highest civilian award of the United States—awarded only months before she died. Despite Hepburn's work on behalf of suffering children, we remember Hepburn only for her slim figure, fashion sense, and iconic movie roles. This illustrates our tendency to overlook virtue and service and remember people for only one aspect of their lives.

What about Eve, the first woman? What comes to mind when you think of her? A nude woman posing in strategically placed shrubbery? A naive ditz talking to a snake? A Scripture-twister? A seductress? A temptress? A dejected sinner draped in animal skin?

Did you picture a believer in Jesus? A woman of faith persevering in the face of intense pain and disappointment? You should.

The first images of Eve that come to mind for most of us are of her activity related to the Fall. Few of us remember her for the first recorded statement of faith in Scripture. Few realize she professed faith at all. In the collective memory of Christianity (and the world), the first woman is a failure and a warning. Eve is a negative type for all women to follow. Eve's deception certainly sounds a warning. But that is not all we should find in the life of our first mother.

In Eve, we see a woman of whom the world was not worthy. In Eve, we find a woman who received the Gospel in faith. We find a woman who persevered in her faith, even through the most painful of circumstances.

The Enemy of the Woman

Have you ever had one of those days when it feels like the whole world is against you? Does it ever feel like you woke up to find Satan sitting on your chest? Do you ever wonder if sin, death, and the gates of hell might be aiming their full forces at you? If you do, you're not alone. Imagine how the woman might have felt hearing the Lord's words to the serpent in Genesis 3:15:

> I will put enmity between you and the woman,
>   and between your offspring and her offspring.

The New Testament identifies the serpent with Satan (Revelation 12:9). Satan (the devil) is a fallen angel, the chief of the enemies of God. He is a liar and a murderer, and specializes in accusing the people of God (John 8:44; Revelation 12:10). Satan has no power in himself to eternally harm people. Therefore, he uses temptation and deception to lure people into sin, which brings the wrath of God. Then he throws their sin before God, insisting that they receive what they deserve—death.

The serpent had already bested the woman once. She was dressed in a fig-leaf loincloth, hiding in the bushes, and cowering in shame because Satan deceived her into transgressing. If one deception and the sin of her husband could bring this, what might the serpent do next? It is no wonder she will hate the serpent.

Due to the unique role the woman will play in the promise to follow, the serpent has a special hatred for her. Satan does not hate women because they are of ultimate value. Satan hates women because Jesus is ultimate—Jesus will arrive as a child born of a woman.

This is why Revelation 12 casts the story of redemption as that of a pregnant woman pursued by a great red dragon. As she cries out in the agony of birth, the dragon crouches at the birth canal, ready to devour this child. This child—the offspring of the woman—is "one who is to rule all the nations with a rod of iron" (v. 5). Satan hates this particular child, whose arrival marks the devil's defeat (Revelation 12:10): "Now the salvation and the power and the kingdom of our God and the authority of his Christ have come, for the accuser of our brothers has been thrown down, who accuses them day and night before our God."

The word *offspring* (sometimes translated "seed") is a word that can be either singular or plural—and sometimes, both. The offspring of the woman becomes both. It is ultimately Jesus. But united with him in faith, believers in Jesus become the "offspring" of the woman. Thwarted in his attempt to abort her offspring, the serpent sets his sights on "the rest of her offspring." Who are they? "Those who keep the commandments of God and hold to the testimony of Jesus" (Revelation 12:17).

Her "offspring" does not refer to all her descendants; even in the most immediate context, it cannot. Some of her children will be the offspring of the serpent. Cain is the seed of the devil; a murderer of the seed of the woman (1 John 3:12). Thus, the serpent's offspring are not demons, but those who do not put their faith in the promised redeemer (John 8:44). The woman's "offspring" then are those who believe the good news of a promised redeemer (Revelation 12:17). These offspring hate one another and are at war. The Bible tells the story of this war. We see this in Genesis (Cain and Abel, Ishmael and Isaac, Jacob and Esau, Joseph and his brothers), in the Old Testament (Israel and the nations), in the Gospels (John 8:43–45), and in the church (1 Peter 5:8; Ephesians 6:11–12; 1 John 3:12–13; Romans 16:20).

Likewise, in a broader sense, "the woman" does not refer only to Eve. It refers to her in the immediate context. It also refers to all women who bear or nurture children of faith as history unfolds. This is why the world hates, abuses, and destroys women as history unfolds. The serpent is attempting to thwart the birth of the Messiah. This is why the Law the Lord gives to Israel honors and protects women. The Law is preserving Israel until the King is born.

This is also why children threaten serpent-servers (like Pharaoh and Herod). This is why these men murder children. This is why Israel's Law protects and defends children, even in the womb (Exodus 21:22–23). In the offspring of the woman is the destruction of the serpent and his offspring.

To be at war with an ancient demonic dragon is a scary thing. But there is a hint of good news, even in these lines. To be at war with the Lord's enemy is to be on the Lord's side. And the Lord does not promise war alone—he promises victory.

The Salvation of the Woman

Death entered the world through the man's sin. Salvation enters the world through the woman's son. The Lord tells the serpent, speaking of the woman's offspring (Genesis 3:15),

> he shall bruise your head,
>   and you shall bruise his heel.

The war between the serpent's offspring and the woman's offspring will culminate in a battle between the serpent himself and one particular offspring—a son. In the ensuing conflict, damage will be done to the serpent's head and to the offspring's heel. We get a picture of a snake biting a man's heel, delivering a lethal injection of venom. In return, the man crushes the serpent's head.

This is the story that unfolds in Cain killing Abel—only to see the seed resurrected in the line of Seth. This is the story of Israel's sons selling Joseph into slavery, where he is buried in a dungeon and resurrected to rule. This is the story of Pharaoh killing and enslaving Israelites, only to have his head crushed in the collapsing waters of the Red Sea.

Ultimately, this is the story of Jesus Christ. Satan entered one of Jesus' disciples, came for him with a mob, and lied to murder the offspring of the woman (John 13:27; 14:30). They crucified Jesus, hanging him on a tree as a sign that he was under God's curse (Galatians 3:13). Jesus died.

Little did the serpent know that the death of the woman's offspring would bring the death of the serpent. Jesus said of his crucifixion, "Now is the judgment of this world; now will the ruler of this world be cast out" (John 12:31). By removing the curse of sin, the cross stripped Satan of power. No longer can he accuse God's people because we have an advocate with the Father, Christ Jesus the righteous (1 John 2:1). Jesus lived without sin; he deserved no curse (Hebrews 4:15). He died for our sins (1 Corinthians 15:3–5). His death was a "propitiation" (1 John 2:2). This means that his execution satisfied God's justice and brought God's favor. In his resurrection, God declared Jesus to be the perfect and well-pleasing offspring (Romans 1:4; Matthew 3:17).

Through his victory, Jesus' people become children of God (John 1:12; Galatians 3:26; 1 John 3:1). *In Jesus, believers become true "offspring of the woman."* The dragon makes war against us (Revelation 12:17). Though he seeks to devour us, we defeat him through firm faith in Jesus (1 Peter 5:8–9). "They have conquered him by the blood of the Lamb and by the word of their testimony, for they loved not their lives even unto death" (Revelation 12:11). As we wait in faith, the Word promises that "the God of peace will soon crush Satan under your feet" (Romans 16:20). One day, resurrected with Jesus, we "will reign forever and ever" (Revelation 22:5).

The promise of victory over sin, death, and the power of the devil is good news indeed! You may find your identity in your past sins, your inadequacies, your body type, your social status, or how your life looks on social media. But the Gospel speaks a better word than these. The Gospel grants us a new identity. When a woman believes the Gospel, she is no longer a sinner in God's eyes; she is righteous. She is no longer cloaked in shame; she hears God declare, "This is my beloved daughter in Christ, with whom I am well pleased." She is no longer defined by the world's standards of beauty; she shines with the glory of God. Her standing is no longer determined by fickle social circles; she is a victor in the war against Satan. She will soon crush his head and reign with Jesus forever.

And better still—all this is ours in its entirety by grace, received through faith in the promised One. It has been this way from the beginning.

The Faith of the Woman

"Are Adam and Eve in heaven?" It's a perennial question for bed-time stalling and youth group lock-ins. And it is an important one. Will we get to meet our first parents in glory? The answer is yes!

The Lord's grace overflows in Genesis 3. Before he ever pronounces the consequences of their sin, he gives humans the promise of a savior. Before he drives the humans out of the Garden, he draws them to himself in faith.

Immediately after recording the ultimate consequence for sin, Moses does a strange thing. He records the man's naming of his wife. Then he moves on to the Lord making garments of skin for them both. What's going on here?

The Lord had promised that "in the day that you eat of it you shall surely die" (Genesis 2:17). He reinforced that after the Fall to Adam: "You are dust, and to dust you shall return" (Genesis 3:19). But in between, he promised the woman children, a child who would defeat the serpent. This raises a question: How would they have children if they would die that day?

This brings tension to the story. Will Adam trust that God is merciful? Will he believe that God will allow them to live for a time and have children? Will he believe the promise of a redeemer?

Then we read, "The man called his wife's name Eve, because she was the mother of all living" (Genesis 3:20). This is an act of faith. He did not believe that God would strike them dead immediately. He believed that God's grace had intervened between him and God's wrath. Adam trusted that he and his wife would live and have children. He believed that she would be the mother of all the living. He had faith that the seed of the woman would come to redeem them.

To this faith, God responded by making garments of animal skins. Their leafy loincloths were insufficient to hide the shame of their nakedness. They were unsuitable for life in the harsh world outside the Garden. So the Lord slaughtered an animal and clothed them through its death.

Adam received God's salvation by grace through faith. God's saving promises are always received and applied by faith. Abraham believed the Lord, and the Lord counted this faith to him as righteousness (Genesis 15:6). Likewise, we are declared righteous, given God's Spirit, and adopted as sons through faith in Jesus (Galatians 2:16; 3:14, 26).

The First Statement of Faith in History

Eve shared her husband's faith. Theirs are the first recorded statements of faith in history. In fact,

> *Eve's statement of faith are the first human*
> *words recorded after the Fall.*

Sometime after they left the Garden, "Adam knew Eve his wife, and she conceived and bore Cain." She said, "I have gotten a man with the help of the Lord" (Genesis 4:1). Though conceived through intercourse with her husband, Eve knew this was a gift of mercy. This offspring was born "with the help of the Lord." Eve had faith that God was helping her according to his promise. Eve believed. "And blessed is she who believed that there would be a fulfillment of what was spoken to her from the Lord" (Luke 1:45).

Notice that Eve used the covenant name of God—"the Lord" (printed in small caps in English translations for the Hebrew name "Yahweh").

> *Eve is the first recorded human being to speak*
> *the divine, covenant name of God.*

The words of this believing woman have served as the confession of faith of God's people throughout history. To believe the Gospel is to say with Eve, "We have gotten a New Adam—Jesus the Messiah—with the help of the Lord!"

The Perseverance of the Woman

Faith does not bring our best life now. The promise is not a life of prosperity. Grace does not guarantee a life of comfort.

Genesis moves us from Eve's profession of faith to bitter suffering. She had two sons—Cain and Abel. Cain did not have faith. Abel did (Hebrews 11:4). You know the story—Cain killed Abel. But think of this from the perspective of a mother.

Imagine that you are a mother. You have only two sons. One son murders the other. The living son continues in his bitterness and goes "away from the presence of the Lord" (Genesis 4:16). His descendants excel in worldly accomplishments but do not know the Lord. Instead, they boast of wickedness and trust in themselves for salvation (Genesis 4:23).

How would you feel? How would you bear the persistent pain of a dead child and wayward son? Would you continue to believe that the Lord is gracious and merciful? Would you have faith that God will keep his promise of salvation? Would you believe that God is for you? Would you persevere in faith?

Eve did.

"Adam knew his wife again, and she bore a son and called his name Seth, for she said, 'God has appointed for me another offspring instead of Abel, for Cain killed him'" (Genesis 4:25).

Eve may have been deceived once, but do not label her "easily deceived." Put your stereotypes aside. Her statement is an incredibly perceptive insight regarding the nature of the "offspring of the woman." It is a statement of intelligent, Word-of-God-interpreting, promise-believing faith.

Eve called Seth "another offspring." Why did she need "another" offspring? What does she mean by that? Cain was still alive. But Eve knew that Cain was not the *promised* offspring; he was a murderer, the offspring of the serpent. Abel was her offspring, a worshiper of the Lord through faith. But Abel was dead now. She knew she needed "another offspring." She trusted that such was what the Lord appointed.

Her offspring, passing from Seth to Enosh, became the people of faith—"the offspring of the woman." "To Seth also a son was born, and he called his name Enosh. At that time people began to call upon the name of the Lord" (Genesis 4:26). Cain went "away from the presence of the Lord." Seth's descendants "call upon the name of the Lord." They are the first people to worship using the name Yahweh. (This probably means some formal or widespread use, as Eve has already called him "Yahweh" in Genesis 4:1.) This righteous line is linked with the faith and confession of Eve.

Beginning with Eve, the Bible presents a long line of women, faithful helpers, who believe the promise. They oppose the serpent. They speak the Gospel and nurture faith in those under their care.

The Hope of the Woman

We see a remarkable change in Eve. Her first recorded words are a conversation with a serpent, ending with her deception in the Garden. Outside the Garden, her first recorded words are a confession of faith. She now recognizes the schemes of the serpent. She perseveres through pain and disappointment with eyes on the Lord and hope in his promise.

Like every human, God created the woman with great worth—in his image and likeness. In one sense, that worth remained after the Fall because she is still the image of God. Yet in another way, the woman became "worthless," taking the serpent's venom under her tongue (Romans 3:12). Like Adam, she failed and refused to enjoy and reflect the worth of God. Instead, she exchanged the glory of God for a lie (Romans 1:22–27; 3:12).

Perhaps you identify with the sinful and "worthless" Eve. You hang your head in guilt over past deception and flagrant sins. You cower in shame due to abuse and betrayal. You are captive to fear due to pain and loss in a cruel, harsh world. You struggle to believe because of the lies and broken vows. Hear this: There is hope.

The Lord offers life-transforming hope to every woman who will listen.

The Lord transformed Eve from a deceived woman of shame into a persevering believer and the mother of all children of faith. The Lord transformed Eve from "worthless" to a woman "of whom the world is not worthy" (Hebrews 11:38). She continued to be part of the "very good" priestly alliance she was created for.

How did he do this? Through the power of the Gospel, received by faith.

We remember Audrey Hepburn for her classic roles and iconic style, yes. But let's also remember her for her humanitarian service and sacrifice for the good of others.

Likewise, let's remember and learn from Eve's deception. But more than that, let's remember God's promise and grace to Eve. Let's remember the transforming power of the Gospel applied through faith.

Celebrating Women and the Gospel

How does this teach us to celebrate the worth of women—both unbelievers and Christian?[1]

What should you see when you see an unbelieving woman? Perhaps her sin and shame are evident in her scars, in her actions, in her reputation. Maybe they hide under a veil of self-righteousness and religious slavery. Regardless of her external appearance, see a human being who has worth as the image of God. See a woman who has "become worthless," deceived by the lies of Satan, the world, and the flesh. But mostly, see a woman who can become a woman "of whom the world is not worthy." See a woman who is not beyond the grace of God in the saving promises of Jesus Christ. See a woman who may one day shine in glory and rule with Christ the King. Then tell her the Gospel.

What should you see when you see a Christian woman? You should not see a snare, a temptation, and a pitfall. You should not see an object of sexual gratification, a threat to power, or a crafty usurper. You should see a mother and a sister, a family member in the faith. See someone who, regardless of her past, wears the righteousness of Jesus Christ. See someone who God adopted as a child—a fellow heir of the kingdom—someone who is still commissioned to be the necessary help that is needed as we fight against the evil one. See someone who the Spirit of God fills and gifts for service as a blessing to the world, the church, and her home. See a woman who will one day rise from the dead to reign with Jesus forever. Tell her that's who she is. Tell her the Gospel.

─────── **DISCOVERING A WOMAN'S WORTH** ───────

1. It's easy to collapse a person's life history into just one event. Has that ever happened to you? Have you ever wished that people would forget about that one foolish thing you did and would see you for who you are now? How might that change the way you think about Eve?

2. Eve did fall into the deception and trap of the serpent in the Garden. But the first words we hear her saying after her fall are words of faith. Remember that the first words spoken in the world after the Fall are words of faith spoken by a woman. How does this change your perspective on Eve?

3. In light of the fact that we all fail to walk in truth and avoid deception, it's important to remember that Eve (like the rest of us) was made in the image of God. How does that change how you think about yourself and how you think about other women, both unbelieving and believing?

4. Summarize what you've learned in this chapter in four or five sentences.

———————————— DIGGING DEEPER ————————————

1. Eve is given the promise of a godly seed. Why is that hope so important to her? Can you think of other women in the Bible who longed for a godly seed, a son?

2. What does it mean to be made in the "image of God"? How do you think both men and women bear that image? Is there any difference?

3. Eve is with all the righteous women of all time awaiting the new heaven and new earth. How does this truth encourage you, even though you may have acted foolishly or been deceived?

FOUR

The Worth of Women in Israel's History

The Lord commanded Moses to give us an
inheritance along with our brothers.
Joshua 17:4

Israel's History: Deliverance through Weakness

There are several times in my life when time seems to drag on interminably: One of them is when I (Elyse) am flying home from a conference. Every time I look at my watch, I can't believe it's only been ninety seconds since the last glance. Really? How can that be? *Maybe there's some sort of time warp that occurs when you fly*, I think. *Perhaps flying 500 mph at 30,000 feet causes time to slow down or reverse.* Well, I'm not sure what it is that happens, but I'm convinced it's something.

Everyone knows what it's like to wait for something. Whether you're a child waiting for your birthday gift, a young professional anticipating the day you finally get the job you've longed for, or a mom-to-be longing for the birth of a child, waiting for a promised event is so difficult. *I just want to be home in my bed. . . . When did this flight change from being across the country to around the world?* Sometimes we wait for things for so long it seems as though the promised event was just an illusion. Especially if you've only heard a promise that was made thousands of years ago. *Maybe the promise was never really given. . . . Perhaps it was misunderstood.*

Eve had spent her life awaiting the Conquering Son who would reverse the curse. She longed to see her folly undone; she told her daughters about the promise they should cling to. But she died without ever receiving him . . . and so did they. Even so, mother after mother passed along the promise to their daughters: *You might be the mother. . . . You might give birth to the One who will turn this mess around.* Over and over through generations of women, over 2,000 years, women hung on to the promise: Maybe they would be the one to give birth to a Son who would remake the world and banish all the darkness. But it had been so long, and still no deliverer had been born. And the promise grew weaker and the light dimmer; the promise faded.

The Promise Renewed

Before the Lord called them, sixty-five-year-old Sarai and her seventy-five-year-old husband, Abram, lived in Ur. Like the people around them, they were moon worshipers. Not only had they lost the worship of the true God, the entire summary of Sarai's life was that she "was barren; she had no child" (Genesis 11:30). Even if she had heard of the promised birth of a deliverer, she didn't have any hope it would come through her. She had waited and waited but had finally accepted the truth: The moon she worshiped was cold and lifeless—like her womb. Was there a long-awaited promised One? Two thousand years is a long time to wait for something spoken in a lost garden long ago.

The unexpected promise that began, "And I will make of you a great nation" (Genesis 12:2), didn't come to two likely candidates. They weren't known for their righteous allegiance to the creator God. They weren't known for their fertility. No. They were idolaters who lacked the ability to do the one thing everyone expected: procreate. God's promise: *You will have a son. I will make you into a great nation.* Abram's god? The moon. Sarai's reality? Barren and childless.

Into this hopelessness, the Lord promised a son who would transform this solitary couple into a multitude of people no one could count. But Sarai's biological clock had not only stopped ticking; it lay rusted and in pieces inside her empty uterus. Perhaps when she first heard the promise that the Lord had spoken, she had tried to believe. She had followed Abram from her home in Ur, agreed to his dangerous and cowardly demands that she lie about their relationship, but it seemed impossible after all these decades, all these months that screamed, "It's over!" In fact, it was over, *humanly speaking.* It had been two thousand years since the first promise was made and twenty-five years since the promise of a great multitude had been believed. She had continued to try to believe; both she and her husband had tried to figure out a way to get it done,[1] but she needed to hear the promise again.

But, now called Sarah, she didn't need to hear the voice of a mere human. So on one particular day, through her tent door, the Lord spoke to her. In his mercy, he wanted her to know that this promise was for her, so before he reiterated it to Abraham he asked where Sarah was. Don't be confused; it wasn't as though the Lord was wondering about her whereabouts, but rather he wanted to reassure her that he knew she was listening (Genesis 18:9). The Lord again promised to intervene in Sarah's life; what was impossible would happen. Eve's promised seed would be born through a very senior citizen. God still loved her and would use her. Sarah the aged would miraculously conceive and become Sarah the joyous mother. She would have a son, and through his descendants, the serpent finally would be crushed. The promise would come true—and through her!

We all know how Sarah responded when she heard this promise: Like her husband before her (Genesis 17:17), she scoffed. We would have too. *As if I'm going to have pleasure with old Abraham after I'm all worn out.... As if ...* Again, to reiterate the fact that the Lord was speaking to her, he let her know that he not only heard her laugh but understood it. He showed her who he was and what he was capable of. He said, "Is anything too hard for the Lord?" (Genesis 18:14). She who was called barren and childless would become the joyous mother of a nation.

Nothing Is Too Hard for the Lord

It's vital that every believing woman and man hear the Lord's declaration: No matter what wonderful scenario you might be waiting for, if it's God's will, nothing is too hard for him. No matter how long you've waited or how many times you've failed, or how many times you've compromised or given in to sinful manipulation and unbelief, nothing is too hard for the Lord. Get this:

> *The Lord's ability to do the impossible is first declared in regard to what he will do through a barren woman.*

It might be easy to think that Sarah had disqualified herself. She had faithlessly abused her slave girl, Hagar, by forcing her to have sex with her husband. And then, when Hagar turned up pregnant, she added to her sin by mistreating her. And yet, God spoke his promise to her: *I can accomplish the impossible—yes, even through you.* If you think it's too hard, too impossible, too wonderful, that's just the sort of thing God loves to accomplish, especially if you know that you don't deserve his help.

The Lord used an idolatrous, manipulative, unkind, scoffing, barren, and unbelieving woman (just like us?) to accomplish the impossible. In fact, using weakness like Sarah's seems to be a favorite thing of his. We know that because another woman also heard these same words. But this woman wasn't old and worn out, she was young and virginal. Her uterus was empty too. Not because she didn't ovulate regularly but because she had never had sex. But the promise came to her, just as it had come to Sarah and to Eve before her. "You're going to be the one to give birth to a promised Son!" When Mary questioned the angel's prophecy that she would have a child, he proclaimed, ". . . nothing will be impossible with God" (Luke 1:37). Don't miss the import of this! It's the *same message* in nearly identical circumstances: A woman's weakness is insignificant in God's plan. In fact, her weakness seems to be his favorite avenue for blessing.

But does that mean anything?

> *In both the Old Testament and the New Testament,*
> *God's ability to accomplish the impossible*
> *is first spoken in relation to women.*

Yes, one scoffed and the other humbly bowed. But one had known years of betrayal by both her husband and her body, while the other may have found it easier to believe because she was young. Nevertheless, it would be God who would work in and through them to miraculously crush the head of the serpent, against all odds. When they looked at themselves, their own power or ability, or even the strength of their faith, they knew that if God was going to accomplish his plan, he would have to do the impossible. Yes, they both questioned God's ability to work against nature, but then they both believed. "By faith Sarah . . . *considered him faithful who had promised*" (Hebrews 11:11, emphasis added). Then two thousand years later, through the power of the Holy Spirit, Elizabeth announced the same thing about Mary, "Blessed is she who believed that there would be a fulfillment of what was spoken to her from the Lord" (Luke 1:45). Together, both Sarah and Mary believed that the God who could accomplish the impossible would accomplish it through them, through their frail, finite, failing bodies and their faltering faith. The prototypical faithful females under the old and new covenants heard the same thing: *Nothing is impossible for the Lord.*

Not By Might, Nor By Power

When Paul wrote that God chose the weak to shame the strong, of course he was speaking of the weakness of the crucified Son. It is the Son who displayed the glory of God's strength by working through weakness. This is why he saves us through a crucified Messiah. And why he works through woman—and the weakness of her body—to bring about that Messiah. God chose to provide him through the weakness of a woman. In fact, the entire plan of salvation rested on the weakness of a woman's body. God shockingly circumvented the lauded strength and virility of man. This truth provides a counterpoint to the manly-man movement prevalent in some Christian circles today. The kingdom of God isn't established through guys doing tricks on motorcycles or wowing the world with pyrotechnic displays. It's born through weak old women and little virgin girls (and their husbands), people like Sarah and Mary (and their husbands) who believe that God will accomplish his good plan through faith. Are men part of this plan? Of course! But it isn't their strength and masculinity any more than it is a woman's strength and fertility that will accomplish it. The Romans had real military might, and yet God used a naked and bloodied man pinioned on a cross to bring their kingdom to nothing, a man who had grown *in utero* within a young girl's body and who drew sustenance from her breast.

In Old Testament times, women viewed their primary role as building God's kingdom through the birth of the promised One. Their entire identity was intertwined with successfully expanding their husband's importance and property by giving him sons and, hopefully, by giving birth to the promised deliverer. This was nearly the entire measure of their success or failure as a faithful woman. *Now, however, since the Promised Son has come, a woman's identity is no longer contingent upon her giving birth to sons.* Of course, that's not to say that having sons or children isn't a blessed vocation for those called to it. It's just that now, because the Messiah has come, a woman's call is to expand God's kingdom through many different vocations. In the same way that the women of old relied on God's ability to use them, even in their weakness and failure, women today can trust that his kingdom will come and his will will be done through them.

Women, no matter where you find yourself in God's plan, he can use you for his great purposes. Perhaps you're a woman who has known years of heartbreak and betrayal. Perhaps, like Eve, you've lost beloved sons to sickness, accident, or folly. Perhaps your beloved son is in prison, and you wonder where you went wrong or why God has allowed this to happen. Perhaps your husband has proven himself weak like Abraham and has tried (maybe success-fully) to coerce you into sin. Maybe, like Sarah, you've coerced your husband into sin, so that you could begin to see the fulfillment of your version of God's promise. Maybe you've had to tell yourself too many times that God is faithful while you suspect that your faith isn't strong enough and you live under what seems to be the Lord's omnipresent frown.

Perhaps you're a woman whose reputation has been ruined (like Mary), or you've known the pain of a sword piercing your soul through mistreatment by people who said they were Christians. Perhaps you've plodded on year after year trying to love a man who is cold and distant or demanding and violent, only to discover that he's never been faithful to you after all. Perhaps the ticking of your biological clock has gotten far too loud and every false sermon you've ever heard about it being God's primary (only?) plan to use you as a wife and mother screams in your conscience of failure and uselessness. My sisters, the true-life stories of Eve, Sarah, and Mary need to speak to you. When all seems completely lost, when the worst you've feared has come to pass, stand on in faith. The Lord sees you and loves you. He wants you to know he's speaking to you and listening to you.

78

My sisters, maybe you have believed that your value to the Lord rested on a relationship to a man. I (Elyse) admit that I've thought that too. In part, because I didn't have a relationship with my father while I was growing up, I wrongly assumed that a relationship with a man would give me value and security. That lie bore all kinds of sinful fruit in my life and eventuated in brokenness and devastation. I wish I could say that I'm now completely free from this deception. As much as I believe that I am beloved, welcomed, and cherished by both the Lord Jesus and my dear husband, Phil, sometimes I still long for the acceptance and approval of other men. I have repented but still sometimes find myself believing that God can only use me as I'm tied to some guy. The lie that the Lord prefers men and only uses women when they're tied to successful men needs to be snuffed out in my life. Is it the same with you?

My brothers, please hear the heart of the women you're called to serve. None of us is perfect. Most of us are far more aware of our failures than you can ever know. We're just like you. We start out life believing that the Lord will use us to incarnate Jesus to the families we're hoping for, and then we end up hiding behind a tent flap scoffing at God's promises. Please don't assume that God rarely uses us or that he only uses those of us who are (1) "smokin' hot"; (2) filled with faith; (3) gently submissive; (4) quiet; or (5) without a strong opinion. Please don't assume that the Lord only uses women as a judgment because men won't step up. Consider that maybe he's using us because that's been his plan from the beginning and he loves using women, especially those who don't quite fit the mold. Please don't assume that every woman who wants to be a part of spreading God's message is looking to take your ministry job. Please don't think that if a woman is friendly and wants to engage you in conversation, it's because she's hoping for a sexual relationship. The vast majority of women I know really don't want to bed you. Are there some women who do? Possibly. But they are not the majority. Most of the women in your church are more like Martha (hustling to serve lunch) or Mary (hoping to learn) than Potiphar's wife, scheming for a lover. What they would like is to have a meaningful conversation with you about things that matter, such as theology. They are hurt and insulted when you refuse to speak to them because they are women or when you automatically assume that they have some hidden motive. Pastors, you denigrate your sisters when you refuse to take into account their opinions or joke about bossy women or fear their voices. Just like you, they want to be treated with respect and to know that their opinions and questions matter to those they are seeking to respect in the Lord. They also want to fulfill their created design to be a helper in every area of life.

You would do a lot to minister to the women in your congregation by occasionally quoting the writing of a woman in your sermons (which would necessitate occasionally reading a woman's writing) or by using non-sports illustrations. You might ask women in your church how your sermons strike them or if they believe that you're interested in building up their understanding or primarily seeking to speak to the guys. Do you even know what women (aside from your wife—don't put this pressure on her!) think that you and the elders of the church think of women?

As a pastor, I (Eric) have had a lot to learn in this area and made my share of mistakes—some out of fear, some out of sheer ignorance. I'm making a serious effort to repent of my shortcomings and to better love my sisters in the local church. One thing I've done recently is to initiate conversations with women in the church about how I, personally, can be a better pastor to them (see Appendix 4 for the letter I sent out). The conversations and meetings that followed were helpful to me. They gave women an opportunity to share observations, experiences, and advice. They also showed me that there are a wide variety of preferences and opinions among women in the local church. The loud, confident voice of one woman (or man) doesn't necessarily represent them all.

Pastors, would you consider initiating such conversations with women in your congregations? If not, why not? What would it hurt? Brothers, your Christian sisters love you and want you to succeed. God has called us to work together in a Blessed Alliance.[2] Please let women help you—after all, it's what they've been called to do. Do you believe that even today, even in your ministries, it is not good for you to be without a helper? Why not determine today to identify women in your congregation you will seek for their opinion? Remember, women were the first ones to hear the declaration that for the Lord nothing is impossible. Perhaps their faith and perspective on the veracity of God's promises are just what you need to hear.

Pastors, you might assert that you believe women are ontologically equal with men in bearing God's image, but how is that demonstrated to them in the way you honor and speak about them publicly? What does your platform on Sunday say? Are they treated with equal respect and deference when there are decisions to be made or projects to be undertaken? Do you seek them out and strongly encourage them to do everything biblically open to them? Do you consider how much you would pay a man to do the work you're asking them to volunteer for and then actually pay them? Women have never been ancillary to God's redemptive story. They have never been secondary or an add-on to God's plan of salvation. They were the conduit through whom he brought forth redemption by faith. He's used them time and again to establish his kingdom and to speak of the power of humble faith. In fact, without the courageous faith of nearly anonymous women, we wouldn't know the story of the second most important man in the Old Testament.

God Used Women to Rescue His Deliverer

We're all familiar with the story of Moses, a man God spoke face-to-face with, as a man speaks to his friend (Exodus 33:11). We know about his great act as Israel's deliverer and lawgiver. But how did he get there?

Now a man from the house of Levi went and took as his wife a Levite woman. The woman conceived and bore a son, and when she saw that he was a fine child, she hid him three months. When she could hide him no longer, she took for him a basket made of bulrushes and daubed it with bitumen and pitch. She put the child in it and placed it among the reeds by the river bank. And his sister stood at a distance to know what would be done to him. Now the daughter of Pharaoh came down to bathe at the river, while her young women walked beside the river. She saw the basket among the reeds and sent her servant woman, and she took it. When she opened it, she saw the child, and behold, the baby was crying. She took pity on him and said, "This is one of the Hebrews' children." Then his sister said to Pharaoh's daughter, "Shall I go and call you a nurse from the Hebrew women to nurse the child for you?" And Pharaoh's daughter said to her, "Go." So the girl went and called the child's mother. And Pharaoh's daughter said to her, "Take this child away and nurse him for me, and I will give you your wages." So the woman took the child and nursed him. When the child grew older, she brought him to Pharaoh's daughter, and he became her son. She named him Moses, "Because," she said, "I drew him out of the water."

Exodus 2:1–10

I (Elyse) am sure you're familiar with this story. Baby Moses. Basket. Princess of Egypt. But this time I want you to read those verses and underline all the personal pronouns (for those of you who went to school in Southern California like me, a personal pronoun is *he* or *she*, etc.). I'll wait here. . . . What did you find? Nearly every personal pronoun is feminine. There's the man taking a wife, and there's the son being born, but aside from that, every other action is accomplished by the women. God's chosen deliverer, his personal friend, was rescued through the plan of a mom, her daughter, and a Gentile princess bathing in the Nile.

As familiar as I've been with this story, I don't think I ever noticed (and certainly never heard any sermons) about how the celebrated savior of Israel was saved by the love, cunning, foresight,

because it's not about people its about what God did

righteousness, and faithfulness of women. In fact, the story of Moses' survival actually began earlier, when two Egyptian midwives refused to submit to Pharaoh's edict and then lied about it (Exodus 1:15–21). How did the Lord respond to them? He "dealt well" with them and "gave them families."

Moses undoubtedly is considered the greatest leader of national Israel. Although he struggled with self-confidence and had trouble believing God could use him, he still led millions of people out of Egyptian bondage and slavery, went toe-to-toe with the most powerful man on earth, and ultimately believed that God would use him to bring his nation into the Promised Land. But again, how did he get there? Here are the names of the women we should hold in high esteem for their Blessed Alliance with Moses and the Lord: Shiphrah, Puah, Jochebed, Miriam, the Princess of Egypt, and her servant girl.

Think about the faith of Jochebed, Moses' mother, who hid her beautiful son from those who would feed him to the crocodiles. Think about the tears she shed and the prayers she prayed as she wove those reeds together and covered them with pitch to make him secure. Think about the courage it took for her to send her daughter, Miriam, Moses' big sister, to follow along at a distance. Did she send Miriam because she thought she couldn't stand the sight of her dear baby being devoured or drowning? Think of the faith and cunning of Miriam, who watched as her little brother, a brother she undoubtedly loved, was taken from the river by the princess. How clever and brave she was to step forward and volunteer her mother as the nurse for her beautiful little brother. I'm astonished that I've never heard any sermons about Miriam aside from the time she struggled submitting to her little brother's leadership. Did she sin then (Numbers 12:1ff)? Yes. (Though we might understand her struggle to submit as the big sister who saved this life!) Miriam was no insignificant person. She was named as a prophetess (Exodus 15:20), was a leader of the nation. Perhaps Miriam had heard the promise of a deliverer, too, and hoped that her brother would be the chosen one to free her people—so she risked her life to protect him and lived her life in service to the promise. Was she sinless? No. But she had believed.

And think about the faith and love of Jochebed, who like Hannah, was happy to have the opportunity to feed her son from her body, knowing all the while that soon he would be taken from her. Unlike Hannah, who could see her son, Samuel, as he grew in the temple, Jochebed knew that once she weaned him, he would join Pharaoh's family. Would she ever see him again? Would he depart from the faith of Israel? Would he spend his life oppressing his people and living in luxury? What faith and love drove her day by day as she rejoiced in his growth and wept over it too? How many of her prayers were answered in the mighty man Moses?

This was not the only time that women saved Moses. Consider Zipporah, Moses' wife, and this occurrence:

> At a lodging place on the way [to deliver God's people] the Lord met him [Moses] and sought to put him to death. Then Zipporah took a flint and cut off her son's foreskin and touched Moses' feet with it and said, "Surely you are a bridegroom of blood to me!" So he let him alone.
>
> Exodus 4:24–26

Okay, I admit that's a weird story. Let me see if I can help you a bit with it. The last time we saw Moses, he was being nursed by his mother and raised in Pharoah's court by the princess. You remember that at some point he murdered an Egyptian who was abusing an Israelite and had to flee for his life. Evidently, the early teaching he heard from his mother made him know that the Israelites were his people and that he should identify with them. So, into Midian he fled, marrying Zipporah, the daughter of Jethro, who was a pagan priest. Zipporah bore two sons to Moses, Gershom and Eliezer. Evidently, Moses had told Zipporah about the command to circumcise male Israelites, and while he may have done so with one, he apparently didn't do so with the other. Perhaps Zipporah had resisted this strange ritual that marked God's people, but it's certain that Moses knew about it. The command that the covenant-sign be placed on God's people was something he must have learned from his mother. And it's at this moment that the great deliverer, Moses, is again delivered through the shocking action of another Gentile woman, Zipporah. "Moses' failure to circumcise his son could have led to his death, had it not been for his wife's action. Once again, Moses' life is preserved through the actions of another, this time his wife."[3] I'm pretty sure that whatever Zipporah means when she calls Moses a "bridegroom of blood," it's not a term of endearment. In fact, though she had just saved Moses' life through her decisive action, it's safe to assume she left him at that time, or perhaps he sent her away, and she and her sons returned home. Later on, Jethro would bring them to Moses in the wilderness, reuniting the family.

Let's look again at the list of women who took action, some of it illegal, deceptive, violent, but most of all courageous, so that a great deliverer would emerge to shepherd Israel out of slavery into the Promised Land:

- Shiphrah and Puah: Egyptian midwives tasked with killing babies who are rewarded for disobeying Pharaoh's orders and lying about it;
- Jochebed and Miriam: Jewish mother and sister of Moses who disobeyed the king's edict and acted decisively and wisely, thereby preserving Moses' life and protecting him from certain death;
- The Princess of Egypt, and her servant girl: a woman of great political power (who may have been childless) and her servant girl, who acted compassionately and saved a male baby—countermanding the decree of Pharaoh;
- Zipporah, a Gentile woman who did a better job obeying God than Moses did, circumcised her son and saved Moses' life because God had determined to kill him.

I don't think I'm overstating the case that if it were not for these women who decided to act against cultural roles and rules, none of us would know Moses' name today. They were truly members of the Blessed Alliance with Moses, a man who needed their help more than he could ever express.

No Cookie-Cutter Femininity

My sisters, how many times have you stopped yourself from being a strong help, an *ezer* to a loved one, because you thought it wasn't properly feminine? How "feminine" do you think Zipporah was as she took a flint to her son's foreskin? How many times have you stifled your thoughts or failed to speak up because you thought that if you gave your opinion the men in the room would not lead? How many times have you assumed that if you eschewed leading, you would create a leadership vacuum in your home or church that would automatically draw men into leadership?

The biblical femininity movement may have done some good for women who never had mothers or proper female role models. But in trying to militate against radical feminism, it has gone too far and stopped many women from pursuing their callings and has made others, whose vocation led them outside home and hearth, feel as though they had no worth to the Lord's kingdom. In addition, this movement has occasionally forgotten that the primary roles for women, those of wife and mother frequently lauded in the Old Testament, have been expanded to include many other vocations, all with the goal of expanding God's kingdom. The women who preserved Moses' life were strong women—women who knew what it was to go against the norm and who were willing to lay it all on the line for the sake of those they loved.

My brothers, it might be a good time for you to step back and begin to question how you got to where you are in life: How many women sacrificed, laid it all on the line, gave up everything—including their good reputation—took chances and fought with valor so that you could live the life you have now? Is it right and good to honor fathers? Yes, of course, it is! But it was the woman of valor, the excellent *ezer* that Proverbs extols:

> Her husband . . . praises her: "Many women have done excellently, but you surpass them all." Charm is deceitful, and beauty is vain, but a woman who fears the Lord is to be praised."
>
> Proverbs 31:28–30

Brothers, can you name many women who have done excellently? Do you openly and publicly praise women, not merely those whom you might honor on Mother's Day for having eight children and keeping a clean home, but those who go out day after day and strive to make their world a better place? Do you celebrate the ministry success of women—even when it overshadows your own? Do you think that honoring women or praising them publicly will feminize your congregation and make men feel inferior? Pastors, have you ever preached an entire sermon about women of valor? When you have preached through the life and ministry of Moses, have you ever spent an entire sermon highlighting the ways that God used women to accomplish the deliverance of his people? Have you given the *ezers* in your congregation the freedom and room to be the helpers God has gifted them to be?

One thing that I (Eric) have sought to do in congregations I've pastored—so far as I've had the decision-making authority to do—is to include women to the fullest extent possible. Elyse and I both believe that the Bible limits the office of pastor/elder to men who are called and qualified by the Scripture. While our churches may not have a woman exposit and exhort from the Scripture in the weekly assembly of men and women, a wealth of other avenues are available for sisters to exercise their gifts and for the congregation to see their faces and hear their voices. Here is a small sampling of what I do to include women in our body:

- include women in our worship services
- advocate for women serving as deacons, collecting offerings, distributing Lord's Supper elements
- ask women to pray in public
- invite women to read Scripture in the service
- have women lead liturgical readings
- ask women to write the liturgy, choose songs, and plan services
- have skilled women leading service music and music teams
- encourage women to be included in leadership decisions and planning teams
- ask women for interpretive insights, illustrations, and applications when planning to teach
- look for areas where our language and habits exclude women and change it

Again, I have failed more than I've succeeded. But I hope I'm stumbling forward; I'm grateful for the sisters who are patient with my mistakes and encouraging in my successes.

In the next chapter, we'll take time to look at some of the Old Testament laws, especially those that seem to discriminate against women, but in the meantime, consider the women God used to accomplish his will.

——— DISCOVERING A WOMAN'S WORTH ———

1. Before the birth of Jesus Christ, the promised Deliverer, every woman of faith believed her primary calling

consisted of giving birth to sons, in the hopes that one of them would be the Messiah. How has that belief changed since the coming of the Christ? What does that mean about how women should view their vocations now?

2. We've looked at the lives of ten women in this chapter. Which ones were most meaningful to you? Which have begun to change the way you think about what it means for a woman to be her husband's helper (*ezer*)?

3. We've asked some pretty penetrating questions about your perspective on women and their roles in this chapter. Which ones aggravated you? Which ones convicted you? Which ones did you just ignore?

4. There are numerous other women named in the Old Testament who should have a place in this chapter. Can you think of any? How did they go outside of societal or religious norms to fulfill their call as a helper?

5. Summarize what you've learned in this chapter in four or five sentences.

DIGGING DEEPER

1. Read the story of Hagar from Genesis 16. Why was her life significant? How do you know that God viewed her as worthy?

2. The first song recorded in the Bible is Adam's declaration when receiving Eve from God's hand. The first man we see weeping is Abraham at the loss of Sarah (Genesis 23:1–2). Why do you suppose it is significant that the Bible records

Abraham's grief at the loss of Sarah? Certainly he wasn't the first man who ever cried, so why do you think this is written here?

3. Do we ever mourn the loss of *ezer-helpers* in the church? Do we believe that God's pronouncement that it is "not good" for the man to be alone has any bearing on the church today? Why or why not?

FIVE

The Worth of Women in Israel's Law

Woman, where are they? Has no one condemned you?
John 8:10

Have you ever read anything in the Bible that made you wonder whether Moses (or God) had a problem with women? I (Elyse) will admit that I have. Because we've read the Bible lots of times, we've come across passages that gave us pause. Have you ever felt that way? I admit that it would be easy to read through certain passages and wonder about God's disposition toward women. Does he actually think women have worth? Or are they more like an unfortunately necessary nuisance or the proverbial fly in the ointment? If you already suspect that women are the cause of all the brokenness in the world, then it would be easy to read portions of the Old Testament, especially the parts that contain his laws, and assume that God regrets making them. For instance, there are rules about uncomfortable things like menstrual uncleanness, how only males are called to the priesthood, and one very strange rule about husbands who are jealous of their wives. There are prophecies about whores and warnings about adulteresses. There are even instructions seemingly about how a husband can easily dump his wife. It really does seem that women are being singled out as worthless or even dangerous, and except for that promise to Eve about a deliverer, one might be tempted to wonder if the world that God "so loved" (John 3:16) included only one gender. Do women have worth in God's eyes?

As I'm sure you've already seen, the premise of this book is that God views women as worthy, as an essential part of his plan to redeem people. His salvation plan began before he created the world when he chose women and men to be his dearly beloved children (Ephesians 1:4). He revealed this plan in seed form to Eve (Genesis 3:15) and then, through many centuries, he gradually made himself, his nature, his holiness, and his grace known. God's plan comes to us as both a story and as commands. The stories about God's people, their failures and successes, and the rules about how they are to live are meant to reveal God's plan of salvation through the coming Messiah. Both the stories *and* the laws are necessary to show us who he is, what he's done, and what we need to believe to live for him.

Unclean Women

Under the Mosaic Law, women were considered unclean during their menstrual cycle (see Leviticus 15). What should we make of this?

To begin with, it's important to note that because both women and men were counted ceremonially unclean after a bodily discharge (Leviticus 15:32),[1] this rule isn't only aimed at women. Also, this isn't the only rule about blood. The rules about blood, whether from menstruation or the slaughter of an animal for food, are found throughout the Bible. Why do you think this is? It is because God so highly values life. Blood has great significance to him, as Leviticus 17:11 states, "the life of the flesh is in the blood." Because blood conveys life, it isn't to be treated as trivial. The slogan at my local blood bank, "Give the Gift of Life," makes this point. Because God so highly values life, he doesn't want us thinking that something this important is inconsequential. So this law about uncleanness isn't about a woman's inherent uncleanness *per se*, but rather about the value of all blood and life, yes, even women's.

Further, Israel was taught that blood had value to cleanse from sin. Usually, when the people of Israel sinned, the guilty party had to offer an animal's shed blood for cleansing from guilt. In fact, the connection between blood and the cleansing of sin is something we Christians continue to recognize. We sing, "What can wash away my sin?" and then answer, "nothing but the blood of Jesus." That's because the blood of Jesus still "cleanses us from all sin" (1 John 1:7). Rules about coming in contact with any bodily fluid, including blood, were meant to point us toward the Seed of the woman whose shed blood would make us clean. "In him we have redemption through his blood, the forgiveness of our trespasses, according to the riches of his grace" (Ephesians 1:7). Blood is not trivial, and we shouldn't get used to seeing it.

Also, don't forget that Israel has just come out of Egypt and would soon be surrounded by other violent cultures that didn't value life but relished the sight of blood. These cultures were quite accustomed to seeing blood in corrupt practices as part of their worship,

> Like the other ceremonial regulations, these laws of personal purity regarding genital discharges distinguished Israel from the other nations. Obedience to these laws would particularly work as a deterrent to intermarriage with other peoples who had no desire to subscribe to these sexual dictates . . . these regulations would exclude fertility rites and cultic prostitution (practices characteristic of Israel's neighbors).[2]

So the rules about ceremonial uncleanness of women aren't meant to demean women, their reproductive cycles, or their bodies, but rather to remind us about the sacredness, the uniqueness of all life, women included.

An Unclean Woman Meets Jesus

Now that you have a more positive perspective on this strange law, let's look to see if we can find Jesus' ministry superseding it. To begin with, in Mark 7, Jesus did away with rules about ritual uncleanness by declaring that it is only sin that originates in the heart that can defile a person (Mark 7:20). In Mark 5 we meet a nameless woman who had a discharge of blood for twelve years. We don't know how old she was or if she was married or single. All we know is that she had "suffered much under many physicians, and had spent all that she had, and was no better but rather grew worse" (Mark 5:25–26). This woman had been condemned to a life of shame and censure. Everyone knew she was unclean, everyone avoided her. Blood was sacred and set apart for holy use, but her issue made it common and disgusting.

Have you ever had to spend time in bed, quarantined from friends and family? I know that the few times I've had to, the time seemed to drag by interminably. There aren't a lot of punishments worse than solitary confinement, but that's what this poor woman's existence had been like for a dozen years. Let's think for a moment now about her life: She had tried desperately to get well. She had exhausted whatever resources she had and undoubtedly endured the worst kinds of pain and humiliation at the hands of the ancient medical practitioners.

Aside from whatever physical pain she may have suffered, she deeply longed to think of herself as normal, not someone people turned away from in disgust. *Unclean, shameful, destitute, alone.* She undoubtedly wondered why God was punishing her like that— or maybe she thought she knew. Because she was ceremonially unclean, she hadn't felt a touch, a hug, a kiss for twelve years, nor had she been allowed into the temple. She couldn't enter into worship, even to offer a sacrifice, or to try to get back in good standing with the Lord. She was completely out of options. But then she had heard reports about a rabbi who welcomed unclean women, so she gathered up her courage and, in one extreme act of faith, snuck up behind him. She touched him. And then . . . she was well. She knew her touch should have made him unclean, but she was willing to risk his ire. *What would all the holy men (and women) say to her if she were discovered? What censure and shame would be heaped on her because of this audacious act?* She was willing to face it all. She was that desperate.

If you want to know what God's heart toward women who are ceremonially unclean is, here it is: Not only did Jesus not turn her away or censor her for touching him, he did more than heal her body. *He made her clean.* He forced her to come to him out of the shadow of her shame and admit her scheme and desperate need of him. How did he respond? He called her "Daughter." Don't miss the importance of this: She's the only one he ever referred to in this way. This beautiful term of affection, *my dear daughter,*[3] must have amazed and melted her heart. She was finally healed, but more than that, she was clean, she was welcomed, she was made new. "She came as an outcast of men, Christ called her daughter."[4] She would have settled for his merely being her healer—a better physician than she had ever known. And he would be that for her, but so much more: He wanted her to know his love.

Please notice that this woman went outside the bounds of societal decorum by touching a man, especially in her unclean state. But she didn't ask for permission. She certainly knew that she was doing something that would have caused revulsion and censure. And yet, by faith she persevered. And she was rewarded for it. It was almost as though she stole her healing and Jesus was not only okay with that, he honored it.

Women, what does this tell us? It tells us that Jesus welcomes audacious faith. It tells us that we can presume upon his love and press into his goodness without fear of his censure. It tells us that he's comfortable around us—even those of us the world or the church looks at as unworthy or unclean. Women, come to him in faith. You are welcomed.

Brothers, what do you learn from this? You can know that you are welcomed by the Lord too. He isn't put off by your uncleanness or reputation for failure. Jesus never worried about being made unclean by us because he's got enough holiness to cleanse us all. So flee to him and encourage the women you know to join hands with you and run to him. Don't push them away.

Faithless Husbands and the God Who Protects Wives

By the time Moses delivered God's laws to the Israelites, divorce was already so commonplace that rules had to be made to regulate husbands' behavior toward their wives and to curb their abuse of power. In order to stop men from glibly divorcing their wives, this law was given:

> When a man takes a wife and marries her, if then she finds no favor in his eyes because he has found some indecency in her, and he writes her a certificate of divorce and puts it in her hand and sends her out of his house, and she departs out of his house, and if she goes and becomes another man's wife, and the latter man hates her and writes her a certificate of divorce and puts it in her hand and sends her out of his house, or if the latter man dies, who took her to be his wife, then her former husband, who sent her away, may not take her again to be his wife, after she has been defiled, for that is an abomination before the Lord.
>
> Deuteronomy 24:1–4

This rule was meant to govern and rein in the abuse of power that was commonplace in Israel. Husbands had the power to divorce their wives and they did so regularly. Now, we understand how you might read this and assume that it denigrates women, that it strips them of rights and treats them as chattel. Actually, the opposite is true. Because the structure of that society was weighted so heavily in a man's favor, with only men being able to initiate a divorce, the Lord gave Moses this rule to protect women. "The certificate of divorce protected the woman's rights, providing evidence of her freedom and ensuring that her husband could not claim her dowry."[5] In addition, we should remember that the stories and practices we read about in the Bible are not necessarily to be copied but rather a description of the ways things actually were in a broken world.

It is true that this law allowed a husband to divorce his wife for a seemingly insignificant reason, such as finding something "indecent" in her. No one knows what this "indecency" might have been. The Hebrew just means some sort of shame or nakedness. This, of course, is a very low bar that any man might claim, but still, it is not nothing. The purpose of this law was to stop husbands from just sending their wives away willy-nilly, or slandering them by saying they had deserted the family. The husband had to actually give his wife a legal document, a "certificate of divorce," which would free her to marry someone else. It would also stop him from sending her away and then changing his mind and making her return over and over again. It would stop him from threatening her with desertion or just throwing her out on the street. If he was going to end the marriage, he'd have to write it out for everyone to see. This law was meant to protect women in a patriarchal society bent by sin and the abuse of power, in which they had very few rights. It was meant to give them legal rights in the marriage.

Jesus and Divorce

Knowing what you do about Jesus and his treatment of women, what do you think he thought of this law? Do you suppose he would think it was acceptable to just send one's wife away, exposing her to shame and destitution, if her husband found her displeasing? When you're considering this, don't forget that Jesus knew divorce was something his mother, Mary, would have faced,[6] had an angel not intervened.

Jesus said that Moses had been forced to give this law because of the inherent hardness, stubbornness, and obstinance[7] of men's hearts. In other words, rather than this rule giving a carte blanche for men to divorce their wives at will, it was a form of judgment on husbands who were already mistreating their wives by divorcing them: "Because of your hardness of heart Moses allowed you to divorce your wives, but from the beginning it was not so" (Matthew 19:8). In the beginning, Adam would have loved, clung to, and protected his wife. But now that men's hearts were hardened toward their wives, God had to protect them from those who should have protected them.

That this kind of protection of marriage, and by extension, women, was out of the ordinary is shown by the disciples' nearly laughable response, "If such is the case of a man with his wife, it is better not to marry" (Matthew 19:10). In other words, they were so accustomed to husbands holding all the power in the marriage relationship that they could not fathom a scenario in which marriage was permanent and they would not be able to jettison any woman they found "displeasing." If divorce and remarriage (except in certain circumstances) caused one to commit adultery, then their practice of acquiring and discarding wives at will would have to end. In their upside-down patriarchal world that was a shocking thought. *Maybe we should stay single, then*, they thought.

These rules about divorce were meant to protect and honor women. Neither Moses nor Jesus was encouraging men to misuse, abandon, or divorce their wives. They were stopping men who cavalierly used women up and then jettisoned them. The modern practice of trading in your old wife for a new "trophy wife" shows us that this practice didn't end in the ancient times. Some husbands are still stubborn, obstinate, and hard-hearted and need to be called to repentance.

Jealous Husbands

Another strange ceremonial law is found in Numbers 5, where instructions are given to a husband who suspects his wife of infidelity but has no proof. In that case, the husband was instructed to bring his wife to the priest along with something called a "grain offering of jealousy." The wife would then take an oath of innocence before the priest and drink water containing ink from the words of the curse and dirt from the floor of the tabernacle. If she was innocent, nothing would happen to her, but if she was guilty she would suffer. This was kind of like the first lie detector test and, yes, it really does seem strange.

How does this bizarre law prove that God loves and values women? It proves it because, like the certificate of divorce, it forced a man to actually take action and make a statement rather than just privately accuse or badger his wife. It also forced him to bring his suspicions to the Lord, and not merely badmouth her to his friends. And most important, it forced him to leave her judgment in the hands of God. The Lord knew her heart and her actions and also knew the husband's heart. If the woman was innocent, she could rely on the Lord to be a righteous and gracious judge and protect her honor. And if she was guilty, she could throw herself on God's mercy and grace. But what wouldn't happen to her was being left in limbo, under a cloud of suspicion.

Jesus and a Guilty Adulteress

What did Jesus think of women who were accused of adultery? Let's observe his interaction with one who wasn't just suspected or accused. In John 8 we read the story of a guilty woman who is brought to Jesus for judgment and execution. How would the Lord respond to the Pharisees' desire to stone her?[8] How would Jesus, the only holy Man who had never committed adultery in either thought or deed, respond? Strangely, he responded by writing in the dirt. What did he write? Perhaps he was writing the Ten

Commandments, perhaps he named the accusers' adulteries—we just don't know. We do know that once he said, "Let him who is without sin among you be the first to throw a stone at her" (John 8:7), the men read his words and went away. Then,

> Jesus was left alone with the woman standing before him. Jesus stood up and said to her, "Woman, where are they? Has no one condemned you?" She said, "No one, Lord." And Jesus said, "Neither do I condemn you; go, and from now on sin no more."
>
> John 8:9–11

What does Jesus say to women who have either been condemned by their own actions or the accusations of others? Remember, the only One who has the right to condemn anyone for infidelity is the One who promised, "Neither do I condemn you."

My sisters, Jesus never brings a word of condemnation to you, no matter if others have. You can come to him in humility and need, admit to him your brokenness, and he will never cast you out or shame you.

Let's notice how the religious elite, the leading men of the day, had twisted this law to fit their chauvinism. They said that it was just women, not women *and* men, who should be punished: "Now in the Law, Moses commanded us to stone such women" (John 8:5). Of course, Jesus knew what the Law actually did say, that both men *and* women should be punished (Deuteronomy 22:22). These self-righteous Pharisees condemned themselves when they said that the couple was actually "caught in the act," meaning that they knew who the man was also. But they seemed to have been perfectly content to let the man off while they called for the execution of the woman. How did Jesus respond? "Neither do I condemn you." He refused to let sinful men condemn a sinful woman. Jesus refused to join in their law-twisting misogyny.

Sadly, this is one of the ways misogyny shows itself in the church today. Not that women are being stoned for adultery, but that women are frequently disciplined in ways that men avoid. Rules about mutual love and submission are regularly twisted to fall primarily on women. For instance, I (Elyse) personally know of numbers of circumstances in which a wife came to elders for help with an abusive husband, only to have the elders end up disciplining her for not being submissive enough. I know of a woman whose husband was addicted to pornography and who was blamed by the elders she went to for help because she wasn't sexy enough. I know of women whose husbands cheat on their taxes and refuse to let them see the finances and who have been told to just pray for them and seek to win them in quiet submission. I know of other women who are married to closet alcoholics, who insist that they not tell anyone because that would be being disobedient. Who, when they finally did tell the elders, they were told to stay in the relationship and try to make their husband happy, and not make waves.

Suffice it to say that we shouldn't confuse the way that men applied the Law with God's purpose in giving the Law, which was to uphold holiness, protect women, men, and the family, and demonstrate God's character. For instance, if a man knew that he would face execution if he tried to seduce someone else's wife, he would probably think more carefully about it. If King David knew that he likely would have been stoned for raping Bathsheba, maybe he would not have done so.[9] We might also wonder how many men and women have been ruined by a man's cavalier belief that he is free to do whatever he likes without fear of punishment, while the women who are their prey frequently suffer the shame of unplanned pregnancy, the devastation of abortion, or the burden of caring for a child alone.

Even in the church today, how many men have wounded their wives with their adulterous pornography habits, without much fear of being disciplined? Cases where a man's adultery with pornography was excused because his wife wasn't as slim as he wanted or wasn't as sexually available as he liked are common. Women suffer as they are denigrated by their husband and secondarily by their pastor who should be shepherding them.

Jesus continues to stand against this hateful twisting of God's good laws meant to protect both women and men.

The Male Priesthood

Let's take time now to look at one more instance of seeming misogyny in the Law. The Old Testament is clear that it is only sons of a particular family, Levi, who were to serve in the priesthood (Exodus 28; Numbers 3, 18). Although women were called as leaders (Micah 6:4; Judges 4:4), prophetesses (2 Kings 22:14; Exodus 15:20; Judges 4:4), and wise counselors (2 Samuel 20:16; 14:2), the priesthood was only bestowed upon the sons of Levi. Only men allowed.

While that seems unfair to women, let's not forget that God's choice of a certain family might seem unfair to the majority of men as well. No one who was outside the family of Aaron and Levi would be able to serve as a priest either. Let's face it: God's sovereignty in choosing certain people and passing over others doesn't make sense in our democratic minds. We think that anyone who wants to have a certain vocation should be able to have it. We tell our children, "You can be anything you want to be." But God's kingdom isn't like that. It isn't a democracy; it's a theocracy. That means that he has the right to choose those who may serve him as priests. Of course, that didn't mean that other men and women were barred from loving and serving him or that they couldn't be part of his family. They just weren't tasked with the work of the priesthood, which primarily consisted of caring for and transporting objects of worship.

Our Great High Priest

Why were men from a certain family chosen for the priesthood? As we consider this question it is helpful to remember that the point of all the history and Law throughout the Bible is the promised Son, Jesus Christ, the Messiah. Because he said that Moses wrote about him (John 5:38, 46), we can assume that the composition of the priesthood tells us about him, and it does. Jesus is the chosen Son (Luke 9:35). He didn't seize this calling for himself, rather it was given by his Father sovereignly (John 5:37; Hebrews 7:21).

But here's where our study gets really interesting. In the same way that we've seen Jesus recast the law concerning unclean or immoral women, demonstrating his superiority to the written code, he didn't just enhance this rule, he completely refashioned it. This decree had restricted the priesthood to the sons of Levi. But Jesus wasn't a Levite. He was from the tribe of Judah. Certainly, if it were the plan to keep this rule in play, it would have been easy for God to have sent his Son as part of the tribe of Levi, but that wasn't his plan. And there's a reason for that: Jesus' Judaic ancestry is meant to show that the former Levitical priesthood and the Mosaic Law itself were being set aside because of their "weakness and uselessness" (Hebrews 7:18). All of the rules about priests only coming from a certain family were being superseded. Jesus was a different kind of priest, one who was inaugurating and guaranteeing a "better covenant," a new and better law (Hebrews 7:22). Jesus came to fulfill all the Law, even the one calling chosen males to service (Matthew 5:17). Jesus is the embodiment of every facet of the better priesthood: He offers himself as the sacrifice, lives a perfect life, bestows cleansing and righteousness on his people, while at the same time interceding with the Father on our behalf. This better covenant is now open to everyone, both women and men, as all believers, male and female, are now members of the "chosen race" the "royal priesthood" (1 Peter 2:9).

The End of the Law

What that means is that all of those laws about food and drink, festivals or Sabbaths, only Levites being called to serve God, are no longer in effect (See Colossians 2:16). These laws were just "a shadow of the things to come" (Colossians 2:17) and "pointed to a future reality that was fulfilled in the Lord Jesus Christ."[10]

The Mosaic Law continually reminded the people of their sin but offered no lasting cleansing. Even if you tried really hard to please God and avoid anything that would make you unclean, you would eventually fail—your body would betray you. No matter how careful you were to eat in a certain way or celebrate yearly feasts, no one was able to do so flawlessly. Sacrifices and offerings to cover sin had to be offered over and over, and yet the people were never free of guilt because just as soon as one offering had been made, another would be necessary. All Christians, both women and men, can rejoice that they are no longer under the Mosaic covenant. Indeed, we have something so much better. We have been given perfection, and all without our law-keeping.

> For since the law has but a shadow of the good things to come instead of the true form of these realities, it can never, by the same sacrifices that are continually offered every year, make perfect those who draw near. . . . For by a single offering he has perfected for all time those who are being sanctified.
>
> Hebrews 10:1, 14

Christians are now freed from the law as a way to appease or earn merit from God. We are completely forgiven and counted completely righteous because of the perfect law-keeping and substitutionary death of Jesus. That truth applies to both women and men. In the same way that we have been equally created in God's image, we are now equally saved, forgiven, and adopted into his family. This is great news. We are brothers and sisters equal in his sight, heirs with one another of the "grace of life" (1 Peter 3:7).

Sisters, I hope that you've learned now how to read the Old Testament in light of what Jesus has done. The rules there are not meant to confuse or condemn you. Rather, they are there to help you see what Jesus has done for you. They are there to help you see how beloved and protected you are and how, like a strong older brother, Jesus protected women from every form of misogyny. He is the True Israelite, the One who fulfilled all that the Law called God's people to be. Yes, he calls us to live lives in dedicated service to him, but he also understands our weaknesses and sin. You can rejoice in him and trust his love.

My brothers, I trust that you've come to see how Jesus cared for women in his day—women who were powerless and in need of protection. Jesus grew up under the Law, learned the Law, embodied the Law and that means that he protected and cared for women (as the Law did). The ultimate evidence that the Law was not misogynistic is the fact that Jesus, who fulfilled the Law, was no misogynist. I hope that you have seen how he comforted an unclean and an immoral woman, and how he didn't automatically support the religious leaders in their quest to twist the Law and shame a woman. And I hope that you have seen how the ministry of our faithful High Priest has abrogated all the Mosaic Law and thrown the doors open for women to serve alongside you in the proclamation of this great Good News. How might you respond?

———— DISCOVERING A WOMAN'S WORTH ————

1. Have you ever felt confused or uncomfortable with the Mosaic Law? If so, how?

2. What does the story of the woman with a bleeding disorder teach you? How did Jesus uphold the Law while showing us its true purpose?

3. What does the law on jealousy teach you about God? Can you see how this is actually a positive?

4. What does the story of the adulterous woman teach you? How did Jesus uphold the Law while showing us its true purpose?

5. How does Jesus' genealogy teach us about the better covenant God has made with us? How is that good news?

6. Summarize what you have learned in this chapter in three or four sentences.

DIGGING DEEPER

1. Read Leviticus 27:3–4. Does this strike you as denigrating to a woman's worth? Why or why not?

2. Read Exodus 21:7–11. Explain how this law actually protects women.

3. Read Deuteronomy 24:1–4. How do these laws about divorce protect women?

4. Read Ezekiel 16. Although this is a chapter about an adulterous woman, how should we read it today? Was it actually aimed at casting aspersions on women in general? Who was it aimed at?

SIX

The Worth of Women in Israel's Worship

And Miriam sang to them:
"Sing to the Lord, for he has triumphed gloriously;
the horse and his rider he has thrown into the sea."

Exodus 15:21

Ah. At last. My (Elyse's) favorite time in the worship service. Time for the bread and the wine. The pastor broke the bread and poured the wine and reminded us that because Jesus' body and blood were broken and poured out for us, we were welcomed at his table. The song leader began playing Sandra McCracken's hymn, "We Will Feast in the House of Zion,"[1] and I started to weep. "This is his body broken for you." Take the cup. Go back to your seat and wait while everyone is served. I watched as the young, tatted, and broken congregation filed up to receive this best of all gifts and I couldn't control my joy. *Yes, I too will feast at the House of Zion. I will sing with my heart restored. "He has done great things. . . . We will sing and weep no more."* I'm his. I'm theirs. He's mine.

There have been many times over the nearly five decades that I've been a Christian that I've been overwhelmed by Christ's nearness and love. I frequently lift my hands in worship—because I can't fly around the room . . . *yet*. I know what it is to rejoice and to be shocked at the truth that I'm invited to *that* table, where I'll feast with sisters and brothers—and One Brother in particular—forever! I know what it is to dance (at least in my heart) because he's delivered me from my soul's enemies. I'll bet you do too.

For millennia, women have been rejoicing at the goodness of God. We're not the first ones and we won't be the last. In the new earth, we will spend forever dancing and singing for joy. Yes, we will sing, and weep no more! Imagine that! We are safe. Our deliverance has been accomplished. It's done!

The Worshiping Women

But life was different for the Israelites in Egypt. It had been centuries since they had known a day without master or whip. They had experienced decades of want, pain, and despair. They were slaves who had watched as their infant sons were devoured by crocodiles. They had felt the flesh-mutilating lash of their harsh masters. Deliverance was a pipe dream. Nothing ever changed. The promise of a deliverer still wasn't fulfilled. Slaves they were born. Slaves they would die. There was no hope. God had forgotten them, it seemed. Their cries for help went nowhere. They were alone.

Then, after 400 years of silence, a deliverer finally arrived proclaiming that God had heard them. They would be safe. They would be free. They followed Moses as he led them out into their new life. But then they were backed up against the Red Sea. What had seemed like answered prayer started to look more like a cruel trick. Had their hope been in vain? Had God forgotten them again? Would they despair forever? After a terrifying night caught between their enemy and the sea, a way of escape was opened and "the people of Israel walked on dry ground through the sea, the waters being a wall to them on their right hand and on their left" (Exodus 14:29). The water, the very source of their terror, became subservient to their deliverance. They had been remembered after all.

And from the shore they watched with incredulous joy as their Savior delivered them and annihilated their enemy (Jude 1:5). As the bodies of the Egyptians washed up at their feet, the women could no longer control their emotion. After all, they had sobbed for their lost sons and their husbands' wounds every night. Their dark days had turned into years as whole generations of women prayed and prayed for fulfillment of the promise and now, finally, the Lord had answered them. God had heard their cries for help (Exodus 3:7–9). They were free! The tables were turned! Their enemy lay dead at their feet! In response, Moses led all the people in a song of praise,

> I will sing to the Lord, for he has triumphed gloriously;
>   the horse and the rider he has thrown in the sea.
> The Lord is my strength and my song,
>   and he has become my salvation;
> this is my God, and I will praise him. . . .
> The Lord is a man of war;
>   the Lord is his name.
>
> Exodus 15:1–3

And then, in great joy and overwhelming gratitude, Miriam picked up a tambourine and started to dance. And,

> All the women went out after her with tambourines and dancing. And Miriam sang to them:
>   "Sing to the Lord, for he has triumphed gloriously;
>   the horse and his rider he has thrown into the sea."
>
> Exodus 15:20–21

Miriam, a woman who had shepherded her baby brother down the Nile, lost him to Pharaoh's court and the wilderness, and had stood by while her parents and all whom she loved broke under the brutal rule of the Egyptians, did something that we have no record of before this time. She was so overjoyed, she couldn't stand still. Moses' song was good, but singing, even joyful singing couldn't capture her exuberance. So she led her newly freed sisters in a dance. Of course she did. Who could stand still and merely sing piously at a time like this? God hadn't forgotten them! The deliverer had come! They were finally free!

This is the first dance of worship in the Bible.

And it was led by a woman.

Are you surprised by Miriam's display of joy and gratitude? I'm not. Over the years, I've watched women declare devotion and love through more than softly spoken words because words simply weren't sufficient. I've seen them weep for joy as they sang words of praise. Other times they have lifted their hands and sung boldly with all their hearts. We read of other women who anointed the One they loved with kisses and perfume (Matthew 26:6–13; John 12:1–3; Luke 7:36–38). Perhaps because they feel their devotion so keenly or maybe because they are not trying to prove that they're in control (and not emotional), women in both the Old and the New Testament are known for extravagant acts of worship. Hannah for one.

A Woman Who Excelled in Prayer and Song

First Samuel opens with the well-known story of Hannah. Like other women we've talked about, Hannah's identity was wrapped up in her ability to give birth to the promised son. And like Sarah before her, she'd failed. Of course, she also longed to bear sons who would carry on her husband's name and thereby ensure the family's inheritance. So in light of the family's need, Hannah's husband, Elkanah, had taken another wife. Elkanah's unlawful,[2] though pragmatic, marriage to Peninnah wasn't meant to hurt her, although every time she saw one of Peninnah's children playing on her husband's knee, she was deeply wounded. No, Elkanah did love her, even though he idiotically overestimated the value of his love and underestimated her devastation (1 Samuel 1:8). Peninnah was able to give birth to many children, and if that wasn't enough to crush Hannah's heart, she loved to rub Hannah's face in it (vv. 6–7). Perhaps Peninnah mourned her loveless marriage and lashed out at Hannah because of it. In any case, Hannah's heart was broken, but still she persevered on in faith.

On their yearly trip to worship in Shiloh, we get to see Hannah's heart of worship. Unlike the priests who ministered there, Hannah had come to give herself wholly to prayer and willing sacrifice. Eli, the head priest at the time, had turned the service of the temple over to his two debased, gluttonous, and drunkard sons, who sexually molested the women who had come to serve at the gates of God's house. The Bible calls them "worthless men" who "did not know the Lord" (1 Samuel 2:12). Into this cesspool of externally religious immorality, a broken and barren woman of faith came. Hannah was

> deeply distressed and prayed to the Lord and wept bitterly. And she vowed a vow and said, "O Lord of hosts, if you will indeed look on the affliction of your servant and remember me and not forget your servant, but will give to your servant a son, then I will give him to the Lord all the days of his life."
>
> 1 Samuel 1:10–11

As an aside, it's important to note that Hannah's addressing God as the "Lord of hosts" (1:11) is the "first time this particular title is found in a prayer in Scripture."[3] In doing so, she's indicating her trust in the power and dominion of God over every created force.

Hannah's pious prayer was observed and misinterpreted by Eli, who saw her mouth moving but didn't hear her words. He assumed that she was drunk and rebuked her. But unlike his sons, she wasn't drunk.

> Hannah answered, "No, my lord, I am a woman troubled in spirit. I have drunk neither wine nor strong drink, but I have been pouring out my soul before the Lord. Do not regard your servant as a worthless woman [like his sons], for all along I have been speaking out of my great anxiety and vexation."
>
> 1 Samuel 1:15–16

Hannah's devotion stands in stark contrast to Eli's failure. He refused to rebuke his sons and honored them above the Lord, seeking rather to please them and keep their good will. Hannah, out of her brokenness and devastation, was willing to give up the very thing that she most desired out of a love for and trust in God. Hannah's prayer was answered and, "the Lord remembered her. And in due time Hannah conceived and bore a son, and she called his name Samuel" (1 Samuel 1:19–20) whose name means "heard of God."[4] God heard this worthy woman's prayer. He hears our prayer, too.

Hannah's Song

Hannah not only shines as an example of prayer in a time of religious darkness, her song is a beautiful example of a woman's calling to worship God for his kindness in exalting both her and his kingdom. Like Mary's song of rejoicing at the conception of her Messiah (Luke 1:46–55), Hannah worships the "God who reverses human fortunes by his mighty power . . . who protects the faithful."[5] And along with David's prayer, which together bookend First and Second Samuel, Hannah's lyric of praise rejoices in God for his holiness, faithfulness, protection, and strength. Hannah is definitely rejoicing in the answer to her prayer and the lifting of her shame, but she's also demonstrating deep theological acumen and gifting as a writer of divine poetry. She uses the answer to her personal prayer to "rejoice in the triumph of God for all his people."[6] And her song was inscripturated for both men and women to read and learn from. As Jerram Barrs writes, "There is no notice at the head of the song: 'For women and children only.'"[7] Women should feel encouraged to use all of God's kindnesses to us as spurs to both public and private worship.

Brothers, are you asking the Lord to help the women in your care to express their faith in the Lord and the songs he's given them publicly? May it never be said that any pastor or elder would denigrate a woman's song or testimony, when offered in faith. Do you make a place for women to pray publicly?

Deborah's Song

Like Miriam before her, the prophetess Deborah led Barak and probably other warriors in a post-war song of deliverance (see Judges 5). "So may all your enemies, perish, O Lord!" she sang, "But your friends be like the sun as he rises in his might" (Judges 5:31). Deborah knew that Jehovah was her mighty friend, so she sang. That Deborah led this time of worship is shown by the fact that the Hebrew word for "sang" here is a "feminine singular form."[8] That means the song was hers, and that Barak (and probably other warriors) just joined it. She is the first person to employ prophetic language about the stars fighting for Israel. Deborah led this time of worship because she could not restrain her joy and relief at her nation's deliverance. The Bible doesn't say that Deborah danced, like Miriam, but I wouldn't be surprised if she did. Would you? Singing and dancing before the Lord is part of Jeremiah's prophesied response to God's salvation,

> For the Lord has ransomed Jacob
> and has redeemed him from hands too strong for him.

They shall come and sing aloud on the height of Zion,
    and they shall be radiant over the goodness of the Lord
        . . .
their life shall be like a watered garden,
    and they shall languish no more.
Then shall the young women rejoice in the dance,
    and the young men and the old shall be merry.

Jeremiah 31:11–13, emphasis added

Women Have Always Worshiped

It would be easy to read the Bible, especially the Old Testament and miss the impact women had in the worship life of God's chosen people. Have you ever had such good news that it made you jump up and down for joy? Have you ever just broken out in song because the event you've been hoping for finally happened, or deliverance was yours at last? I have. I've had times of worship when I was so overwhelmed by some precious truth or the nearness of the Lord that I've lifted my hands and wept for joy. I've heard the same thing from women who worship their Lord on the way to work—some of them to a job they love, others to one that wasn't their choice. And yet, he is there with them, stuck in traffic, stuck in mundanity or purpose, consigned to a life that may be something different than the one they dreamed about as a young girl or the very thing they've always dreamed of.

I've talked with sisters who show up faithfully at school every day, teaching and learning and praying in between classes that their hearts would be freed and fed by the One who loves them, while they plod on in faith, trusting that the Lord is guiding them in this too. And I've heard from women who wept for joy as the Lord met them in the chemotherapy clinic—as poison was being pumped into their bloodstream while life was being imparted to them through his Spirit and the songs they sang in faith. I've stood with widows who were finding that the Lord really was their Husband and other single women who longed to serve him in their

114

calling and were finding the intimacy they longed for in him. All of them knew times of extravagant worship, whether they knew the deliverance they longed for or not. All of their hearts poured out words of gratitude and trust. Sometimes in vocations at home with babies. Many times on the subway or in the airline seat while they tried to find the Lord in their craziness. And sometimes they danced.

Women have been worshiping and will worship into eternity. And of course, a woman's song will be heard in the New Earth as the church, *the bride*, gives voice to the salvation that's finally hers (Revelation 7:9–10). No one will censure her then. No one will chide her for her extravagant devotion (John 12:5). No one will say, "Calm down, ladies. You need to be more respectful. God's not interested in your emotional responses." In fact, as I've perused the Bible looking at women and their worship, I haven't found any place where women were scolded by the Lord for emotional responses to his grace. No, they were always invited in, always encouraged, always welcomed. I have heard words of censure, but never spoken by the Lord. Never a, "Tsk, tsk, ladies. Calm down and be more respectful."

Worshiping through the Psalms

The Psalms are the hymnal of God's people. They are a collection of prayers, laments, and songs written by men but spoken and sung by women and men. Even during Old Testament times, both genders were welcomed as those who proclaimed in song, percussion, and dance God's great deliverance. They were worshipers.

> The Lord gave the command;
> a great company of *women* brought the good news:
> "The kings of the armies flee—they flee!" . . .
> People have seen your procession, God,
> the procession of my God,
> my King, in the sanctuary.

Singers lead the way,
with musicians following;
among them are young *women*
playing tambourines.
Bless God in the assemblies;
bless the Lord from the fountain of Israel.

Psalm 68:11–12, 24–26 CSB,
emphasis added

Maybe you're a woman who loves to play drums or loves to dance or loves to write lyrics and music. I have a good friend who has taught and taken dance classes her whole life. She feels God's pleasure when she's moving her body and she uses dance as a way to worship. Perhaps your church frowns upon all forms of demonstrative worship, but don't let that stop you. Crank up the praise music in the car or at home and move your body in joyful celebration. It's okay. Play your tambourine or clap your hands or leap for joy. If it's an offering to him, he loves it.

Even though they weren't part of the official priesthood in the Old Testament, women were known for worship and service in the temple. Exodus 38:8 and 1 Samuel 2:22 speak of women who ministered or served at the entrance of both the tent and temple. What did these women do? The Hebrew word translated "served" is used in other places to refer to the work of the Levites. This practice was carried into New Testament times, where we find a servant girl on guard at the door when Jesus is being questioned (John 18:16). We shouldn't be surprised by this—after all, both Eve and Adam were tasked with guarding and protecting the Garden. Why would guarding the temple be any different?

Although we can assume that their serving and ministry included caring for the physical needs of the buildings, we know that isn't all they did. Many women gave financially to the work. Exodus tells us that they donated their mirrors for the construction of the bronze basin in the tabernacle where they served. Women have always been involved in giving to the church. In fact, when Moses gave the command for the people to contribute to the congregation in the wilderness,

> So they came, both men and *women*. All who were of a willing
> heart. . . . All the men and *women*, the people of Israel, whose
> heart moved them to bring anything for the work that the Lord
> had commanded by Moses to be done brought it as a freewill of-
> fering to the Lord.
>
> Exodus 35:22, 29, emphasis added

In fact, their offerings so exceeded the need that Moses had to
restrain the people from giving. God had miraculously delivered
them. They responded by generously giving. Both women and
men did this in worship. Whether you have access to great sums of
money or just a widow's mite, your gifts are seen and welcomed
by the Lord. I have a friend who has inherited significant wealth.
She's used most of it in the Lord's work and has a beautiful lodge
she opens for people who need respite. Whether it's a donation to
a church or work in your honorable vocation, all of this is worship to the Lord.

Do you like to make beautiful things? Some women love to craft
quilts while others love to craft beautiful pictures and poetry on
Instagram. I used to love to paint but now most of my time is spent
painting with words. My dear friend Julie designs and fabricates
stained-glass windows. Sometimes these are done for churches, but
many times they go into someone's home or business. I know that
every time she completes a project she's offering it in thankfulness
to the Lord. She's beautifying the world, making it a better place.

Many women love to scrapbook and create records of the life
of their family. Other women delight in making a beautiful meal—
mixing colors and flavors to bless those they love. In the same way,
the women of old used their hands to create cloth to beautify the
tabernacle, "All the *women* whose hearts stirred them to use their
skill spun the goats' hair" (Exodus 35:26, emphasis added). Well,
I don't know anyone who spins goats' hair, but I do know women
who write music and beautify spaces they inhabit in their cities.

I (Elyse) have the wonderful privilege of attending women's con-
ferences numbers of times each year. I love looking at all the ways

the women express their love of their sisters by making yummy food, arranging music, writing skits, gathering door prizes, and welcoming visitors—including me! Honestly, I can tell how involved women were in the planning and lead-up to the conference by how beautiful and welcoming the space is. Are these things necessary for the ministry of the Word that I do? No. But neither were the blue and purple and scarlet pomegranates and golden bells that decorated the edge of the priests' robes (Exodus 28:33–34). God loves for us to rejoice in beautifying the spaces he has made. It's okay to use our imagination, and it's all for his glory. The way women express love for Christ and the fulfilling of their call doesn't have to happen in the church. It can happen in corporate offices, in dental offices, on construction sites—and it does.

But it's not just decorating that we do either. I have numerous friends who counsel in the church and in their offices—bringing the wisdom of Christ into the brokenness around them. As all these women pour out their lives, they're worshiping. I have another friend who is a CPA by day and our church's Bible study leader at other times. Her work at our church is important—she's like those women who ministered at the door of the temple in the Old Testament—but that church-based work isn't any more important than the good work she does as a CPA. Our vocations, if they are offered "as unto the Lord," are holy worship (see Ephesians 6:5–7 and Romans 12:1).

And, for some, it can happen in the home. As I write this, it's nearly Christmas, and my mother, Rosemary, is in the process of dying. She's very frail and weak and has lost most of her memory. She doesn't remember from day to day that it's December, but the other day when I went to see her and wore some sparkly jingle bells, she remarked at how much she loved looking at them. And so, with the help of my brother, Rick, we put together some festive decorations to cheer her and remind her of this happy season. As much as any other act of worship, I believe that our efforts were a sweet-smelling aroma to the Lord. Every time a woman loves her neighbor because she's been loved, she's worshiping. No matter what that looks like. A believing woman who serves food in a school cafeteria or prepares blankets for refugees on our borders is serving Christ. She's a worshiper.

Worship is way more than service in the temple. Yes, it is that, but it's more. As *ezers* we pray, sing, give, create, file, lead, clean, teach, drive, speak, spin goats' hair, and yes, even dance, and we remind our brothers that all of life is holy and to be lived in love for God's glory. We're getting the world ready for the new earth.

This makes me think of verse 3 of "Brethren, We Have Met to Worship":

> Sisters, will you join and help us
> Moses' sister aided him;
> Will you help the trembling mourners
> Who are struggling hard with sin?
> Tell them all about the Savior,
> Tell them that He will be found;
> Sisters, pray, and holy manna
> Will be showered all around.[9]

Women Were the Backbone of Israel's Familial Worship

In ancient Israel, women prepared the home for the Sabbath celebration. Their expression of worship focused on the ways they planned for the Sabbath rest. If they weren't prepared, their family would suffer; so they couldn't decide to take Fridays off and go for a stroll through the fields or check out what was happening at the city gates. The worshiping woman "looks well to the ways of her household and does not eat the bread of idleness" (Proverbs 31:27). And she ministers at the gates of her home getting the family ready for worship.

In addition, women also prepared for every annual celebration from Passover to Pentecost. Their children, the generations to come, would learn about the Lord's salvation and sustaining grace through the seemingly mundane work of cleaning out the leaven, preparing the herbs, reciting the story. As they kneaded the dough for the bread they baked, they would present the first part of it as a contribution to the Lord (Numbers 15:19). Bread baking was an act of worship. Day-to-day life was shaped around the worship of Jehovah, and the women oversaw that.

The beginning and end of life was also in their hands. From birthing and naming the next generation of worshipers,[10] to caring for them through all their lives, and then burying those they loved, women expressed their worship every day in everyday ways. Because they were in charge of gathering and preparing herbs and spices for the burials of those they loved, they had to be willing to become ceremonially unclean as they sought to try to beautify the ugly reality of death and decay.

Although Jewish women weren't called to the physical sign of the covenant, circumcision, women were equally consecrated and dedicated to the service of the Lord. They were part of the covenant community and were as integral in the worship and life of the nation as any man. The success of the national religion depended upon them just as much as upon any man.

Throughout the entire body of Old Testament literature, we find women as joint-heirs of God's covenant of salvation. They are welcomed into the worship of the tabernacle and the temple. They know how to lead in song and in prayer. They know how to give, and their gifts are just as important as any man's gift, whether it's an Egyptian mirror or a widow's mite.

I love the fact that we live in a time when many vocations are open for women, vocations that expand the stereotypical roles we've been called to. Phil and I have been married for 40-plus years, and during that time I've held many different roles. When our kids were young, I sometimes worked as a janitor at night to help supplement our income. I also homeschooled the kids for a number of years. Before that I taught in the Christian schools where they attended because we could not have afforded it otherwise. Then, when they were getting older, I was trained in biblical counseling and began my writing career. At this point I've written and published around two dozen books and travel about fifteen weekends per year, taking the message of the gospel of grace around the world. These are not your typical callings for a woman, but it is the calling of the Lord. I'm glad to do it, and it's my expression of worship to him.

Brothers, we pray that this chapter has helped you to think about how to include and rejoice in your sisters' gifts and contributions. We pray that you would begin to see women you perhaps have devalued stepping up and using their gifts—at your invitation and encouragement. That you would pray that your heart and eyes would be opened to the gifting God has provided for you and your church.

Women, all of this is to say that you shouldn't see your faith as a straightjacket that forces you into one particular calling or one particular way of worshiping. Men, how has the Lord blessed you and your church with rejoicing women? Have you ever taken time to hear their stories of faith or asked them to share them with the congregation? If someone were to pick ten leading women from your congregation, would you know what they were praying about? You have been called and welcomed into God's family: a family that is full of women who worship and who work for God's glory in all sorts of ways. So open your mouth and your hand and speak and sing and, yes, dance.

—— **DISCOVERING A WOMAN'S WORTH** ——

1. Who was the first person recorded in the Bible to have danced in worship to God? What do you think is the significance of that?

2. Who was the first person recorded in the Bible to have prayed to God as "the Lord of Hosts"? Do you think there is any significance in that?

3. Deborah was a woman who led a song of victory after leading the warriors in the defeat of their enemies. Do you think that is significant? Why or why not?

4. The Old Testament mentions some women who worked at the door to the sanctuary and others who played percussion instruments and sang. Do you ever think of women being employed in these pursuits? Does this encourage you?

5. Summarize what you've learned in this chapter in four or five sentences.

DIGGING DEEPER

1. The first recorded song in the New Testament is Mary's song (Luke 1:46–55). Why do you think that's significant? Read her song and compare it to the songs of Miriam (Exodus 15) and Deborah (Judges 5).

2. What is your favorite worship song? Write out the lyrics that are particularly meaningful to you. What is it about those words that speaks deeply to your soul?

3. Take time now to consider the ways in which God has delivered or protected you in your life. Even if you don't think of yourself as a lyricist or a poet, try to write a song of victory to the Lord.

SEVEN

The Worth of Women in Israel's Wisdom

Does not wisdom call?
Does not understanding raise her voice?
Proverbs 8:1

Margot Lee Shetterly's 2016 book *Hidden Figures* recounts the "Untold Story of the Black Women Mathematicians Who Helped Win the Space Race." It features African American women—such as Katherine Johnson, Dorothy Vaughan, and Mary Jackson—who worked as "human computers" at NASA in the 1940s through the '60s. These women proved essential in several missions, including the Mercury mission, John Glenn's orbit around Earth, and the Apollo 11 flight to the moon. Despite this, they were often segregated from men and white women. Until the publication of Shetterly's book in 2016, the black female contribution to the space race was largely unknown and overlooked.[1]

In the same way, it's easy to read the Scriptures and overlook the surprising ways that wise women contributed to the story of our redemption.

The Wise Women of Proverbs

King Solomon, a man known as Israel's wisest king, tells us that
as a child he had learned wisdom from his mother (Proverbs 1:8;
6:20–22). Who was that woman? Bathsheba. She was a woman
who at the very least had been sexually assaulted by King David,
who had suffered the loss of her beloved husband, Uriah, yet still
persevered as a primary voice of wisdom in her son's life. She
sought to prepare him for his life as a ruler, something she had
negotiated with his father, David.[2] Did Solomon always live wisely?
No, of course not. But he did admit that he valued his mother's
teaching,

- "Hear, my son, your father's instruction, and forsake not
  your mother's teaching" (Proverbs 1:8).
- "My son, keep your father's commandment, and forsake
  not your mother's teaching. Bind them on your heart always; tie them around your neck. When you walk, they
  will lead you, when you lie down, they will watch over
  you; when you awake, they will talk with you" (Proverbs
  6:20–22).

The wisdom that Bathsheba sought to instill in her son was
the "skill of choosing the right course of action for the desired
result. In . . . Proverbs, it denotes skill in the art of godly living."[3]
In other words, wisdom is the desire and ability to live out one's
core commitments to the Lord in everyday circumstances; it is the
skill of choosing the right course of action that will best eventu-
ate in demonstrating love and commitment to God. So Bathsheba
and other wise women who loved the Lord continually observed
how things work, the general grain of the world, and learned to
understand how certain actions affect those whom they love and
their walk with God. Wise women view life through the grid of
the blessing that the Lord bestows on those who seek to walk in
godliness and who are committed to his will, and they think about

the ways that those whom they love, whether family or friends, can live the blessed life, no matter what the cost.

Did Solomon have a wise woman or wife to whom he listened and who would guide him as he ruled? We don't know of any. And so, in many ways we can see how the one who had enough wisdom to recite his mother's and father's teaching didn't actually take it to heart. Even so, from the very beginning of Proverbs, the book of practical wisdom he wrote, to the very end, the wisdom of women figures prominently. In fact, Proverbs is bookended in praise of wise women. It opens with Solomon extolling his mother's teaching and ends with a different unknown king, Lemuel, reciting the oracle about wise women his mother taught him. From her he learned how to rule wisely and choose a discerning woman for his queen. Like the women in our last chapter, this prudent queen is known for her worship.

> Charm is deceitful, and beauty is vain,
>   but a woman who fears the Lord is to be praised.
> Give her of the fruit of her hands,
>   and let her works praise her in the gates.
>
> Proverbs 31:30–31

Oh no! Not Proverbs 31 again!

If that was your response when you saw where we were headed, we don't blame you. We know that many women feel intimidated by this description of wise womanhood, but you really shouldn't. Rather than seeing it as an exhausting punch list of one day's work, we should view it as a portrayal of the relationships this woman of valor[4] fights and works for in her life. She isn't afraid to be strong and she looks at the days to come and laughs with confidence because of her faith in her God. Her words are full of wisdom, and by her kindness and industry she demonstrates the goodness of God. Although she's a queen who helps her husband as he rules, her primary goal is the expansion of God's kingdom. This wise woman shouldn't intimidate us, she should encourage us. She shows us that the wise woman has many doors open to her and can walk through them courageously. Although this oracle is directed toward a son making a wise choice of his queen, that doesn't mean marriage is the only way a woman can live a life of valor. Maybe she doesn't have husband or a family, maybe she waits tables or cleans offices at night. Those things don't define her. Rather, she's a woman who is praised because she fears the Lord and she has skills that she uses for the furtherance of God's kingdom and the benefit of her loved ones. For instance, I've got a valiant friend who is a cytotechnologist. She gets up very, very early, works until midday looking at cells under a microscope, and then counsels in the evenings. She's working on a PhD in biblical counseling in her "spare time." All of her work is worship, and she is an excellent wife, worth more than rare jewels, though she isn't married—at least not to any mere human. She is wise and worshipful, even though she's serving the Lord in what might be viewed as nontraditional ways.

Proverbs 31:10–31 is actually a beautiful acrostic poem composed by a mother who taught it to her son so that he could recite it by rote for others. What is the priceless woman like? She cares for her household and makes it a center of ministry for the poor as Rosaria Butterfield commends in *The Gospel Comes with a House Key: Practicing Radically Ordinary Hospitality in Our Post-Christian World*. Or she can be a wise businesswoman who deals in goods and real estate and oversees her household workers with care and diligence. Remember, this description of what an excellent wife is like is authored by a mother looking to protect her son from folly and provide for her grandchildren and her nation. Unfortunately, Solomon ignored this wise and godly counsel (if he even knew of it) and in doing so, brought the nation down (1 Kings 11:1–8).

Lady Wisdom

Another female presented in Proverbs is Lady Wisdom. To men and women she calls,

O simple ones, learn prudence;
  O fools, learn sense. . . .
Take my instruction instead of silver,
  and knowledge rather than choice gold,
for wisdom is better than jewels,
  and all that you may desire cannot compare with her.

Proverbs 8:5, 10–11

"I have counsel and sound wisdom," she says. "I have insight; I have strength" (Proverbs 8:14). Lady Wisdom calls young men to listen to her, "Blessed are those who keep my ways" (8:32). We frequently hear women being equated with folly and gullibility, as though women are more susceptible to deception than men, but that's not how the Bible describes them. "The Old Testament does not teach the rational, emotional, and spiritual inferiority of women. Rather, it teaches the equality of women and men as persons made to reflect the likeness of God."[5] Of course that doesn't mean that there aren't silly women. Of course, there are. Just as there are silly men. But silliness and gullibility are not the primary descriptors the Bible uses to talk about women.[6]

Women of Surprising Wisdom

It would be easy to think that being a woman of wisdom of necessity means embracing certain traditional roles and actions. But now we're going to look at the lives of three women of wisdom who don't fit traditional expectations: Tamar, Abigail, and Jael. Of course, we could have looked at Queen Esther, who wisely overcame her people's enemy and his planned genocide, or Ruth, who wisely chose a husband to raise up a son for her deceased husband's name, but we want you to see that a woman's wisdom sometimes shows up in very unexpected ways. Tamar, Abigail, and Jael should be remembered for their wisdom, for their skill in discerning the right way to act, and their resolve to risk their own lives in service of it. Each of them was brave, able to discern and

127

pursue the right course of action, and valued truth and goodness more than their own comfort.

Tamar

If you were going to make a list of wise women from the Bible, we're guessing that Tamar (of all people!) wouldn't be on it. Let us remind you of her story, from Genesis 38:6–30: Tamar was a Canaanite, daughter-in-law to Judah, one of the twelve sons of Jacob. Her marriage to Judah's son, Er, was a disaster. We don't know a lot about him, but we do know that he was "wicked in the sight of the Lord." He was so wicked, in fact, that the Lord "put him to death" (Genesis 38:7). Tamar not only lived through a horrid marriage, but also through Er's death and her widowhood. What it meant in those days was that without a male heir, the very name of her husband would cease to exist. In addition, a childless widow wouldn't inherit her husband's property. She would be left desolate, and her husband's name would soon be forgotten. In addition, her desire to give birth to the promised deliverer would be thwarted. And so, out of care for the significance of the husband's name continuing and the hope for a deliverer, the Lord commanded what is known as the Levirate marriage: A widow would be given to her husband's brother so that she would have sons by him, and the man's name would continue. In light of this, Judah gave Tamar to his second-born son, Onan, so that he would raise up a son to take the place of the firstborn. But Onan was wicked as well. As Er's brother, Onan shared Tamar's responsibility to rescue Er's name from extinction, but he was as bad as his brother. Whenever he had sex with her he would "waste the semen on the ground, so as not to give offspring to his brother" (Genesis 38:9).

> Apparently he repeatedly degraded her by using her for his pleasure, then denying her the opportunity to conceive. One can only imagine how appalling and humiliating his actions were for Tamar, all the more since she had entered into this second marriage for the

sake of honor and family loyalty. To make matters worse, she was powerless to do anything about Onan's cover-up.[7]

Using Tamar in this way was "wicked in the sight of the Lord," so God put him to death also (Genesis 38:10).[8]

At this point, after the loss of two of his three sons, Judah told Tamar to return to her father's house and wait until his youngest son, Shelah, was old enough to marry. Tamar's life was a train wreck. Being joined to God's "chosen people" had brought her nothing but heartache. She had no legal recourse, no son, no one to protect her, and her experience of being married to Er and Onan had to have been abusive to say the least. But Tamar, a faithful Canaanite woman, was also a woman of wisdom who was determined to do the right thing and keep her husband's name from passing into extinction.

Once she saw that Judah would not give Shelah to her, she made a plan. Knowing Judah's character, she dressed herself as a prostitute and went out to do the righteous thing: seek to preserve her husband's name. How did Tamar know that such a scheme would work? She was wise and insightful. Tamar left her illicit encounter with Judah with the two things she needed: her husband's genetic material and her father-in-law's ID. She needed his sperm to save her husband's name; she needed his signet, cord, and staff to save her own life, knowing her father-in-law as she did. This wasn't some torrid tryst for her. Nor was she simply trying to get a child for her own selfish desires. She wisely chose to do what was necessary to see the family line preserved and in the hope of a Messiah. And in so doing, she eventually brought Judah back to his senses.

It wasn't long until Judah heard news of his daughter-in-law's infidelity. His response? He sentenced her (and her unborn children) to be burned. His sentence was far more severe than mere stoning, which the law would have allowed. Perhaps he was secretly glad to rid his family of this albatross of a daughter-in-law. But at this point in the story, once again Tamar demonstrated valiant wisdom. She waited until Judah pronounced sentence on her and then she turned the tables. "By the man to whom these belong, I am pregnant. Please identify whose these are" (Genesis 38:25). Tamar skillfully waited until Judah had condemned her, and in essence himself, before she played her trump card. Like Nathan after her, she announced, "You are the man!" (2 Samuel 12:7).

What was Judah's response when he realized the truth? He declared, "She is more righteous than I, since I did not give her to my son" (Genesis 38:26). It would be easy to read Judah's response as a statement of comparison: "She's a better person than me." But that's not what it is. It actually means, "She is righteous, not I."[9] Or as The Message reads, "She's in the right; I'm in the wrong."[10] Judah isn't saying that he's a little righteous and she's a little more righteous. After all, what in any of Judah's actions could he classify as righteous? Tamar was more righteous than Judah not simply because he had engaged in prostitution and condemned her for the same thing. He was guilty of selling his brother Joseph into slavery. He was guilty of not caring about preserving his son's name. And he was guilty of seeking to execute her in the most agonizing way for doing the same thing he had done. On the other hand, Tamar was willing to face disgrace and death to do the right thing, while he sought pleasure for himself. She sought to safeguard the family. And miraculously, through the birth of her twins, Perez and Zerah, both of Judah's wretched sons had their legacy preserved.

What did the people of ancient Israel think of Tamar? When Boaz took Ruth to be his wife (fulfilling the Levirate law), the people said,

> We are witnesses . . . may your house be like the house of Perez, whom Tamar bore to Judah, because of the offspring that the Lord will give you by this young woman.
>
> Ruth 4:11–12

Tamar's name was invoked in blessing to the house of Ruth and Boaz. Like Tamar, Ruth would find the blessing of having her dead husband's name continue. And, of course, the line of King

David and the Messiah were preserved through her as well. Tamar "wasn't called righteous for her gentle and quiet spirit. She was righteous by being strong and assertive. She was a godly leader."[11] And she was wise.

The Beauty and the Beast

In 1 Samuel 25, we are introduced to another wise woman, Abigail, who was married to an unquestionably nasty man, Nabal. Nabal was very rich and was known for being harsh and demanding. He was undoubtedly as abusive to Abigail as he was to all his servants. Abigail was a woman who is described as "discerning." She had a wealth of deep understanding. She had learned how to coexist with a beast like Nabal.

On one particular day, Nabal's shepherds were shearing his sheep when David's men, who had been protecting them from attack, came and asked for some provisions. What they asked for was not a lot, just "whatever you have at hand" (v. 8). It was certainly reasonable for them to ask for and was within Nabal's power to give. But being the kind of man he was, he both refused their request and insulted them. "Who is David? Who is the son of Jesse?" he asked. In other words, he was saying, "Who does this nobody think he is?" David, furious at Nabal's response, determined to respond with violence.

Fortunately, one of Nabal's servants relayed the story to Abigail. Because this probably wasn't the first time they had asked her to intervene because of her husband's foolishness, Abigail immediately went into action. She quickly put together an offering of food and drink. Without her husband's knowledge or permission, she hurried out to intercept David and put herself in harm's way to stop David from making a costly mistake. Throwing herself on the ground before him, she said,

> On me alone, my lord, be the guilt. . . . Let not my lord regard this worthless fellow, Nabal, for as his name is, so is he. . . . But I your

servant did not see the young men of my lord, whom you sent. . . . Please forgive the trespass of your servant. . . . My lord shall have no cause of grief or pangs of conscience for having shed blood without cause or for my lord working salvation himself.

1 Samuel 25:24–25, 28, 31

Like Tamar, Abigail was willing to risk everything to prevent an evil from happening. Like Hannah, her testimony stands in contrast with worthless men around her. She was willing to face her husband's wrath. And she was willing to declare wisdom to a man who was intent on wiping out everyone in her house. She was brave, strong, and discerning. John Calvin writes that she is like the "valiant woman of Proverbs 31."[12]

David sees that Abigail is a wise woman, employing skills of evaluation, action, and perception. He says, "Blessed be your discretion, and blessed be you, who have kept me this day from bloodguilt and from working salvation with my own hand!" (1 Samuel 25:32–33). So David received her gifts and repented of his decision to wipe out Nabal and his servants. "Go up in peace to your house," he said. "See, I have obeyed your voice, and I have granted your petition" (1 Samuel 25:35). In this situation, David wisely chose to listen to and obey a wise woman's counsel. He and his army stood down.

When Abigail returned home, Nabal was holding an elaborate feast and was very drunk. In wisdom, she chose not to tell him what she had done right then. She understood that this wasn't the right time, but when he woke up the next day, "when the wine had gone out of Nabal" (v. 37), she did. Abigail was willing to face his rage, possibly in the hope that her wisdom would serve to change his character. Instead, he must have been so angry with her that his blood pressure skyrocketed for "his heart died within him, and he became as a stone" (v. 37). Then "about ten days later the Lord struck Nabal, and he died" (v. 38).

Like Tamar, Abigail was content to try to do the right thing even though her husband was a worthless fool. When it came to letting someone incur sin and cut off her family line, she acted. In wisdom she gathered together everything necessary to appease her enemy. She acted without her husband's knowledge or permission. She directed David in the way of righteousness. The Bible doesn't censure her for her actions. Rather, she's called a woman of discernment. And King David was better off for obeying her voice.

What does Abigail's story teach us? It teaches us that though Christian wives are called to submit to their husband's godly leadership, that doesn't mean that they should stand quietly by and do nothing while their husband foolishly brings destruction on himself and others. Undoubtedly Abigail knew that Nabal wouldn't approve of her actions with David, but there was more at stake here than Nabal's approval or censure. Lives were at stake, so she acted.

The Wise Warrior

Remember the definition of wisdom? We suggested that wisdom consists of "skill of choosing the right course of action for the desired result; the skill in the art of godly living." Let's consider now the wise warrior Jael. We first meet Jael in Judges 4. Deborah has led Barak and Israel's warriors in a successful fight against the Canaanites, and in particular against the commander of the Canaanite army, Sisera. This powerful man who had command of 900 chariots of iron fell before a woman and all of Israel's forces. Then, at the end of the battle, when not one of Sisera's warriors was left alive, he fled on foot to the tent of Jael.

Jael knew what kind of man Sisera was, so she valiantly met and even welcomed him into her tent. "Turn aside, my lord; turn aside to me; do not be afraid," she said (Judges 4:18). Exhausted and disheartened, he was glad to have a place to rest and hide. He lay down on the floor, and Jael covered him with a rug. He was undoubtedly hungry and dehydrated. "Please give me a little water to drink," he asked. "So she opened a skin of milk and gave him a drink and covered him" (v. 19). He needed something to drink, but she gave him something more, something that would satisfy his hunger as well. As he began to relax under her care, he asked another favor: "If anyone comes looking for me, please lie and tell them I'm not here." This great warrior asked a woman to protect him. She said she would, but she was lying. She had another plan for him, of course. She waited until she was sure he was asleep and

> Jael the wife of Heber took a tent peg, and took a hammer in her hand. Then she went softly to him and drove the peg into his temple until it went down into the ground while he was lying fast asleep from weariness. So he died.
>
> Judges 4:21

Soon Barak, who was pursuing Sisera, came to Jael's tent and she invited him to come and see the man he was chasing. His enemy, Sisera, lay dead with a tent peg through his skull. Deborah and her warriors celebrated Jael's victory that day. Consider the courage and cunning it took for her to do what she did. She had no guarantee that Sisera wouldn't awaken and kill her. But she bravely acted, so Deborah sang this song about her heroism:

> Most blessed of women be Jael,
>   the wife of Heber the Kenite,
>   of tent-dwelling women most blessed.
> He asked for water and she gave him milk;
>   she brought him curds in a noble's bowl.
> She sent her hand to the tent peg
>   and her right hand to the workmen's mallet;
> she struck Sisera;
>   she crushed his head;
>   she shattered and pierced his temple.
> Between her feet
>   he sank, he fell, he lay still;
> between her feet
>   he sank, he fell;
> where he sank
>   there he fell—dead.
>
> Judges 5:24–27

Deborah continued her lauding of Jael's bravery by mocking Sisera's mother's concerns: She imagined her looking out of the window waiting for her son's return and wondering at how long the battle had taken. She comforts herself, "Have they not found and divided the spoil?—A womb or two for every man" (Judges 5:30). Don't miss the meaning of this. Sisera and his hordes were known as men who would not only plunder villages they conquered but would also rape the women. "A womb or two . . ." Indeed. Jael had a tent peg with Sisera's name on it.

Perhaps you're a woman who is in the military and you've heard that's not a proper occupation for a woman. Deborah and Jael have an answer for that. I'm not saying that military life isn't hard, and perhaps particularly so for women, but that doesn't mean that women are incapable or unnecessary or that godly women should be barred from working there. If your gifting and vocation tends more toward courageous action, then pursue that. Remember that Proverbs 31 is a hymn like the ones that would be sung about David's mighty men of valor. You can live as a wise woman while you discern valid threats from your office on the Internet or in the cockpit of your F-14. I know a Christian woman who works for the FBI, who seeks to protect her country from terrorist threats. Women, you are free to discern what kind of vocation the Lord is calling you to and he will use you as you work in wisdom for his glory.

Throughout the entire body of Old Testament literature, we find women as joint-heirs of God's covenant salvation. Many are defined by their ability to discern the right course of action and to complete that action, even when they face censure, wrath, or death. I love the fact that there are many women who enjoy being homemakers, who love being stay-at-home moms, and who seek God's wisdom on a daily basis as they strive to ensure their family's well-being. But I also love the fact that we live in a time when other vocations are open for women, vocations that expand the roles we've been called to.

You have been called and welcomed into God's family: a family that is full of wise women who work for God's glory in all sorts

Worthy

of ways. Remember that the wise woman recommended by Lemuel's mom in Proverbs 31 is not lauded because of her physical beauty. This song of a valiant woman "glorifies the good works of a woman in the ordinary affairs of family, community and business life—good works which for all of their earthiness are rooted in the fear of the Lord."[13]

───────── **DISCOVERING A WOMAN'S WORTH** ─────────

1. Read Proverbs 31:10–31. If you've read this passage before, how have you thought about it? How do you think of it now? Does reframing it as a heroic song of a valiant woman help you see it as more encouraging?

2. We looked at the lives of three wise women: Tamar, Abigail, and Jael. Have you ever thought about them as being particularly wise? What is it about their lives that challenges and encourages you?

3. Where are you personally called to live a life of wisdom? How much time have you spent asking the Lord to give you wisdom in your vocation? How can your wisdom in these different contexts help expand the kingdom of God?

4. Summarize what you've learned in this chapter in four or five sentences.

───────────── **DIGGING DEEPER** ─────────────

1. There are women who fill the role of counselor in the Old Testament. These women were known for their wisdom,

136

and men relied on them. Who were they and what do we know about them? (See 2 Samuel 14; 2 Samuel 20.)

2. How has the discussion of Tamar, Abigail, and Jael challenged your previous thoughts about what a wise woman is like?

3. Have you ever thought the book of Proverbs was dismissive or insulting to women? Has your opinion changed during this study? Why or why not?

EIGHT

The Worth of Women in Jesus' Birth

Blessed is she who believed that there would be a
fulfillment of what was spoken to her from the Lord.

Luke 1:45

In April 2009, *Britain's Got Talent* featured contestant Susan Boyle. The singer introduced herself as an unemployed, unmarried forty-seven-year-old. She lived with her cat and had never been kissed. She aspired to be a professional singer as successful as Elaine Paige. When she appeared on stage, the audience both laughed and cringed. They rolled their eyes, shook their heads, and covered their faces. They winced at the disaster they assumed would soon unfold. "[T]hey saw a thick-waisted, middle-aged woman with Freida Kahlo eyebrows and Brillo pad hair, and the members of the audience could be seen rolling their eyes and smirking. They could not conceive that so plain and postdated a package could contain so lovely a voice."[1]

No sooner had the first notes left her mouth than the audience recognized her talent. They erupted in applause. The judges' jaws dropped in unison. Simon smiled. Judge Amanda Holden remarked, "I am so thrilled because I know everybody was against you. I honestly think we were all being very cynical, and I think that was the biggest wake-up call ever."[2]

Boyle would not win *Britain's Got Talent*, taking second place in the finals. Even so, she went on to a recording and touring career. She performed for royalty, sang Mass for the pope, and had a stage musical based on her life.

Boyle's story touched the hearts of millions. It also exposed the superficial judgments of the broader culture. No one expected so much from someone who looked like so little.

Think about the kingdom of God. What will it look like? When it is threatened, who will rescue it? Who will be in it? Who will proclaim it? What does it look like to serve in it? What kind of person comes to mind when you think of someone God uses to advance, proclaim, and serve in his kingdom?

Think about your church. What does spiritual growth and vitality look like? When your church is in danger, who will God use to rescue it? Who would your ideal church include? Who tells others about Jesus? What does it look like to serve? What kind of person comes to mind when you think of someone God uses to advance, proclaim, and serve in his church? Did you think of women? You should.

If you did think of women, what do you think of when you think of a "woman of God"? What does she look like? Where did she come from? Do you think of women who have been abused or raped? Involved in incest? Prostitution? Women who have been publicly shamed and stigmatized as unclean and sinful? Who are childless, barren, or widowed? Who suffered horrific pain? You should.

God chooses women with painful pasts to advance, proclaim, and serve in his kingdom. We see this no more clearly than in the events leading up to and surrounding the birth of Jesus Christ, the King.

In this chapter, we will walk through the birth of Jesus and the events leading up to it. We will see that God has a vital role for women to play. And not just women—but women the world would never expect.

God Uses Surprising Women to Advance His Kingdom

We saw in Genesis 3 that God promised to bring redemption through "the offspring of the woman." As we wait for this promised redeemer, we "watch the woman." Each could be the mother of the Messiah.

As the Old Testament progressed, God's promise narrowed. He promised Abraham an "offspring" who would become a great nation. This offspring would bless all the nations of the earth (Genesis 15, 17). Thus, we look for the offspring of Abraham to come through Israel, the offspring of Abraham. Then God promised David an "offspring" who would reign over his kingdom forever (2 Samuel 7:12–16). Thus, we look for the offspring to come through David's line. We are looking for the "offspring of the woman" . . . and Abraham . . . and David.

As the New Testament opens, Matthew labors to show us that this offspring is Jesus. He does this by recounting Jesus' genealogy (Matthew 1:1–17). "The book of the genealogy of Jesus Christ, the son of David, the son of Abraham." As the list of names unfolds, a pattern emerges. "X was the father of Y, and Y the father of Z," each time moving from father to son.

Matthew interrupts that pattern four times before arriving at Joseph and Mary. Each variation is significant, designed to reveal something about the King and his kingdom. Each interruption includes a woman. Each woman is surprising, associated with scandal and shame. Each furthers the lineage of the promised "offspring of the woman." God uses her to advance his kingdom.

The first woman encountered is Tamar, whose story we find in Genesis 38 and read about in chapter 7. Widowed by the death of her wicked husband Er, the responsibility to give her a child fell to her brother-in-law Onan. The Lord killed Onan for refusing to father a child with Tamar. She appealed to Judah for another husband, who failed to provide a son to marry her. So, Tamar took matters into her own hands. Disguised as a prostitute, she had sex with her father-in-law and bore twin sons—Perez and Zerah. Despite injustice, shame, and the social stigma of incest, Tamar advances the kingdom.

NO, God did

The second woman we meet is Rahab (Joshua 2). A prostitute, she provided lodging for Jewish spies on a reconnaissance mission. The king of Jericho sent a message to Rahab demanding that she bring out the men. But Rahab knew of the Lord's redemptive power and believed that the Lord would destroy Jericho. So she lied to the king, hid the men, and provided them a safe escape. In gratitude, the spies promised to spare her and her family when Israel invaded. Through her faith, Rahab's actions advanced the kingdom (Hebrews 11:31).

The third woman we meet is Ruth, a Gentile, whose story takes place during the period of judges. Ruth married a Jewish man whose family fled to Moab during a famine (instead of trusting the Lord). Soon her father, husband, and brother-in-law all died. When her mother-in-law returned to Bethlehem, she encouraged Ruth to remain in Moab. Naomi understood that returning to Bethlehem meant that Ruth would never remarry. After a decade of marriage, Ruth had no children, indicating barrenness. Furthermore, Mosaic Law forbade Jews from marrying Ammonite or Moabite women (Deuteronomy 7:1–4). The Law banned those who did (and their offspring) from entering the assembly of the Lord (Deuteronomy 23:2–3). Still, Ruth trusted the Lord and returned with Naomi to Bethlehem.

Through courageous faith, Ruth walked into Bethlehem, facing life as an unwanted outcast. A courageous and strong woman, she took responsibility for leadership, protection, and provision in the home, going out to the fields to glean to feed herself and her mother-in-law. Through faith, she slept on the threshing floor and expressed her willingness to marry Boaz. Through all this, Ruth rescues the line of the offspring and advances the kingdom.[3]

The fourth woman we meet is "the wife of Uriah." By this title, Matthew highlights the sordid details of Bathsheba's union with David. Given the authority and power inherent in a king, David's actions qualify as rape. Remember, rape doesn't have to be an assault at knifepoint. It is any sexual intercourse that occurs without consent. Upon discovering her pregnancy, David attempts to cover it up. Eventually, he murders her husband and quickly marries her. Though this son would die, they would have other sons. One would become Israel's wisest king, through whom the Messiah would come. Through Bathsheba's pain, the kingdom advanced.

What is Matthew teaching us? The kingdom advances through unexpected and unlikely people. God works through women such as these. Mistreated, wrongly accused, shamed. Stigmatized, bearing a reputation for wrongdoing, and unclean. Barren and bereaved, unwanted and abused. And this is only a small selection. We could include others, such as the undesirable, unloved Leah, who is forced on Jacob (who never loves her) but gives birth to Judah, giving her the honored status of a distant grandmother to the Messiah.

These women point to the truth that the kingdom would arrive through a Savior like them. Unexpected and unlikely. Mistreated, wrongly accused, and shamed. Stigmatized (as a bastard child) and given a reputation for wrongdoing (drunkard, glutton, sinner). Declared unclean (hung on a tree under God's curse; Galatians 3:13). He was barren, bereaved, unwanted, and abused (beaten and crucified).

These women teach us about the unexpected and unlikely people of the Messiah. Jesus identified with the mistreated, the shamed, the stigmatized. He was a friend of the sinful, the unclean, the barren, the bereaved, unwanted, and abused—many of them women. He died for sinners on the cross so that they could be forgiven. He rose from the dead so that the shameful could be transformed and adopted as children of God.

No one ought to wonder at this Messiah or the people he seeks and welcomes. The whole Bible prepared us for this. Those surprised at who he befriends are those who haven't paid attention to the Old Testament.

Women, do you see yourself in any of these women? Do you fear that your sinful choices and shameful past make you unfit for kingdom work? That your darkest secrets or public reputation prevent God from working through you? You shouldn't. God chooses the weak and foolish things of the world (like a crucified Messiah) to shame the strong and the wise (1 Corinthians 1:21–31). Do you believe that God can and does work through you to do great things in his kingdom? You should. He saves through the shame of the cross. He transformed a Middle-Eastern terrorist into the author of half the New Testament. He can and will use you.

Husbands, how do you view your "wife with a past"? Do you see her through the lens of her history—sexual sin, intoxication, promiscuity, abuse, self-righteousness? Does it hold you back from valuing her in the present? Her past is her *past*; it is neither her *present* nor is it her *future*. Her past is what happened; it is not what is happening; it is not what will happen. If she is in Christ, she is a new creation. "The old has passed away; behold, the new has come" (2 Corinthians 5:17).

Reader, do you expect God to use women to advance his kingdom? Do you seek the kind of women through whom Jesus arrived? On a mission trip in college, a friend encouraged me to share the Gospel with a group of rough-looking young people on a park bench. I resisted and made up excuses. In truth, I doubted that they were likely to get saved. I wanted to look for a more likely target. My friend saw through it. "Eric," he said, "the Gospel is for those people too. God *can* save them."

What kind of women do you pursue in your evangelism, discipleship, and fellowship? What kind of women do you want in your small group or on your church leadership team? What kind of woman do you envision reading Scripture during the service? What does a women's Bible study teacher look like? What kind of woman makes it in the pictures on your church website? What kind of women do you dream of your sons marrying? Do they have a shameful past? Were they notorious sinners? Have they suffered trials that continue to haunt them? Do they have scars they cannot hide beneath the latest fashion trend and a makeover? Does the world (the religious included) look down on them, look past them?

Do you dream of your church, your family, and your circle of friends including women who look like Jesus? Despised and rejected by men, women of sorrows and acquainted with grief, and as ones from whom men hide their faces?

Jesus values such as these. He came to seek them and to make them his own. To despise them is to despise our Salvation.

God Uses Women to Proclaim the Kingdom's Arrival

Imagine that you are on a committee to announce the appearance of a long-expected and famous king. Your task is to select the heralds to make the first announcements of his arrival. Who would you choose? Would you pick someone attractional and contextualized to the values of your culture? Would you select someone famous, powerful, influential? Someone with clout? Someone whose word the culture valued, trusted, and accepted? Would you pick people who reflect what the king is like, who typify his kingdom?

God displays the countercultural nature of the kingdom in its first heralds. We often note that humble shepherds were the first to receive news of the Savior's birth. Gentile wise men visited from afar. The kingdom is for the poor and a blessing to the nations. But before gift-bearing magi and shepherds watching their flocks by night, there was someone else. There were women—unlikely and humble, grace-receiving and promise-believing, courageous and kingdom-proclaiming women.

God proclaimed his kingdom through unlikely and humble women. Luke's gospel opens with a focus on two unlikely and humble women—elderly Elizabeth and the virgin Mary.

Luke introduces us to a priest named Zechariah and his wife, Elizabeth. Despite their noted righteousness, they had no child. The prospect of a child seemed impossible; Elizabeth was barren, and they were old.

It is difficult for us, a twenty-first-century audience, to grasp the lowliness of Elizabeth's position. She says that the Lord gave her a son "to take away my reproach among people" (Luke 1:25). She bore reproach—disgrace and insults—because of her barrenness. There would have been whispers among the neighbors. *What sin had she committed for the Lord to withhold children from them? Poor Zechariah, burdened with a barren wife!*

The next woman we meet is Mary. In her own words, she was a woman of "humble estate" (Luke 1:48). She had no station in life that made her a woman to whom people would listen. Though given the honor of being the mother of the Messiah, it would not be without a lifetime of shame. Unwed (but engaged), the virgin would conceive a child by the Holy Spirit (Luke 1:28–35). The Messiah would be born to an unwed mother, presumably through immorality. Jabs about immorality and an "illegitimate child" would follow her and her son for decades (John 8:41).

These are not the types of women to whom the world was likely to listen. But this was not a King and a kingdom that the world was likely to receive. Are you willing to let God's choice of these women transform who you expect him to use today?

God proclaimed his kingdom through grace-receiving and promise-believing women. An angel of the Lord appeared to Zechariah in the temple. He declared that Elizabeth would have a son, whom they were to name John. This child would be a mighty prophet, preparing the people of God for the arrival of the Messiah. Zechariah, the righteous and honored priest, responded in unbelief.

But Elizabeth, humble and barren, responded by confessing grace. "Thus the Lord has done for me in the days when he looked on me, to take away my reproach among people" (Luke 1:25). She knew that he had "looked upon" her—a phrase denoting that he noticed her and showed her grace. We hear no hints of unbelief in Elizabeth. She would soon rejoice, believing that Mary carried the baby she called "my Lord" (Luke 1:42–45). When those circumcising her son wanted to name him Zechariah, Elizabeth intervened. "No," she insisted, "he shall be called John" (Luke 1:60). These words are a confession of faith. She believed that her son would be who God said he was—the forerunner of the King.

Likewise, Mary confessed God's grace in the gift of her child. The angel greeted her as "favored one"; she had "found favor with God" (Luke 1:28, 30). She received this proclamation of grace—"Behold, I am the servant of the Lord" (1:38). Elizabeth celebrated Mary's faith—"Blessed is she who believed there would be a fulfillment of what was spoken to her from the Lord."

The first two recorded confessions of faith in the Old Testament were from the lips of Eve (Genesis 4:1, 25).
It is fitting that the New Testament's first two recorded confessions of faith are from women, daughters of Eve by faith.

God had promised Eve an offspring to redeem her; she believed he was doing that. God had promised Mary and Elizabeth offspring—the Redeemer and his forerunner. These women received the promise with faith.

Luke is teaching us the Gospel. The grace of God has visited us in the person of Jesus Christ, crucified for our sins and raised from the dead. God welcomes into his kingdom all those who receive this grace through faith.

Friend, this offer is not restricted to a class—the strong, the beautiful, the respectable, the wealthy, the free. It is not limited by sex or ethnicity. It is open to any and all who receive the grace of Christ in faith. This is a message to preach and to sing to all who will listen! May our lives, our churches, our homes, and our witness reflect this glorious truth.

God proclaimed his kingdom through courageous and kingdom-proclaiming women. The courage of both Elizabeth and Mary is admirable. Imagine the courage it took to declare that her son would be named "John." Since Zechariah could not speak, those gathered were going to call the boy after his father. But Elizabeth spoke up, believing that her son would be who the Lord said he would be, and named him in obedience.

Imagine the courage it took for Mary to submit to the news of an unplanned, unwed pregnancy. She had likely seen the ostracizing of unwed mothers. She had heard the whispers and clucking of tongues. But she trusted her God and called herself his servant.

These courageous women became the first to proclaim the arrival of the Messiah on earth. Mary went to visit Elizabeth (Luke 1:39–56). At the sound of Mary's voice, the baby leapt in Elizabeth's womb. The Holy Spirit filled her, and she exclaimed, "Blessed are you among women, and blessed is the fruit of your womb! And why is this granted to me that the mother of my Lord should come to me?"

> *Elizabeth's is the first recorded statement recognizing the Messiah's arrival on earth.*

Mary responds in song (Luke 1:46–55). Her poetry is not only an insightful piece of biblical theology.

> *It is also the first hymn of the new covenant people of God.*

We should mention one more woman. An elderly widow, Anna "did not depart from the temple, worshiping with fasting and prayer night and day" (Luke 2:36–37). She was a prophetess, one through whom God spoke with spontaneous utterances. At the moment they presented infant Jesus in the temple, Anna "began to give thanks to God and to speak of him to all who were waiting for the redemption of Jerusalem."

> *Anna, a woman, becomes the first human to proclaim the birth of the King in public.[4]*

How fitting that women are the first to proclaim the one promised to come through the woman! How appropriate that God chose women who looked like his kingdom and his Son—humble, unexpected, gracious, brave, and full of faith.

Friend, God calls and uses women to proclaim the Gospel. Regardless of differences in practice, every believer should celebrate this truth. Heralding the Good News is a charge that the reigning Lord has given to every believer (Matthew 28:18–20). We have no right to overlook or exclude any believer in this task.

As a young pastor, I (Eric) didn't know what to do with women who wanted to speak to me about our faith. I don't mean women who had questions. I mean women who had something to say to me from the Bible. My theology told me this was acceptable. But inside I grew uncomfortable, suspicious, resistant, tentative.

When I thought of leadership development, I thought of equipping men to be pastors. I trained men in interpretation, theology, preaching, and church leadership. I left training and equipping women up to other women. (After all, I reasoned, Titus 2 says training women is the work of women. I failed to notice it did not limit that work to women alone.)

Brothers, we ought not to be suspicious of our sisters. We ought to celebrate them. We ought not to be uncomfortable with a woman encouraging us with the Gospel. We ought to be thankful. We ought not to be resistant when a woman corrects our theology or practice. We ought to be grateful. We ought not to be tentative when women ask for training, equipping, and opportunities to share their gifts and wisdom. We ought to be excited!

These sisters are not seeking to usurp their pastors. They are not despising their brothers. They are not man-haters who want to roast us over an open fire and serve us up with an apple in our mouth.[5] They are daughters of the Father and sisters of the King who want to help us in the work of the kingdom. They are our mothers and sisters, heirs with us in the grace of life. *Together*, we are "a kingdom and priests to our God" (Revelation 5:10). When their gifts serve you, you are not failing at biblical manhood—you are fulfilling it.

God tasked the first humans with subduing the earth and exercising dominion together. God put the first man in the Garden and tasked him with priestly service—a ministry that he could not fulfill alone. This work required a helper—the woman—an *ezer*. When we invite women into the work of ministry, we are fulfilling God's design.

Do you see women as strategic partners in proclaiming the Gospel? Do you follow God in pursuing humble and unexpected women? Do you encourage women to share Jesus with others and teach them to follow him? Do you look for grace-receiving, promise-believing women to equip for strategic kingdom work?

Do you have a place for women to exercise their gifts for the edification of your church? Is there a place in your church for the fulfillment of God's new covenant promise—"I will pour out my Spirit on all flesh; your sons and your daughters shall prophesy" (Joel 2:28)?[6] Is there a place for a woman to share her insights, concerns, warnings, and corrections? Is there a place for a woman to correct "an eloquent man, competent in the Scriptures," who has "been instructed in the way of the Lord," is "fervent in spirit" and speaks and teaches "accurately the things concerning Jesus" (Acts 18:24–25)?

Brothers, are you willing to listen to an Anna when she speaks to you of God's redemption? Sisters, are you ready to step forward and say, "No, this is how it should be," like Elizabeth?

Do you give women difficult tasks that involve risk or danger and call for courage? You should. God does.

God Calls Women to Share in the Suffering of the Kingdom

In Jesus' infancy, Simeon told Mary, "a sword will pierce through your own soul also" (Luke 2:34–35). No doubt her heart was metaphorically pierced as she saw her firstborn pierced and dead on a cross. But her suffering started before then. The stigma of her pregnancy aside, she would be forced into exile to escape the wrath of King Herod. Herod, threatened by the news of a newborn king, ordered the murder of all the male children in the area of Bethlehem ages two and under. Mary and Joseph fled with Jesus to Egypt. Hundreds of other mothers were not as fortunate.

Matthew said that this fulfilled what was spoken through the prophet Jeremiah (Matthew 2:18): "A voice was heard in Ramah, weeping and loud lamentation, Rachel weeping for her children; she refused to be comforted, because they are no more."

Jeremiah spoke those lines in a bit of prophecy proclaiming the Lord's intention to turn the mourning of his people into joy. He follows that sentence with these words (Jeremiah 31:16–17):

> Thus says the Lord:
> "Keep your voice from weeping,
>   and your eyes from tears,
> for there is a reward for your work,
> declares the Lord,
>   and they shall come back from the land of the enemy.
> There is hope for your future,
>   declares the Lord,
>   and your children shall come back to their own
>   country."

The weeping mothers should dry their eyes, for their children will come back home. Jeremiah compared the Israelites in exile to "Rachel weeping for her children . . . because they are no more." This is an odd reference since none of Rachel's children died before her. She died after giving birth to her second son. Jacob buried her on the way to Bethlehem. It is after the account of her death and burial that Genesis turns to the story of her son, Joseph. He is eventually sold into slavery in Egypt. Eventually, Jacob and his other sons go to Egypt to escape the famine, leaving Rachel in her grave.

Jeremiah sees Rachel as symbolic. She weeps as her children pass her tomb on their way to dwell in a foreign land. But one day, when they return, she shall be comforted. God calls women to share in the suffering (and the comfort) of his kingdom.

It is notable that this is precisely what happens in Matthew 2:20–21. When it is safe, an angel commands Joseph to "take the child and his mother and *go to the land of Israel*." The true offspring of Abraham—*Jesus*—came back to his own country. The promise of comfort was beginning to be fulfilled.

But until that comfort is fulfilled in the return of Jesus to raise the dead in a new heavens and new earth, the weeping continues. Women suffer to advance the kingdom.

Think of the women we've seen so far—Tamar, Rahab, Ruth, Bathsheba, Elizabeth, Mary, Anna. God used each to advance his kingdom. He worked through them—specifically, through their sufferings. Each woman shared in suffering for the advance of the kingdom. Each will one day be comforted.

Women, when you picture serving the kingdom of Christ, do you imagine suffering? Or do you have a sanitized and romanticized vision of kingdom service? Do you think that following Jesus in singleness or marriage, in mothering or barrenness, in being a wife or widow or divorcée will be easy? Being a woman is a calling to blood, sweat, and tears.

Men, does it seem chivalrous to exclude women from painful missions work and possible suffering? It's not. Do you think "biblical manhood" means excluding women from potential suffering for the kingdom? It doesn't.

We'd all like to avoid suffering. But that is not how God works. God calls women to the work of his kingdom—to the painful, bleeding, sobbing, suffering work of his kingdom. He sends them on risky, dangerous, deadly missions. Think of Amy Carmichael, Lottie Moon, Elisabeth Elliot, and the thousands of women in church history who chose to walk into danger and death for the sake of the Gospel and the service of others. God is still doing this.

We should include women in the hard stuff, in the dangerous stuff, in the painful stuff. Brothers, don't fear that your sisters are too weak for this suffering. They're stronger than you'd ever imagine. They've been suffering hardship since Adam and Eve left the Garden.

These women aren't alone. The King—the Suffering Servant—loves them and gave his life for them. He will never leave them or forsake them. He promised to be with them always, even to the very end. The promise that sustained our sisters in the past will sustain them today, brothers. They are in better hands than our own.

——— DISCOVERING A WOMAN'S WORTH ———

1. Discuss the opening story about Susan Boyle.

   a. In what ways are your views and expectations of women superficial and stereotypical?

   b. What do you picture when you think of a "woman of God"? What does she look like? Where did she come from?

   c. Think about your church:

      i. What does spiritual growth and vitality look like?

      ii. When your church is in danger, who will God use to rescue it?

      iii. Who would your ideal church include?

      iv. What kind of person comes to mind when you think of someone God uses to advance, proclaim, and serve in his church?

2. Discuss the women in Jesus' genealogy.

   a. Women, do you see yourself in any of these women?

   b. Do you fear that your sinful choices and shameful past make you unfit for kingdom work? Why or why not?

c. Do you fear that your darkest secrets or public reputation prevent God from working through you? Why or why not?

d. Do you believe that God can and will work through you to do great things in his kingdom? Why or why not?

e. What kind of women do you pursue in your evangelism, discipleship, and fellowship?

f. What kind of women do you want in your small group or on your church leadership team?

g. What kind of woman do you envision participating in your Sunday service?

h. What does a women's Bible study teacher look like?

i. What kind of woman makes it into the pictures on your church website?

j. What kind of women do you dream of your sons marrying?

k. In all these categories:

    i. Do they have a shameful past?

    ii. Were they notorious sinners?

    iii. Have they suffered trials that continue to haunt them?

    iv. Do they have scars that they cannot hide beneath the latest fashion trend and a makeover? Does the world (the religious included) look down on them, look past them?

l. Does your church seek the kind of women through whom Jesus arrived?

3. Summarize what you've learned in this chapter in four or five sentences.

——————— **DIGGING DEEPER** ———————

1. Discuss the ways that Elizabeth, Mary, and Anna proclaimed Jesus' arrival.

   a. Men: How do you react to women encouraging you with the Word of God? Correcting you? Do you welcome it? Why or why not?

   b. Women: Are you willing to speak about Jesus to others? Do you feel free to encourage your brothers in Christ with what you know about Jesus? Are you willing to correct theology and practice? Why or why not?

   c. In your church, is there a place for women . . .

      i. to exercise their gifts for the edification of others?

      ii. in your church's evangelism and missions efforts?

   d. In your church, are women truly partners and helpers in service of the kingdom? Why or why not?

2. Discuss the various ways the women we looked at suffered.

   a. Women: Do you see suffering as an inevitable part of serving Jesus? Why or why not?

   b. Men: Are you willing to invite women into difficult and dangerous ministry? Why or why not?

   c. Does your church welcome women into the hard stuff? The dangerous stuff? The painful stuff? Why or why not?

NINE

The Worth of Women in Jesus' Life and Ministry

They marveled that he was talking with a woman.
John 4:27

The office of president of the United States of America is often considered the most powerful in the world. Yet, sadly, its history is littered with the mistreatment of women.

In the final month of the 2016 United States presidential election, a video surfaced in which then-candidate Donald Trump is heard describing his attempts to seduce a married woman. He goes on to boast about grabbing women by their genitalia. In his apology, Trump described the talk as mere "locker room banter."[1] Trump would go on to be elected the forty-fifth president of the United States.

In January 1998, accusations broke that Bill Clinton, the forty-nine-year-old president of the United States, had carried on an illicit sexual relationship with a twenty-two-year-old White House intern, Monica Lewinsky. He famously denied it, stating, "I did not have sexual relations with that woman. . . . The allegations are false."[2] In the course of the fallout, President Clinton would admit to the sexual relationship. He would serve out the remainder of his term and remain a beloved figure in the Democratic Party. Miss Lewinsky would be diagnosed with post-traumatic stress disorder resulting from the ordeal. The trauma of this "inappropriate abuse of authority, station, and privilege" continues to affect her twenty years later.[3]

The devaluing of women is not limited to the political sphere. Kathy Ireland came to fame as a model before becoming an entrepreneur whose companies are worth over two billion dollars. Despite her business success, she faced opposition in her efforts to develop and sell her office equipment line. She was told that no one would buy business furniture from women.[4] She writes, "America's largest companies would develop home furniture with us, even home office. Not business furniture. Felt it would offend men."[5] Though welcome in thirteen consecutive *Sports Illustrated* swimsuit editions, when it came to the business world she wasn't allowed even to *design* a seat at the table, simply because she was a woman.

Beyond politics and business, we need not look far to find women devalued in every realm of life. Hollywood and the "casting couch." Professional athletes abusing women. Musicians objectifying women. Restaurants known for the size of their waitresses' breasts.

Sadly, the church is not immune. In May 2018, author and Bible teacher Beth Moore published a blog post titled "A Letter to My Brothers."[6] It details "what it's been like to be a female leader in the conservative Evangelical world." Here's a portion of what she has experienced:

> I've ridden elevators in hotels packed with fellow leaders who were serving at the same event and not been spoken to and, even more awkwardly, in the same vehicles where I was never acknowledged. I've been in team meetings where I was either ignored or made

fun of, the latter of which I was expected to understand was all in good fun. I am a laugher. I can take jokes and make jokes. I know good fun when I'm having it and I also know when I'm being dismissed and ridiculed. I was the elephant in the room with a skirt on. I've been talked down to by male seminary students and held my tongue when I wanted to say, "Brother, I was getting up before dawn to pray and to pore over the Scriptures when you were still in your pull ups."

She goes on to outline her experiences with public accusations:

> . . . several years ago when I got publically maligned for being a false teacher by a segment of hyper-fundamentalists based on snippets taken out of context and tied together, I inquired whether or not they'd researched any of my Bible studies to reach those conclusions over my doctrine, especially the studies in recent years. The answer was no. Why? They refused to study what a woman had taught.

And her experiences with some male theologians and church leaders:

> About a year ago I had an opportunity to meet a theologian I'd long respected. I'd read virtually every book he'd written. I'd looked so forward to getting to share a meal with him and talk theology. The instant I met him, he looked me up and down, smiled approvingly and said, "You are better looking than _____." He didn't leave it blank. He filled it in with the name of another woman Bible teacher.

From the throne of Israel to the Oval Office, from the business executive to the pastorate—no location, no office of authority is immune to misogyny and sexism, to objectifying, abusing, and devaluing women.

Jesus Christ is the Son of God (Mark 1:1). He was born king (Matthew 2:2). All authority was entrusted to him (John 3:35;

Matthew 11:27; 28:18). So how will this king use his position, power, and authority in relation to women? How will he speak to women and listen to them? How will he treat them when alone with them? How will he touch them, welcome them, protect them?

Beyond king, Jesus is God in the flesh (John 1:1, 14). He is God with us (Matthew 1:23). To see Jesus is to see God the Father (John 14:9). What then can we learn about how God views and values women from watching Jesus?

In this chapter, we'll examine the life and ministry of Jesus, seeing how the perfect man valued, loved, and honored women.

What We Don't See in Jesus

Let's start with what we *don't* see. We admit that arguments from silence can be tricky, deceptive even. Nevertheless, there is value in noting what is not found in Jesus' life and ministry, especially in light of what we see in too many in positions of power.

We see no hint of impropriety with women on the part of Jesus. We find no indication that women were uncomfortable in his presence.

Jesus demonstrates no concern for how loving and engaging with women would impact his reputation, hinder his ministry, be misinterpreted (maliciously or innocently), or cause alarm in others (especially the religious). He gives no indication that he views women across the board as snares, sexual objects, and seductresses.

We do not hear Jesus engage in "locker room talk." Nor do we see genuinely inappropriate or unwelcome touch (though he did not shrink from receiving touch that alarmed the religious of his day).

Perhaps this is why we read of no female enemies, but many devoted female followers. "Against the background of the failure of the male disciples the devotion and courage of the women shine out . . . they remained there to the end, demonstrating by their very presence their continuing loyalty to their crucified Lord. It is worth noticing that there is no mention of any woman at any time taking action against Jesus; all his enemies were men."[7]

Charles Spurgeon notes, "We have no record of any unkindness to our Lord from any woman, though we have many narratives of the loving ministry of women at various periods in his life."[8] In fact, at his trial, a woman is the only one to defend his righteousness (Matthew 27:19). All his recorded opponents are men.

We don't find the devaluing, objectification, abuse, or marginalization of women in the life and ministry of Jesus. If these actions and attitudes had no place in the life of the perfect human and King of Kings, they certainly have no place in our leadership, our workplaces, our locker room talk, our homes, our cultures, or our churches. The reign of Christ roots out and replaces all of this with something better.

What is that better thing? What do we see about the value of women in the life of Christ?

What We See in Jesus

Jesus noticed women. On one occasion, Jesus sat down in the Court of Women (the farthest women could enter into the temple) and watched people put their gifts in the offering box (Mark 12:41–44; Luke 21:1–4). He noticed a woman who may have been easy to overlook—a poor widow. Not only did he notice her, but he also called others to see her, praising her example as being greater than all the others.

Jesus dignified women as fully human.[9] On another occasion, as Jesus taught in the synagogue, he noticed a woman suffering under demonic affliction with physical results, a condition she'd endured for eighteen years (Luke 13:10–17). Jesus called her to himself, touched her, and healed her. When the ruler of the synagogue rebuked the people for seeking healing on the Sabbath, Jesus rebuked him, "You hypocrites! Does not each of you on the Sabbath untie his ox or his donkey from the manger and lead it away to water it? And ought not this woman, a daughter of Abraham whom Satan bound for eighteen years, be loosed from this bond on the Sabbath day?" Jesus has no patience for a man who values an animal more than a woman.

Notice how Jesus dignifies this woman. He sees her, speaks to her, touches her. He defends her value as a human being and a member of God's family—"this woman, a daughter of Abraham." He shames those who value their animals more than her.

Jesus enjoyed the company of women. Women were counted as his acquaintances and traveling companions from his earliest moments of public ministry to the foot of the cross (John 2:12; Luke 23:49). These "many" women ranged the social scale from Mary Magdalene (out of whom Jesus exorcized seven demons) to Joanna to the wife of Herod's household manager (Luke 8:1–3).

Each gospel notes a group of women (some named and others unknown) present at Jesus' crucifixion, which "followed him and took care of him" (Mark 15:40 CSB; cf. Luke 23:49; Matthew 27:55–56; John 19:25). Scholar James Edwards comments on Mark's expression:

> The imperfect tenses of both verbs in Greek indicate not occasional or sporadic accompaniment and service, but the continued presence and service of Jesus throughout his ministry. These and "many other women" have done what Mark throughout his Gospel has defined as discipleship: following and serving Jesus. Only angels (1:13) and women (15:41) are said to have ministered to Jesus in Mark. . . . A Roman centurion makes the first Christian confession, and women, although not Jesus' most notable followers, have been among his most faithful.[10]

Jesus did not shrink from spending time alone with women— even scandalous women. Once, while passing through Samaria, Jesus sat down at a well, wearied and thirsty. His disciples had gone into town to fetch food, leaving Jesus alone. A Samaritan woman approached the well, whom he immediately engaged in conversation. When his disciples returned sometime later, "they marveled that he was talking with a woman" (John 4:27).

Jesus initiated a theological conversation with a Samaritan woman at a well. In Jesus' day, almost every word in that sentence was scandalous.

First, the initiative—Jesus *initiated* the conversation. "His taking the initiative invited the accusation of acting in a flirtatious manner. Jewish men usually did not speak to women in public."[11]

Second, the location—a *well*. This may not seem significant to modern readers, not much more than conversation around the water cooler. Andreas Köstenberger explains the cultural significance of the location: "The fact that Isaac's and Jacob's prospective wives were met at wells (Genesis 24:17; 29:10) created the sort of precedent that would further have cautioned devout Jews. The precedents were taken to suggest that, unless one is looking for a mate, one should avoid speaking to women in public, especially at wells, which were known to be places where men could 'pick up' women."[12]

Third, the subject—he was with *a woman* at the well. A rabbinical saying taught: "A man shall not be alone with a woman in an inn, not even with his sister or his daughter, on account of what men may think. A man shall not talk with a woman in the street, not even with his own wife, and especially not with another woman, on account of what men may say."[13] *Jesus, apparently, did not shrink from conversation with women due to fear of what other men might think or how it would "ruin his witness."*

Fourth, the ethnicity of the woman—a *Samaritan*. Jews avoided Samaritans in general, fearing ritual defilement. "Probably this fear was intensified when the Samaritan was a woman: within a generation Jewish leaders would codify a law (Mishnah *Niddah* 4:1) that reflected longstanding popular sentiment, to the effect that all 'the daughters of the Samaritans are menstruants from their cradle' and therefore perpetually in a state of ceremonial uncleanness."[14]

Fifth, the activity—he engaged in conversation—*theological conversation*—with a woman. Rabbinical teaching discouraged men, under the threat of hell, from engaging in lengthy conversation with women. "He who prolongs conversation with a woman brings evil upon himself, ceases from the words of the law, and at the last inherits Gehanna."[15]

More than that, rabbinical tradition viewed the *theological instruction* of women a particular waste of time. "Some rabbis went so far as to suggest that to provide their daughters with a knowledge of the *Torah* was as inappropriate as to teach them lechery, *i.e.,* to sell them into prostitution."[16]

Nevertheless, the traditions of men do not dissuade Jesus. In *Through His Eyes: God's Perspective on Women in the Bible*, Jerram Barrs observes:

> Jesus treats the Samaritan woman as a rational and thoughtful person. He should know, of course, for he is the Creator of women as persons, persons who are just as much the image of God as any man he has made. As the Creator of women he is fully aware of her intellectual abilities and her capacity to learn and discuss theology. No teacher (and no man) had ever spoken to her in this way before. But Jesus enters into a theological discussion with her.[17]

With that context in mind, imagine how this woman must have felt when a man invited her into a conversation about life and theology, taking her seriously both in his listening and his replies. "No man had ever before addressed her as a social equal."[18] Perhaps, no man (or woman) had ever addressed her as a human being. Jesus went to where all the women were not to seek the woman all the women were not seeking.

> *The Samaritan woman (whose ethnicity embodied both Jew and Gentile) was the first person to whom Jesus revealed himself as the Messiah. She was also the first person he tasked with taking that message to a non-Jewish audience.*

Jesus was ministered to by women. Jesus revealed his vulnerability to women and allowed them to serve his needs. At the well, "Jesus shows his vulnerability and need to the Samaritan woman—he is tired and thirsty. . . . He dignifies her by acknowledging his need of something she can do for him. He shows his vulnerability to her. He is thirsty and tired, and she can help him."[19] In doing so, Jesus honors her humanity by acknowledging his own.

Lest we think the request for a drink at the well was merely a one-time vulnerability aimed more at evangelizing a soul than quenching a real thirst, we should note how often women served Jesus. In Mark's gospel, "only angels (1:13) and women (15:41) are said to have ministered to Jesus."[20] In his gospel and the book of Acts, "Luke was fond of pointing out the role of women in service to Jesus," with at least nine significant notes of service (Luke 1:5–80; 2:36–38; 8:1–3; 23:49, 55; Acts 9:36–42; 12:12–17; 18:24–28; 21:9).[21]

The women who continually followed Jesus are the only recorded source of income for Jesus' itinerant ministry, providing for him "out of their means" (Luke 8:1–3). They "took care of him" (Mark 15:40–41 CSB) and "looked after him" (Matthew 27:55–56 CSB), as other women did on several occasions (Matthew 8:15; Mark 1:31; Luke 4:39). Jesus even received the hospitality of a female homeowner when "a woman named Martha welcomed him into her house" (Luke 10:38–42). This is remarkable because "in Jesus's day, a Jewish rabbi or religious leader would never receive hospitality by a woman this way."[22]

Some men may enjoy the company of women, but only as an occasion to demonstrate their own strength and wisdom, their ability to protect and provide. They would never dream of being served by—much more, depend upon—a woman. Jesus' manhood was not so fragile.

Jesus touched and was touched by women. If a side-hug in the church foyer makes you uncomfortable, you might want to skip this one. Jesus' interactions with women often included touch. He touched women. Jesus healed Peter's mother-in-law by touching her hand (Matthew 8:14–15, Mark 1:29–31). Why does this matter? "The only point that concerns Matthew is Jesus' compassion for yet a third category of people who were viewed as second class citizens within Judaism, namely, women. . . . Touching women in this fashion was banned by at least some Jewish traditions."[23] Such traditions forbade a man to touch the hand of a woman, "not even to count money from his hand to hers."[24]

Likewise, Jesus allowed women to touch him without rebuke, sometimes quite scandalously (Matthew 9:18–26; Mark 5:21–43; Luke 8:40–56). As Jesus dined at the home of a Pharisee, a woman entered (Luke 7:36–50). This itself was not scandalous, such meals being semi-public affairs at which uninvited guests might stand around the edges to observe. She stood at Jesus' feet and, overwhelmed with the grace he'd shown her in forgiving her sins, began to weep.

Tears fell from her cheeks, landing on his feet, wetting them. So the woman let down her hair and began to wipe the tears from Jesus' feet. This act alone would have prompted the rebuke of most Jewish men, as "a Jewish lady never unbound her hair in public. This was apparently seen as a mark of loose morals."[25] "Apparently, for a married woman to let down her hair in public constituted grounds for divorce."[26] How much more scandalous for a "woman of the city," a "sinner."

Going even further, she kisses Jesus' feet before anointing them with oil. Consider the intimacy of this touch as this woman bends down to place her lips to the feet of the Messiah. Jesus, to the dismay of his host, does not rebuke the woman. He not only receives her intimate touch, but he also praises it, holds her up as an example of hospitality. He admonishes the failure of his (male) host and sends her away in peace.

On another occasion, his friend Mary did something similar (John 12:1–8; see also Matthew 26:6–13; Mark 14:3–9). One author notes, "The fact that Mary (who probably was single, as no husband is mentioned) here acts in such a way toward Jesus, a well-known (yet unattached) rabbi, was sure to raise some eyebrows."[27]

But Jesus is not concerned about how receiving this woman's touch may appear to outsiders, may stimulate gossip, or may "ruin his witness." He cares about this woman.

Jesus was always appropriate with women—gentle, gracious, and compassionate, though never condescending. Though culturally scandalous, Jesus showed no impropriety with the woman at the well or those who washed his feet.

Jesus showed compassion to women in their suffering. He healed sick women (Matthew 8:14–15; Mark 1:29–31; Luke 4:38–39). When the Lord saw a widow mourning her only son, "he had compassion on her" and raised him from the dead (Luke 7:11–17). When a woman fell at his knees, fearful and trembling at being found out for touching his garment, he offered gentle reassurance—"Take heart, daughter; your faith has made you well" (Matthew 9:18–26; Mark 5:21–43; Luke 8:40–56). Observing a woman in the synagogue, afflicted by a demon for eighteen years, bent over and unable to straighten herself, Jesus called her, touched her, and healed her (Luke 13:10–17). When a Canaanite woman begged for mercy, Jesus not only delivered her demon-oppressed daughter, he praised her faith (Matthew 15:21–28). He entered into the weeping of Mary over the death of her brother Lazarus; he was deeply moved and wept with her—and then raised her brother from the dead (John 11:1–44). When speaking of the last days, he spoke with awareness of and compassion for the demands on pregnant women and nursing mothers (Matthew 24:19; Mark 13:17; Luke 21:23).

Jesus had time, touch, and tears for women.

Jesus rebuked, disagreed with, corrected, and forgave individual women. Jesus' gentleness with women should not be mistaken for condescension. He did not treat his female friends with disdain.

Jesus gently challenged his own mother (John 2:4). He directly disagreed with and corrected the Samaritan woman's theology (John 4:1–26). The Lord addressed Martha's anxiety and corrected her choices (Luke 10:38–42). When a woman proclaimed that the greatest blessing a woman could desire was to be the Messiah's mother, Jesus corrected her; the greater blessing is to hear and obey him (Luke 11:27–28).

Jesus also forgave women. He said to the sinful woman who anointed his feet, "Your sins are forgiven" (Luke 7:47–48). Though this statement may seem unremarkable to those of us familiar with the forgiveness of sins offered in the Gospel, consider what it says about her personhood. Her standing with God is not determined by her connection to a man, whether a husband or a father (or the men who used her). She is fully human; she stands before God as her own person—once a sinner, now forgiven.

Jesus included women in his parables and illustrations. Consider the characters we meet in Jesus' teaching. Women grinding at the mill (Matthew 24:41; Luke 17:35). Virgins waiting for the arrival of the bridegroom (Matthew 25:1–13). A woman making bread (Luke 13:20–21). A woman searching for her lost coin (Luke 15:8–10). A persistent widow seeking justice (Luke 18:1–8). The Lord did not limit his illustrations to the men. He included women carrying out the tasks common to them in that culture, often casting them as positive examples of kingdom virtues.

Jesus even used the idea of protective motherhood to illustrate himself and his compassion toward Israel (Luke 13:34–35; Matthew 23:37–39). "Jesus' words betray great tenderness and employ maternal imagery. God transcends gender and displays attributes that humans often associate with women, as well as those commonly associated with men. Here Jesus wishes he could gather all the recalcitrant 'children' of Israel, to love, to protect, and nurture them like a mother hen does with her baby chickens."[28] Perhaps this is why Paul and Timothy would be comfortable comparing their ministry to a nursing mother (1 Thessalonians 2:7).

Jesus used his platform to protect and dignify women, opposing misogyny and sexism. The Lord forbids treating women as physical objects to lust after. In fact, he condemns the objectification of women as an evil worthy of hell (Matthew 5:27–30). He condemns the neglect of mothers (Matthew 15:4–6; Mark 7:8–13). He protects women from unjust divorce (Matthew 5:31–32; 19:3–12; Mark 10:11–12; Luke 16:18).

Jesus taught, discipled, and dialogued with women. Jesus did not shrink from engaging women in significant theological discussions (see John 4:1–26; 11:1–44). He interacted with women as intelligent, rational, intellectual people.

When Luke notes that Mary "sat at the Lord's feet and listened to his teaching," he communicates something more than her seating location (Luke 10:39). In Acts 22:3, Luke records Paul testifying that he was "educated *at the feet* of Gamaliel." In her posture, Mary "takes the place of a disciple by sitting at the feet of the teacher."[29] Jesus' willingness to allow women to listen to his teaching and to become part of his ministry went against the rabbinic practices of his day.[30] "Our Lord, from the beginning, loves and includes women among his disciples and in his fellowship."[31]

This discipleship extended to meaningful ministry, such as the task of proclaiming his resurrection to others (Matthew 28:10). "Many in the church today need to recover more of the biblical witness concerning God's dealings with women. He is an equal opportunity dispenser both of his grace and of contexts to serve him."[32]

At the beginning of the chapter, we asked how Jesus—the perfect Man, the King of all—would use his position, power, and authority in relation to women. This brief survey of his life and ministry sought to answer that question, which Dorothy Sayers summarizes poignantly:

Perhaps it is no wonder that the women were first at the Cradle and last at the Cross. They had never known such a man like this Man—there never has been such another. A prophet and teacher who never nagged at them, never flattered or coaxed or patronized; who never made arch jokes about them, never treated them as either 'The women, God help us!' or 'The ladies, God bless them!'; who rebuked without querulousness and praised without condescension; who never mapped out their sphere for them, never urged them to be feminine or jeered at them for being female; who took their questions and arguments seriously; who had no axe to grind and no uneasy male dignity to defend; who took them as he found them and was completely unselfconscious. There is no act, no sermon, no parable in the whole Gospel that borrows its pungency from female perversity; nobody could possibly guess from the words and deeds of Jesus that there was anything "funny" about women's nature.[33]

What we see in the life of Jesus—his teachings, actions, and attitudes—is what true humanity is supposed to look like. It is what the kingdom of God looks like. To the degree that such is lacking in our cities, workplaces, and families, to that degree the reign of Christ still needs to have its full effect. Moreover, if the church is the body of Christ, then these things must be included in the marks of a healthy church. To the degree that such is lacking in local church culture, perhaps then, so is Christ.

——— DISCOVERING A WOMAN'S WORTH ———

1. Apparently, Jesus didn't have any qualms about meeting with or talking to women. How do you reconcile this with the common belief these days that men should avoid such meetings?

2. List some of the things we said we don't see in the life and ministry of Jesus. Which ones are most meaningful to you? Why?

3. We listed eleven things that we can see in Jesus' ministry with women. List the three that are most meaningful to you. Why did you choose as you did?

4. Women: How have these items built your faith in God's love and welcome of you? Men: How have they opened your eyes to ways you can minister to women?

5. Summarize what you have learned in this chapter in four or five sentences.

───────── DIGGING DEEPER ─────────

1. Although it may be wise to be careful about meeting with people we are not married to, can you think of any reasons why a hard-and-fast rule about this may be harmful? Denigrating? Can you think of any ways this rule might be employed without harm?

2. In Genesis, the woman was created to be the helper, one who would model the helper nature of God. In what ways do we see the women in the Gospels helping the Second Adam, Jesus?

3. What gospel women have gotten a bad rap? After considering the way Jesus interacted with them, how might that be changed?

TEN

The Worth of Women in Jesus' Death and Resurrection

*And truly, I say to you, wherever the gospel
is proclaimed in the whole world, what she
has done will be told in memory of her.*

Mark 14:9

Amongst terrorists in the Middle East, this young man stood head and shoulders above his peers. He prided himself on a noble ancestral lineage. He learned from the best—an esteemed teacher in the strictest of schools. His zeal knew no bounds, propelling him to become the preeminent religious zealot of his day.

He watched approvingly as a mob gathered around a Christian man, lobbing large stones at him until he died. He breathed out threats and murder against the church in his region. He stalked Christians—capturing men and women, shackling them and handing them over to the authorities for punishment. He hated Christ.

He hated the church. He made it his life's ambition to wipe Christianity off the face of the earth. This man, Saul of Tarsus, would go on to write the majority of the New Testament letters.

The Apostle Paul (as he would sign his letters) said of himself, "I was a blasphemer, persecutor, and insolent opponent [of the Lord]" (1 Timothy 1:13). Left to himself, he would have gladly continued down that road. But as he traveled it, the Lord intervened, knocking him off his high horse and setting him on a new trajectory. "I received mercy," Paul wrote, "and the grace of our Lord overflowed for me with the faith and love that are in Christ Jesus. The saying is trustworthy and deserving of full acceptance, that Christ Jesus came into the world to save sinners, of whom I am the foremost" (1 Timothy 1:13–15).

At this point in the book, whether you're a man or a woman, we hope you've come to better grasp the value of women. But we also hope you've begun to understand how you have failed to value women—something both men and women can be guilty of doing. The example and perfection of Jesus should convict us all.

For some, the failure may be egregious. You may be guilty of the vilest and most dehumanizing acts against women. You've sexually molested, raped, physically assaulted, emotionally abused, trafficked, or murdered women or girls. You've remained silent as these things happened to a woman or girl.[1]

For others, the failure may be more socially acceptable. You've objectified the female body, using or offering it as an object of pleasure divorced from a valuable human being. You've discriminated against, demeaned, condescended to, or stereotyped females—all in the name of "common sense," tradition, or "just a joke." You've stood by silently as you watched women being mistreated.

For others, the problem may be pride. You know that you've done these things. But to admit it and to change seems too costly. Like Saul, you've built your reputation on such behavior. Perhaps you're a pastor, manager, coach, or parent whose words, actions, or passivity have been hurtful to women. You fear that to admit such would ruin your reputation or cost you your job. You regret how you've been, but you're feeling the tug of self-justification and self-preservation fighting your desire to repent. And so you won't.

If we're honest with ourselves, we must admit that we have all failed to glorify God in the way we have treated women. These acts of spiritual and sometimes criminal wickedness (along with so many more we do not have time to list) may be committed by either a man or a woman. Misogyny is not a one-sex problem. We, Elyse and Eric, can both testify to our own guilt in devaluing and harming women in our thoughts, words, and deeds—both done and undone.

Is there a solution? Is there justice for victims? Can the worst offenders find redemption? Can we find freedom for honesty and repentance? Is there any provision for forgiveness? Can we see hope for transformation and change? The answer to each of these questions is a resounding yes! For, as Paul wrote, "The saying is trustworthy and deserving of full acceptance, that Christ Jesus came into the world to save sinners, of whom I am the foremost."

In this chapter, we follow the Lord Jesus Christ down a road remarkably different than that followed by Saul of Tarsus. The way of the cross was a road of shame, suffering, service, and self-sacrifice. He walked it for sinners—for sexists, chauvinists, and misogynists. He traveled it for sufferers—for the marginalized, the abused, and the oppressed. He became what they are so that they could become what he is. At this point, it should not surprise us to learn that women—women who were both sinners and sufferers—were present every step of the way, representatives of those whom he came to seek and to save.

The Way of the Cross

"You know that after two days the Passover is coming, and the Son of Man will be delivered up to be crucified," Jesus told his disciples (Matthew 26:2). The Passover to which Jesus referred was the annual festival Israel observed to remember their rescue from

Egypt. The Israelites had been enslaved for hundreds of years, and the Lord raised up Moses to deliver them. After a series of plagues, one final blow would convince Pharaoh to let the Lord's people go. The Angel of the Lord would visit the land, striking dead the firstborn in every household—both Israelite and Egyptian. The Israelites were instructed to slaughter a lamb—one for each home—and paint the doorways to their homes with its blood. When the Lord visited the land that night and saw the blood on the door, he would "pass over" that home. The firstborn would be saved by the blood of the lamb. Now Jesus marched to Jerusalem to be crucified during the Passover, to be sacrificed as "the Lamb of God, who takes away the sin of the world" (John 1:29).

Following the Lamb were women. Overlooked and unexpected, these women see who he is, faithfully follow him, receive his compassion, declare his righteousness, witness his death and burial, see, hear, and touch his resurrected body, proclaim his resurrection, and worship him. Let's walk through the last chapters of the four gospels and see the role these surprising figures play in the final hours of the Messiah's earthly ministry.

A woman prepared Jesus for his burial while men plotted his assassination.

In Matthew 26 we witness three consecutive gatherings, settings, and actions that could not be more different. In the first, "the chief priests and the elders of the people gathered in the palace of the high priest . . . and plotted together in order to arrest Jesus by stealth and kill him" (Matthew 26:3–4).

In the second scene, we find Jesus in Bethany, dining at the house of Simon the leper (whom, it is assumed, Jesus healed). As he reclined at the table, a woman approached (we learn in John 12 that she is Mary, the sister of Martha). She carried an alabaster flask of ointment—pure nard (Mark 14:3)—valued at a year's wages. Such extravagant ointment was "used for solemn acts of devotion. More common household oils were used to anoint guests."[2]

Nevertheless, Mary poured it on Jesus' head and anointed his feet, wiping them with her hair (Matthew 26:7; John 12:3).

This act angered the disciples, causing them to demand, "Why this waste? For this could have been sold for a large sum and given to the poor" (Matthew 26:8–9). Jesus, knowing the disciples' grumbling, defends her actions,

> Why do you trouble the woman? For she has done a beautiful thing to me. For you always have the poor with you, but you will not always have me. In pouring this ointment on my body, she has done it to prepare me for burial. Truly, I say to you, wherever this gospel is proclaimed in the whole world, what she has done will also be told in memory of her.
>
> Matthew 26:10–13

The disciples will always be able to care for the poor; they will not always be able to care for Jesus in this critical hour. This woman did something that could only be done then—she prepared Jesus' body for burial. The Lord praised her actions as a model of devotion for which she will be remembered whenever the Gospel is preached in all the world.

Our third scene unfolds as Judas goes to the chief priests, asking what payment he might receive for delivering Jesus to them. Mary prepared Jesus for burial with ointment worth 300 denarii (a year's wage). Judas prepared to betray Jesus in exchange for thirty pieces of silver.

Why does this woman's presence in the story matter? Notice the bookends of these scenes. In the first, a group of men, distinguished leaders of Israel, gather in the comfort of a palace to plot the assassination of Jesus. In the last, a man seeks those men out to profit from joining their cause. These ghastly actions bookend what Jesus calls "a beautiful thing" (Mark 14:6). In the home of a former leper, a meek woman demonstrates prodigal love for Jesus. It is she—and not the chief priests, the elders, or Judas the apostle—who understands and models true discipleship.

What is the significance of women's presence throughout Jesus' ministry and especially in the last hours of his life? Women were a marginalized social class. Faith would be expected from one of the Twelve, such as Judas and Peter. But it is the women who followed him without betrayal or denial. The chief priests, the elders, and the high priest of Israel should have recognized their Messiah. But a woman anoints the King. The unexpected, despised, rejected Messiah is followed by unexpected, despised, rejected people.

But Jesus does not despise and reject these unexpected disciples. He sees, receives, and affirms them, and promises that they will never be forgotten.

A woman declared the righteousness of Jesus.

The next time we see Jesus, he is in Jerusalem eating the Passover meal with his disciples. During the dinner, Judas departed to arrange Jesus' betrayal. After the meal, Jesus went with his disciples to the Mount of Olives where he pled with the Father to take the cup of his crucifixion away from him. None of Jesus' disciples could stay awake to pray with him, even though he asked them to. Then a great crowd approached, armed with clubs and swords, sent from the chief priests and the elders. Judas identified Jesus to the mob by a greeting and a kiss. When the crowd seized Jesus, "all the disciples left him and fled" (Matthew 26:56). The crowd took him to be tried before the high priest. As Jesus spoke the truth before the highest officials in Israel, Peter, one of his closest disciples, cowered before a servant girl and denied three times that he even knew him (Matthew 26:57–75).

In the morning, the religious leaders delivered Jesus over to Pontius Pilate, who sought to release Jesus because he understood the motive for the arrest was envy. It is now that we hear, "while he was sitting on the judgment seat, his wife sent word to him, 'Have nothing to do with that righteous man, for I have suffered much because of him today in a dream'" (Matthew 27:19). God gave Pilate's wife a troubling sign in her sleep to communicate Jesus' innocence.

This proclamation from an unlikely prophet is not to be overlooked. Though she speaks with significance that she cannot possibly understand, she expresses a truth central to the Gospel—Jesus is a "righteous man." While the religious leaders are clamoring for his execution, a Gentile woman warns that he is the righteous one.

Righteousness is conformity to God's character and standards in all manners. The New Testament confirms that Jesus was "without sin" (Hebrews 4:15); he is "the Righteous One" (Acts 7:52; 22:14), "Jesus Christ the righteous" (1 John 2:1). Jesus never sinned; he never disobeyed God; he always did what was pleasing to the Father (John 8:29).

Why does it matter that this woman declared his righteousness? Again, from an unexpected place—a non-Jewish woman and the wife of the man who will sentence Jesus to death—the truth is revealed about Jesus. Even the pagans knew that he was innocent. This is why, when the chief priests sought false testimony against Jesus, they could find none (Matthew 26:59–60). He was righteous, uncondemnable.

Why does it matter that Jesus is righteous? At the Feast of the Passover, Jesus is led like a lamb to the slaughter (Isaiah 53:7). The Passover lamb had to be "without blemish" (Exodus 12:5). In Christ's death, God would purchase his people "with the precious blood of Christ, like that of a lamb without blemish or spot" (1 Peter 1:19).

Christ went to die as a sacrifice for sins, a substitute for his people. This required that he be perfect. "Christ also suffered once for sins, the righteous for the unrighteous, that he might bring us to God" (1 Peter 3:18).

On the cross, God declared the Righteous One to be a guilty sinner, so that he could claim guilty sinners to be righteous ones. "For our sake he made him to be sin who knew no sin, so that in him we might become the righteousness of God" (2 Corinthians

5:21). On the cross, our sin is reckoned as belonging to Jesus, who is condemned and put to death under the wrath of God for it.

When a sinner repents and trusts in Jesus, the righteousness of Christ is imputed to that sinner, who is justified (or "declared righteous") in the sight of God. As Hebrews says,

> The blood of Christ, who through the eternal Spirit offered himself without blemish to God, [will] purify our conscience from dead works to serve the living God.
>
> Hebrews 9:14

This righteousness is the grounds on which God receives and shows mercy to all manner of women (and men!) whom Jesus loved. The adulteress, the prostitute, the self-righteous, the demon-possessed, the bereaved, the poor, the helpless. No matter the greatness of her sin and shame, nor the insignificance of her class or station—any and all can be forgiven and justified with "a righteousness . . . which comes through faith in Christ" (Philippians 3:9). Praise God for Jesus, "that righteous man!"

Women received the compassion of Jesus, even as he suffered execution.

In his execution, no one showed Jesus any compassion (see Matthew 27:26–49). Pontius Pilate had Jesus scourged.

> Those condemned to it were tied to a post and beaten with a leather whip that was interwoven with pieces of bone and metal, which tore through skin and tissue, often exposing bones and intestines. In many cases, the flogging itself was fatal.[3]

After the flogging, Pilate delivered Jesus to be crucified. The soldiers showed Jesus no mercy. They stripped him naked, then dressed him in a scarlet robe, pressed a crown of thorns onto his head, and put a reed in his right hand as a laughable scepter. They knelt before him and mocked him—"Hail! King of the Jews!" Then they spat on him and struck him on the head.

After mocking him, they forced him to carry the cross beam to which he would be nailed, a beam that would be hoisted in the air, on which he would hang as a condemned criminal until he died. As they watched him, they gambled for his clothing, his only worldly possessions. They nailed a sign above his head, which declared the crime for which he was condemned—"King of the Jews."

The chief priests, scribes, and elders of Israel showed him no pity. Instead, they mocked him. The robbers amongst which he died showed no kindness, joining in the reviling themselves.

Yet in the midst of humiliation and agonizing pain, Jesus remained compassionate. As they crucified him, he prayed, "Father, forgive them, for they know not what they do" (Luke 23:34).

Luke records a striking picture of Jesus' compassion as he walks to the cross (Luke 23:27–31). A "great multitude of the people and of women" followed him. They were "mourning and lamenting for him." Jesus summons the strength and presence of mind to turn and address these women with tenderness, compassion, and exemplary regard for one's neighbor over oneself (Luke 23:28–31).

He tells them, "Daughters of Jerusalem, do not weep for me, but weep for yourselves and for your children." After the cross, Jesus will go to glory. But it is about to get much worse for Israel. The day was coming when the wrath of God poured out on Jesus through these Roman soldiers will be turned on the nation. Jesus asks, "If they do these things when the wood is green, what will happen when it is dry?" By this he means, if they do such things to the King, how will they treat his people?[4]

When this day comes, the people will flee to the mountains and the hills for protection. But such an escape is slowed when pregnant or nursing or carrying small children—making such families easy prey. And so, he says, "The days are coming when they will say, 'Blessed are the barren and the wombs that never bore and the breasts that never nursed!'" Those with no children do not have to watch their children suffer.

Even in the midst of his own agony, Jesus' compassion for his people, for "daughters of Jerusalem," overflows. He does not view these women as maidservants to tend to his aches and pains while he dies. Rather, taking note of unique aspects of womanhood, he loves them, pities them, and serves them in word and deed.

John records what is perhaps the most touching scene in all the life of Christ (John 19:26–27). Hanging on the cross, Jesus noticed his mother and John standing nearby. Mary is likely widowed, in her late forties, with no wealth or source of income. She watches as her oldest son dies. Jesus said to his mother, "Woman, behold, your son!" And then to John, "Behold, your mother!" With these words, he transfers care of his mother to his disciple, providing for her in the hour of his death. John would care for her from then on.

Why do these displays of compassion matter? They demonstrate Jesus' remarkable faithfulness to his people, the unfathomable depths of his compassion. At no point does the love of Christ fail. His own pain cannot tear him away from caring for his flock. Despite their present distress, he knows what is ultimate and seeks their ultimate good at his own loss.

In his words to the "daughters of Jerusalem," Jesus points beyond the immediate circumstances to what is to come. They wept because a man they admired died. Jesus cares enough about them to warn of something worse—the coming wrath to fall on them. We all have sinned. We all deserve the wrath of God. This is why Jesus goes to the cross—to save us from the wrath to come by receiving it in our place (Romans 5:8–10).

> But God shows his love for us in that while we were still sinners, Christ died for us. Since, therefore, we have now been justified by his blood, much more shall we be saved by him from the wrath of God. For if while we were enemies we were reconciled to God by the death of his Son, much more, now that we are reconciled, shall we be saved by his life.

What hope these stories should give us now! If Jesus had the presence of mind to note the unique burden of mothers as he walked to the cross, will he forget them now that he is raised to glory? If the Lord provided for a widow while hanging on a cross, will he fail to provide for them now that he sits at the Father's right hand? If the Suffering Servant demonstrated such compassion toward others in the hour of his own need, will he withhold it from you in yours?

Women witnessed Jesus' suffering, death, and burial.

Of the disciples recorded in the Gospels who followed Jesus faithfully to the end, the Gospel-writers take special note of women. "All his acquaintances *and the women* who had followed him from Galilee stood at a distance watching these things" (Luke 23:49, emphasis added). They followed him to Galilee in the north as he journeyed south to his death in Jerusalem, apparently never leaving him (unless prevented by a location, such as the palace where they tried him).

Jesus' mother, his mother's sister (possibly Salome, the mother of the sons of Zebedee), Mary Magdalene, Mary the mother of James and Joseph, Mary the wife of Clopas—they are named, noted personally for their presence, given places of honor at the foot of the cross (Matthew 27:55–56; Mark 15:40–41; John 19:25). These devoted and courageous disciples did not betray him, deny him, or flee from him. They loved him, even to the end. These female disciples serve as examples of those who take up their cross and follow him.

As a side note, the presence of the women at the crucifixion speaks of the strength of women in general, pushing back against common stereotypes. Reading a draft of this chapter, our friend, Emily Jensen, commented:

> . . . these scenes affirm feminine strength in the face of gore. Jesus did not "protect the weaker sex" by shooing them into the house where they didn't have to see the blood and guts. They were on

the front lines of this epic battle scene where their beloved teacher and Savior took the most brutal hits.[5]

Indeed. It is striking that, by God's design, two of the most "exclusively feminine" activities (meaning: things a female can do that a male cannot) both involve blood—menstruation and child birth. Women deal with blood on a regular basis almost all their adult lives. It is fathers who more often pass out during labor and delivery. When I (Eric) had custodial rotation at my seminary job, only the men balked and complained about having to attend to the feminine product disposal bins in the women's locker room stalls.

Likewise, after Jesus had died, the women accompanied his body to the tomb and witnessed his burial. Joseph of Arimathea was a disciple of Jesus, a dissenting member of the council that condemned him, and possibly the son of "Mary the mother of Joses" who witnessed these things (Mark 15:43–47). He asked Pilate for the body of Jesus and, once granted permission, took the corpse, prepared it for burial, and placed it in his own unused tomb, which he closed with a great stone (Matthew 27:60–61). "The women who had come with him from Galilee followed and saw the tomb and how his body was laid" (Luke 23:55; see also Matthew 27:61; Mark 15:47).

Why does it matter that these women witnessed Jesus' suffering, death, and burial? Their witness verifies the reality of his death. Jesus was not sick or swooning. He was dead. *Dead*-dead. Dead as a doornail, as Dickens might put it. They witnessed the blood and the water flow from his pierced side, verifying his death to the executioners (John 19:34). They saw Joseph take the *corpse* down from the cross (Mark 15:45–46). They witnessed as Joseph and Nicodemus "took the body of Jesus and bound it in linen cloths with the spices, as is the burial custom of the Jews" (John 19:40). They witnessed as Joseph laid the body in a tomb "and rolled a stone against the entrance" (Mark 15:46). They saw, and they knew the truth—Jesus died. These women are named, allowing anyone to interview them about the reality of his death.

Their witness to his death lends credibility to their witness to his resurrection. Several of these women will be named as the first witnesses of Jesus' resurrection. Some will even be tasked with returning to tell his disciples the good news. The fact that they saw him dead—*really dead*—makes them perfect witnesses to the fact that he is alive—*really alive.*

Their witness also gives the ring of truth to the witness of the Gospels in general. In the first century, women were not valued as credible witnesses, particularly in weighty matters. If the authors of the Gospels were interested in fabricating a myth, lying about the death and resurrection of their leader, why give women the central role as witnesses? Why not use characters more valued and trusted in their culture? Why women? Because the authors were not spinning a fable; they were recording true history. This history was not theirs to massage. God, in his sovereign wisdom, ordained that these women were the witnesses, and so they are recorded as such.

Why does it matter that Jesus *really died*? Why is his death, verified by these witnesses, so important?

The death of Jesus is an indispensable component of the Gospel. The Apostle Paul will write—

> Now I would remind you, brothers, of the gospel I preached to you, which you received, in which you stand, and by which you are being saved, if you hold fast to the word I preached to you—unless you believed in vain. For I delivered to you as of first importance what I also received: that Christ died for our sins in accordance with the Scriptures.
>
> 1 Corinthians 15:1–3

"Christ died *for our sins.*" This real death is necessary because "the wages of sin is death" (Romans 6:23), and "the soul who sins shall die" (Ezekiel 18:20). But "Christ died for the ungodly. . . . God shows his love for us in that while we were still sinners, Christ died for us" (Romans 5:6, 8). He was "cut off out of the land of the living, stricken for the transgression of [the] people" (Isaiah 53:8). Through this death, we who trust in Christ see that God has "forgiven us all our trespasses, by canceling the record of debt that stood against us with its legal demands. This he set aside, nailing it to the cross" (Colossians 2:13–14).

If Christ did not die, then we are still in our sins, for "without the shedding of blood there is no forgiveness of sins" (Hebrews 9:22). But Christ did die and he "put away sin by the sacrifice of himself" (Hebrews 9:26).

Think back to our first chapters, where we saw men and women placed on earth to exercise dominion, put in the Garden in a priestly role. Think of how they fail as kings and priests to our God. Think of the tragic sentence—"you are dust, and to dust you shall return" (Genesis 3:19). Think of the way we saw women devalued and mistreated as sin and its consequences spread over the globe. And now, think of the promise—the seed of the woman would crush the head of the serpent, ending the curse, restoring creation, and redeeming his people.

In this death, we see the seed of the woman, Jesus, who shared our flesh and blood so that "through death he might destroy the one who has the power of death, that is, the devil, and deliver all those who through fear of death were subject to lifelong slavery" (Hebrews 2:14–15). And so he has.

May remembering his death cause us to sing the chorus from Revelation 5:9–10, 12:

> Worthy are you . . .
> for you were slain, and by your blood you ransomed
>   people for God
>   from every tribe and language and people and nation,
> and you have made them a kingdom and priests to our God,
>   and they shall reign on the earth. . . .
> Worthy is the Lamb who was slain,
> to receive power and wealth and wisdom and might
> and honor and glory and blessing!

Women were the first witnesses to Jesus' resurrection.

In keeping with the women's devotion from Jesus' departure from Galilee to his burial in the tomb, all four gospels record that women were the first to visit the tomb on the first day of the week (Matthew 28:1; Mark 16:1–2; Luke 24:1; John 20:1). They went early in the morning, some while it was still dark, with the spices they had prepared to finish burying their Lord. They arrived to find the tomb open and empty, the stone rolled away from the entrance (Mark 16:3–4; Luke 24:2–3).

Stepping inside, these *women became the first to see the empty tomb.* Angels greeted them, inviting the women to examine the tomb and see that Jesus was not there (Matthew 28:6; Mark 16:5–6; Luke 24:2–4).

The women then became *the first to hear the good news of the resurrection.* "Do not be afraid," said an angel, "for I know that you seek Jesus who was crucified. He is not here, for he has risen, as he said. Come, see the place where he lay" (Matthew 28:5–6; see also Mark 16:6–7). "Remember how he told you, while he was still in Galilee, that the Son of Man must be delivered into the hands of sinful men and be crucified and on the third day rise" (Luke 24:5–7).

Women become the first to see, hear, touch, and worship the Risen Lord.

Matthew records that the women, leaving the tomb to tell his disciples, met Jesus, who greeted them; and they "took hold of his feet and worshiped him" (Matthew 28:9).

John records the tender vignette in which Mary Magdalene encounters Jesus (John 20:14–15). Weeping and convinced that Jesus' body has been moved, she turned to see Jesus in the garden. She does not recognize him initially. Perhaps because she is in shock and weeping, perhaps because he is turned away from her. Either way, she supposes he is the gardener. So she asks where he may have moved the body. Turning to her, Jesus speaks the first recorded name after the resurrection, a woman's name—"Mary."

How appropriate is Jesus' encounter with Mary in the garden! In Genesis 3, a serpent spoke to the woman, deceiving her, leading to her and her husband's sin and exile from the Garden. She heard the promise that the seed of the woman would crush the head of the serpent. Now, in another garden, we find a woman out of whom Jesus had driven seven demons (Luke 8:2). She hears the voice of the seed of the woman, the Risen Lord, who has crushed the head of sin, death, and the power of the devil.

Why does it matter that these women were such early witnesses to the resurrection? It matters because these women knew Jesus well. They traveled with him—eating with him, supporting him financially, taking care of him, learning at his feet. These women knew him. They watched him die, saw his body prepared for burial and laid in the tomb. An imposter would not dupe them. They knew their Lord—and this man, risen from the dead, was their Jesus.

Why does it matter that Jesus rose from the dead?

The resurrection declares Jesus' Kingship. God the Father declared Jesus "to be the Son of God in power according to the Spirit of holiness by his resurrection from the dead" (Romans 1:4). To be the "Son of God" was to be God's chosen King, appointed to reign over God's enemies forever (Psalm 2; 2 Samuel 7:4–16). In raising him from the dead, God declared Jesus to be the all-authoritative Lord and Christ who dispenses the promised Holy Spirit (Matthew 28:18; Acts 2:29–36).

The resurrection vindicates Jesus—that is, it shows him to be in the right (1 Timothy 3:16). The old covenant declared that anyone hanged on a tree was under a curse (Deuteronomy 21:23). If Christ died on the cross and remained dead, it was reasonable to assume that he deserved his death—that the curse remained on him for his sins. If the curse remains on him, then it continues on us.

The resurrection is for the justification of believers. The Gospel declares that "Christ redeemed us from the curse of the law by becoming a curse for us" (Galatians 3:13). His resurrection demonstrates that the curse is ended, our sin and guilt removed. Paul also writes, "[Righteousness] will be counted to us who believe in him who raised from the dead Jesus our Lord, who was delivered up for our trespasses and *raised for our justification*" (Romans 4:24–25, emphasis added). Through faith, believers in Jesus enjoy union with him, so that what is true of him is true of us. If he was delivered up for trespasses, then we have died with him. If he was vindicated in the resurrection, then we are declared righteous with him.

The resurrection guarantees our resurrection. Like Jesus' death, his resurrection is a nonnegotiable part of the Gospel—he died for sin and rose from the dead (1 Corinthians 15:1–5). "If Christ has not been raised, your faith is futile and you are still in your sins" (15:17). If Jesus' resurrection is a sham, then so is our hope.

But that is not the case, for "Christ has been raised from the dead, the firstfruits of those who have fallen asleep" (15:20). The "firstfruits" is the initial portion of the harvest, which gives a foretaste of the remaining yield. As he is, we too shall be.

Christ is risen! He is risen, indeed! Hallelujah!

Women were the first to proclaim that Jesus was raised from the dead.

It is fitting that these women—the first to see, hear, touch, and worship the Risen Lord—should be *the first to be commissioned by the Lord to declare the good news*. They are first sent by the angel in the tomb to "go quickly and tell his disciples that he has risen from the dead" (Matthew 28:7; see also Mark 16:7). As they go, they meet Jesus, who commissioned them himself—"Do not be afraid; go and tell my brothers to go to Galilee, and there they will see me" (Matthew 28:10). Jesus tells Mary Magdalene, "Go to my brothers and say to them, 'I am ascending to my Father and your Father, to my God and your God'" (John 20:17).

The women are obedient Gospel-heralds, becoming *the first humans to declare the resurrection of Jesus* to another (Luke 24:10). "Mary Magdalene went and announced to the disciples, 'I have seen the Lord'—and that he had said these things to her" (John 20:18).

The women also become the *first to be disbelieved when pro-claiming the resurrected Lord.* The women "told these things to the apostles, but these words seemed to them an idle tale, and they did not believe them" (Luke 24:10–11).

Why does the commissioning of women to proclaim Jesus' resurrection matter? As we've said before, the choice of them is startling. "Mark's report that women were the first witnesses to Christ's resurrection was courageous, since the testimony of women as witnesses was not always given credence in the first-century context, especially in a court of law."[6] Nevertheless, Mark recorded it because he recorded what was accurate, not what was likely to sell.

Jesus' choice of these women reminds us of the nature of his kingdom. It is not of this world. The first century regarded the testimony of women as weak, foolish, low, and despised—"an idle tale." But God did not save his people through wisdom and strength. He saved them through the cross, Christ crucified—"a stumbling block to Jews and folly to Gentiles" (1 Corinthians 1:23). Those whom Christ calls into his kingdom and sends out on mission match the message. They are stumbling blocks and foolishness to the world (1 Corinthians 1:26–29):

> For consider your calling, brothers: not many of you were wise ac-cording to worldly standards, not many were powerful, not many were of noble birth. But God chose what is foolish in the world to shame the wise; God chose what is weak in the world to shame the strong; God chose what is low and despised in the world, even things that are not, to bring to nothing things that are, so that no human being might boast in the presence of God.

Sisters, do not doubt the truth of what you have read and learned of Jesus. He is the righteous one who died for sins and rose from the dead. All authority has been given to him. He has commissioned you—as he has commissioned every follower—to go and make disciples of all nations (Matthew 28:18–19). You may feel like a hidden figure, overlooked, under-appreciated, unseen. You may be despised by men and rejected by the world. Nevertheless, the King is with you always, even to the end (Matthew 28:20).

Friends, do not doubt the power of Christ crucified and risen. He came to save sinners—the worst of them. He came to rescue sufferers—from the worst places. Come to him. Confess your sin. Cast off your shame. Be clothed in his righteousness, washed by his blood, forgiven by his death, and transformed by his resurrection. "The saying is trustworthy and deserving of full acceptance, that Christ Jesus came into the world to save sinners, of whom I am the foremost." Hallelujah! Amen!

——— DISCOVERING A WOMAN'S WORTH ———

1. In what ways have you actively or passively sinned against women? Have you repented of this? If not, what keeps you from admitting it? Where do you still need to change? Do you believe that Jesus can forgive you and change you in these areas?

2. What does Jesus' acknowledgement and appreciation of women, particularly his mother, Mary, and Mary the sister of Martha, tell you about his value of women?

3. Why do you think Jesus said Mary's anointing of him would be told everywhere as part of the Gospel story?

4. Who were the last people with Jesus at Calvary? Why is that significant?

5. Who were the first people with Jesus on Easter Sunday morning? Why is that significant?

6. Summarize what you've learned in this chapter in four or five sentences.

DIGGING DEEPER

1. On his way to Calvary Jesus stopped to care for women and warn them. What does that tell you about his care for them?

2. While on the cross, Jesus places his mother into his friend's care. Why is that significant? What does it tell you about his care for you?

3. The first people the angels and Jesus commission to be heralds of his resurrection are women. Again, why does that matter? And why does it matter to you?

4. What does it mean for women to be "Gospel-heralds" today? For the task of proclaiming the Gospel, do you believe we give women

   a. proper equipping?
   b. ample opportunity?
   c. appropriate credibility?

ELEVEN

The Worth of Women in the Church

Go therefore and make disciples . . . teaching them
to observe all that I have commanded you. And
behold, I am with you always, to the end of the age.
Matthew 28:19–20

In a recent internet brouhaha, a woman, undoubtedly thinking she was loving her sisters and standing for truth, said that the best thing a single woman can do to snag a husband (and thereby fulfill God's will for her life) was to avoid tattoos, debt, and sex outside of marriage. Needless to say, she was excoriated on the internet. We're not here to rake her over the coals again. We would agree that being debt-free and not having sexual relations before marriage is a good thing for both women and men. When it comes to tattoos, we're ambivalent. We view them as being adiaphora (spiritually neutral). The reason we're mentioning this blog is because it seemed to assume that the primary (only?) calling in a Christian woman's life is to be married and to have lots of children. We recognize the courage it took for this woman to write her opinions. But we wonder what they have to do with the New Testament church. Even though it reflects the majority teaching Christian women hear, it neglects the earth-shattering truth that since the birth of the Messiah, believing women have been given a new calling. Being a wife and mom is lovely, but it's secondary to the Gospel.

Our New Calling

We've spent a lot of time considering the valuable and frequently shocking roles that women have played in the history of God's redemptive work. We've looked at Eve, her creation in God's image, her devastating fall, and God's promise that a son of hers would reverse the curse of sin. We've seen her valiant Old Testament daughters, women who, like her, were longing for the Messiah, who hoped that perhaps they would be the one who would birth him. We've seen those wise women of faith worship and work and heard surprising stories of their exploits. And we've seen Mary, the one who was chosen by God to give birth to the promised One and watched in awe as she willingly submitted to God's will and a life of suffering. We've considered the brave women who followed Jesus and how he loved and welcomed even the most questionable among them. They rejoiced because the Messiah, the One every pious woman hoped would be her son, had finally arrived. And through his incarnation, sinless life, death, resurrection, and ascension, and the good news of their deliverance from exile, condemnation, and slavery, God's beloved daughters no longer had to wait for him. Like Eve, their mother, through him they were forgiven and reconciled. The long-awaited deliverer had finally come. And because of his birth, pious women everywhere were given a new purpose: *Rather than hoping they would marry and be the one to birth the blessed child, they were to share the news that he had already come.* Both women and men now have the same primary vocation—the Great Commission:

> Go therefore and make disciples of all nations, baptizing them in the name of the Father and of the Son and of the Holy Spirit, teaching them to observe all that I have commanded you. And behold, I am with you always, to the end of the age.
>
> Matthew 28:19–20

A Christian woman's vocation is simple: make disciples and teach them the truth about the One who has come. That doesn't mean that women who are gifted and so inclined shouldn't seek to fulfill this commission in part by raising godly children or loving their spouses in his name. But that particular vocation is no longer primary.[1] Because New Testament women are no longer hoping to give birth to the Messiah, they are now free to look for other ways to take the good news of his work to the far corners of the earth. Yes, of course, they can do this through their marriages and families, but they can also do it through outside employment or ministry; either way, it's up to them and the Lord's unique call on their life. The work of the ministry is now open to all,

> But you [women and men] are a chosen race, a royal priesthood, a holy nation, a people for his own possession, that you may proclaim the excellencies of him who called you out of darkness into his marvelous light.
>
> 1 Peter 2:9

This transformation in calling from motherhood to discipleship is portrayed in Luke's gospel. After hearing Jesus' teaching, "a woman in the crowd raised her voice and said to him, 'Blessed is the womb that bore you, and the breasts at which you nursed!'" (Luke 11:27). Certainly, she was speaking as a pious Israelite woman. *Blessedness comes from producing children!* Jesus' response is jarring: "Blessed rather are those who hear the word of God and keep it!" (Luke 11:28). Think about that. In one sentence Jesus reoriented this woman's theology and perspective on women. *No,* he said. *Giving birth to righteous sons, even the Messiah, is not where blessing comes from. Rather, that comes from hearing and believing the truth.*

From Gender-Exclusive Circumcision to Gender-Inclusive Baptism

Single Christian women no longer have to await motherhood in order to bring others into his covenant people. This shift away from the sole option of motherhood to joining their brothers in disciple-making is seen in part in the change from male circumcision to male *and* female baptism.[2] Whereas in the past, "as a sign of a holy covenant, the circumcision of the head of each family designated that family as belonging to the Lord,"[3] the sign was given only to men. Women were shown to be members of the covenant *only* through their relationship to a circumcised male. But now women are free to enter into the new sign, baptism, whether they are bound to a believing male or not; a woman's circumcised and baptized Husband has already come.

> *The old covenant sign, circumcision, has been replaced by a new gender-inclusive sign, baptism.*

The women we find in the New Testament were called, commissioned, and comforted by Jesus' promise to them, "And behold, I am with you always, to the end of the age" (Matthew 28:20). So, rather than seek a husband and family as a first priority, they committed their lives to him, knowing that his presence would sustain them, and used whatever means they had to incarnate him in the lives of others. Did they do that with their family members? Yes, of course they did. A well-known example of this is Timothy's mother and grandmother, Eunice and Lois. Paul recognized that these two valiant women were the means God used to impart faith to him. Because Eunice was married to an unbeliever, Timothy's instruction was something she undoubtedly did without her husband's help, and possibly even in opposition to him. Eunice joined the ranks of new covenant women who knew that the most important work she could do was to make disciples and teach the faith. And she wasn't the only one. As we'll soon see, she's joined by other women, a surprising number of them single, who made the Great Commission their own and were pivotal to the growth of the church.

We all have the ministry of reconciliation. That's what we're called to. At this point, it's probably a good idea to remember that Jesus never commanded any woman (or man) to marry, that he was supported (as far as we know) solely by women, and that Paul's admonitions to widows and virgins about marrying are given in the context of his overarching rubric that if one is able to live a single life, it's better for devotion to the kingdom and freedom from "worldly troubles" to do so (1 Corinthians 7:8, 28). Additionally, there are only two direct commands about child rearing in the entire New Testament (Ephesians 6:4; Colossians 3:20–21), both addressed primarily to fathers which, if nothing else, should tell us that parenting wasn't a main emphasis in the early church. Are marriage and parenting important topics and ministries? Yes, but they are secondary to the ministry of reconciliation, spreading the news that, "For our sake he made him to be sin who knew no sin, so that in him we might become the righteousness of God" (2 Corinthians 5:21).

In the Upper Room

As we've seen, the Lord Jesus crossed cultural barriers by welcoming women into his coterie. So we shouldn't be surprised to see this practice continue after his ascension. From the very beginning of the New Testament church, women were invited and included.

For instance, on the day of Christ's ascension, his disciples, including Peter, James, and John, began to devote themselves to prayer together. But this wasn't just a men's prayer meeting. With them were a group of people known simply as "the women," a group that included Mary the mother of Jesus (Acts 1:14). Praying there in the upper room were the disciples and the women who regularly traveled with them (Luke 8:2–3), undoubtedly including Mary Magdalene, Mary the wife of Cleopas, Joanna, Susanna, Salome, Mary the mother of John Mark, and others. These women were there when, on the day of Pentecost, the Holy Spirit fell. Tongues of fire rested on them. And they were "filled with the Holy Spirit and began to speak in other tongues as the Spirit gave them utterance" (Acts 2:3–4). Then they went out into the city of Jerusalem, speaking of the "mighty works of God" (Acts 2:11) to all who would listen. Women and men together began making disciples and teaching the Word of truth; they were ambassadors for God.

> *Women prayed in the Upper Room and received*
> *the church's first empowering of the Spirit.*

Brothers, do you regularly invite women to pray with the men? Remember that Paul assumes women will be praying in the public assembly (1 Corinthians 11:5). Do you recognize that women are equal recipients of the Spirit and that he is given to them for the same reason he is given to you—to publish the good news of the Christ?

The First Sermon

It was at this time that Peter delivered the first New Testament sermon. What was his message? He said that what the people were witnessing, the bold proclamation of the good news through men and women, was nothing less than the fulfillment of the ancient prophecy of Joel,

And in the last days it shall be, God declares,
that I will pour out my Spirit on all flesh,
and your sons and your daughters shall prophesy,
   and your young men shall see visions,
   and your old men shall dream dreams;
even on my male servants and female servants
   in those days I will pour out my Spirit, and they shall
    prophesy.

Acts 2:17–18

Don't miss the importance of Peter's use, by the unction of the Spirit, of the prophet Joel's words. In employing this passage, the Spirit was declaring that the New Testament church would be filled with Spirit-empowered women and men. That together, as brothers and sisters of the Christ—no longer waiting for his birth, but rather as his siblings—they would proclaim the good news that "everyone who calls upon the name of the Lord shall be saved" (Acts 2:21). They announced they knew truth about him, "of that we all are witnesses" (Acts 2:32). What were they witnesses of? His life, death, and resurrection. The Gospel's promise is for both genders, in every generation in every place (Acts 2:39), and both genders are empowered by the Spirit to speak it out to everyone who will hear. "Joel draws particular attention to this reality emphasizing it by saying it twice, stating that the Spirit of God will be given to men and women equally, so that all will be able to make known God's truth."[4]

The first sermon preached in the New Testament
church declared that the new era of Spirit-filled
and Spirit-utilized women and men had come.

The First Church in Europe

Then from the seedbed in Jerusalem, the church sprouted and grew outward to Judea, Samaria, even to "the end of the earth" (Acts

1:8). Part of that growth included the conversion and inclusion of a former Pharisee, Paul, whose apostolic missionary work and epistles would dramatically shape the church.

In Acts 16, we read of Paul's second missionary journey and his visit to Philippi. While trying to discern God's will for his travels, he received a vision of a man from Macedonia asking him to come and help him. But when Paul arrived in Philippi, he discovered that apparently there weren't enough believing men there to have formed a synagogue. And so, he and his traveling companions (Silas and probably Luke), sought out others to receive their message. As ambassadors, they went "outside the gate to the riverside, where [they] supposed there was a place of prayer, and [they] sat down and spoke to the women who had come together" (Acts 16:13). What happened next was a continued fulfillment of Joel's promise that all who called upon the name of the Lord (women and men) would be saved. "One who heard [them] was a woman named Lydia, from the city of Thyatira, a seller of purple goods, who was a worshiper of God. The Lord opened her heart to pay attention to what was said by Paul" (Acts 16:14).

Here's the situation: A group of devout women, having no other place to gather for prayer in the city of Philippi, had gone down to the river outside the city on the Sabbath to pray. This had undoubtedly been their normal practice. But what happened next was anything but predictable. Three Jewish strangers began to witness to them about the Christ, and the Lord (who had promised to be with his ambassadors) opened Lydia's heart to hear and respond to the Good News. And thus, the European church was born. Perhaps Paul was surprised that a woman was his first convert, especially because he had seen a vision of a man who needed help, but nothing in the text hints at that. Luke, the one who wrote the account, told the story as though there was nothing strange about it at all. The only record we have is that Paul baptized her and her household, and then used her house as a base of operations and the meeting place of the first European church. Paul thus established one of the leading churches in Europe through the prayer, faith, and ultimately the giving of a group of women. "Clearly, God intended to establish a beachhead for the gospel in Enemy territory on European soil with a band of women."[5]

> *The first European convert to Christianity*
> *was a single woman.*
> *The first European person to receive the*
> *sign of the covenant was a woman.*
> *The first European church was in a businesswoman's house.*

I know that there is concern these days about the "feminization" of the church. And, perhaps that means something.[6] Instead what we learn from this story was that Paul wasn't concerned about girly-churches. He didn't seem to worry that if a woman was his first convert, or if the church met in her home, it meant that men wouldn't come to faith. He wasn't worried about talking with a group of women by a river. He wasn't concerned about staying at what was undoubtedly a single woman's home.[7] He allowed her to prevail upon them, and her position of respect and wealth were a great blessing to him. Rather than pounding his chest declaring his masculinity, he said that he was like a "nursing mother" with the Thessalonians.

Later, when Paul left Philippi and continued on his missionary journeys, the Philippian church continued to partner with him by supporting him financially. We know that Lydia was a very wealthy and successful businessperson, and so undoubtedly, it was she (and the others who met in her home) who supported Paul out of their means, in the same way that Old Testament women and those who followed the Lord Jesus had.[8] Paul testified that the Philippian church was the only one that gave to him and who sent him help for his needs, "once and again" (Philippians 4:15–16; 2 Corinthians 11:9). It was to Lydia and her fellow-believers that the promise, "my God will supply every need of yours according to his riches in glory in Christ Jesus" was originally written (Philippians 4:19). And again, the Philippian church was the only one that supported Paul financially during his eighteen-month stay in Corinth, freeing him from the necessity of tent-making and opening a wide door of ministry.

> *The Philippian church, meeting in the home of a wealthy*
> *businesswoman, subsidized the first preaching of the*
> *Gospel in Corinth and sustained Paul in his ministry.*

How did Paul feel about this church? Was he embarrassed that it met in a woman's home and relied, at least in part, on a single woman's finances? Was he worried about relying too much on a woman and thereby making men feel inferior? Hardly. In his letter to the Philippians, Paul said that he prayed for them and viewed both women and men as partners with him in the Gospel—a partnership that began on the "first day" (Philippians 1:5). What day was that? It was the day that he spoke with those women by the river. He referred to them as those whom he held in his heart and who were partakers of grace with him. His love for and appreciation of Lydia and the church that met in her home was affectionate and warm. Paul would have been impoverished without the help this woman furnished.

But Lydia wasn't the only woman at Philippi Paul cherished as a fellow laborer. Euodia and Syntyche are women he calls "true companions," who labored side by side with him in the Gospel. These were women whose names were written in the book of life (see Philippians 4:2–3). That he would publicly entreat them to get over their differences indicated their importance to the church and to him. He didn't think less of them because they were women; rather he valued the work they did and needed them on the front lines with him as ambassadors spreading the Gospel.

Paul's Greeting to the Roman Church

Was Paul worried about the feminization of the church? Certainly not at Philippi. Nor was he in Rome. Nine of the twenty-eight

199

leaders Paul greeted at the church of Rome were women. In fact, the first person Paul commended to the church was Phoebe, a businesswoman who delivered and probably read his letter out loud.[9] How does Paul describe her? He calls her a servant, or *diakonos*, a word we've transliterated to "deacon." Whether you believe that women can be ordained to a church office or not, like Lydia, Phoebe was undoubtedly a wealthy woman and functioned as a deacon, meeting needs in the church. She served as a "patron," a person who was a benefactor of aliens or the poor who needed assistance. Paul then applauded her because she had been a patron, a helper, to him as well. It's interesting that we have no record of Paul ever telling these women, both of whom probably were unmarried and who were women of means, to find a husband and settle down; to stop pursuing a career and stay home. Instead, Paul tells the church to help Phoebe in whatever way is necessary. This is the language of ministry support. The reason, "for she has been a patron of many and of myself as well" (Romans 16:1–2). She financially underwrote Paul's ministry; he sent her on a costly task and now he's asking the church to financially underwrite her ministry. In doing so, he was laying the foundation for women to be paid in ministry.

Women, let that speak to you. Perhaps you're not married and you think that earning a living is a lesser calling. Or perhaps you don't even want to be married or have a family but have been told that your inclination is contrary to God's plan for biblical womanhood. We know that some women have been told that going to college is a waste of their time and money because God's only call on their life is that of marrying and caring for a family. Take heart: Paul didn't think that way. In fact, he said that being single was actually preferable, and that women like Lydia and Phoebe, who worked outside their homes, were a great benefit to him and to the Gospel. They were to use their careers, whether in the home or the marketplace, in service of the Great Commission, and they were to rest in the truth that whatever way they chose to witness for him, the Lord would be with them.

Paul's Fellow Workers

The second person in Rome that Paul commended was Prisca (or Priscilla), a woman who along with her husband Paul referred to as his "fellow workers in Christ Jesus" (Romans 16:3). This couple faced danger with him and hosted a church in their house. We know that Priscilla herself was strong in theology because she, along with her husband, taught Apollos the "way of God more accurately" (Acts 18:26). Apparently, she had a more prominent ministry role than her husband, because nearly every time their names are listed, her name comes first. She didn't have any problem with correcting someone as gifted as Apollos and neither her husband nor the Apostle Paul had any problem with it either.

My brothers, how do you feel about a woman who is strong in theology? How do you feel about one who is stronger in theology and faith than you or her husband? Do you think that she is more likely to usurp your role or that of her husband? Do you believe that women should keep their theology to themselves (or not even study it, as we have heard), thereby creating a leadership vacuum in the home that their husband will hopefully fill? Do you believe that God may have gifted women in your congregation with an understanding and wisdom that you could learn from? Or do you think that women don't have anything to teach you? Sadly, some seminaries, the places where most pastors are trained, do not employ female teachers at all, and so young men enter the pastorate thinking that women have nothing to teach them. That's sad not only for the women who are shut out of ministry opportunities for which they've been gifted by Christ, but also for the men who could learn from them.

All of God's people, men and women, are to be prepared to listen to and learn from one another. It is the height of spiritual arrogance and a denial of the nature of Christ's kingdom for a man to say that he cannot and will not listen to or learn from a woman. Will such a man remove the words of Deborah or Hannah or Mary from Scripture? . . . He cuts himself off from the wisdom of half of God's people. Peter declares that the prayers of such a man, a man who does not acknowledge that his wife is a joint-heir of the grace of life, are hindered.[10]

What do you think of the single women in your church? Do you view them as less valuable than those who are married? Do you think that there is something wrong with a woman who prefers to be single or who loves her job? What would you think of someone like a Lydia or Phoebe? Would you value her or think that it's too bad that she can't fulfill her "primary calling" to be a wife or a mother? Can you say that you agree with Paul's assessment that it's more beneficial for the kingdom of God for women to be unmarried and thereby devote themselves wholeheartedly to the Lord? Of course that would mean they would need employment to support themselves. Does that challenge your stereotype of femininity?

We don't think it's too much to remind us all again that even someone like the Apostle Paul, whose religious training had certainly taught him the opinion echoed by second-century rabbi Judah Ben Ilai, "I thank God that I am not a woman, a slave, or a pagan," didn't have any hesitation receiving from and building on the support and faith of a woman. Were these women ancient feminists to be feared or were they valiant *ezers*, a gift to be cherished by the whole church? Is God's counsel, "It is not good for man to be alone," applicable only in marriage? Could it also be applicable in your church, in your ministry too?

The Ministry of Women Prophets Continued

You'll remember that there were numerous prophetesses named in the Old Testament. There are in the New as well. In fact, the gifting of women to speak words of "upbuilding and encouragement and consolation" (1 Corinthians 14:3) is assumed by Paul, who said that a woman who "prays or prophesies" publicly must be careful to demonstrate by her attire that she is under godly authority (1 Corinthians 11:5). He addresses the sisters and brothers in Corinth, "When you come together, each one has a hymn, a lesson, a revelation, a tongue, or an interpretation" (1 Corinthians 14:26). Paul is assuming that the Holy Spirit will continue his empowering work in the lives of the men and the women there in the church at Corinth. Women and men are each presumed to have important truth and wisdom that would edify, encourage, and comfort the church, and they were expected to share that truth for the mutual building up of the whole body. It's impossible to think that the Spirit who fell on both women and men on Pentecost and has continued to empower us ever since then would refrain from gifting women in their calling of disciple-making through Spirit-empowered speech.

Silent in the Churches?

Yes, Paul also writes that "the women should keep silent in the churches" (1 Corinthians 14:34), a passage that, if not read in context, has the potential to cause much confusion. We know that Paul cannot mean that women should never speak in church, because he's already acknowledged that women are free to pray and prophesy publicly, as long as they do not dishonor those in authority by the way they dress. Because of his prior teaching, "it is difficult to see this as an absolute prohibition."[11] Furthermore, at a different time, when Paul and Luke both visited the home of Philip, the evangelist, who had "four unmarried daughters, who prophesied" (Acts 21:9), the apostle didn't seek to correct them. We have no record of him telling Philip to get his daughters married or to stop them from speaking the Word of God under the unction of the Spirit. In fact, it seems as though Luke, who wrote Acts, is boasting about them. The ministries of praying and prophesying women that began under the old covenant continues on into the new, with the added dimension of the Spirit enabling and gifting women to be ambassadors and fulfill the Great Commission.

Because the Great Commission has been spoken to all believers, men and women alike, we need to ask whether our churches have opened the door for women to teach and make disciples. Are women who have been gifted by the Spirit to witness to and testify of the coming of the Messiah forced into silence or denigrated when they speak? We need to question whether women who are single have been given a voice and whether, even though we believe that men and women are equally created in the image of God, we demonstrate this belief by inviting worthy women into the non-authoritative speaking ministry of the congregation.

Recalling that the first words after resurrection were spoken by a woman, the first sermon included the promise of the Spirit for women, the first convert in Europe was a single businesswoman, the first preaching of the Gospel in the churches of Achaia were funded by a woman and the church that met in her home, we shouldn't be surprised to discover that the last recorded words of the church are also spoken by a bride, the church in unison with the Spirit, to the Son. Those words? "Come." From beginning to end, from Mary's "Behold, I am the servant of the Lord; let it be to me according to your word" (Luke 1:38) to the bride's prayer, "Come, Lord Jesus, we long for you," the voices of women have joined together with their brothers under the power of the Holy Spirit in one ageless chorus of praise to their King.

─────── DISCOVERING A WOMAN'S WORTH ───────

1. In Old Testament times, women were expected to birth sons, in the hopes of birthing the deliverer and in order to establish their husband's name. How has that changed in the New Testament?

2. Have you heard that God's plan is primarily for women to marry and have children? After reading this chapter, what

do you think? Do you think there is any significance to
Paul's relationship with Lydia and Phoebe, single women
who may not have raised children?

3. When Paul, then the Pharisee Saul, was seeking to extin-
guish the Gospel, he dragged off "men and women and
committed them to prison" (Acts 8:3). He "persecuted this
Way to the death, binding and delivering to prison both
men and women" (Acts 22:4). What do these verses tell
you about the importance of a woman's ministry of the
Gospel?

4. What is the calling that is on all women, single or married? How do you fulfill that calling in your life?

5. The mother of James and John came to Jesus and asked
that her sons be elevated to positions of authority. Why
do you think she did this? What was wrong with her
thinking?

6. Summarize what you've learned in this chapter in four or
five sentences.

DIGGING DEEPER

1. "It seems incredible . . . for a former Jewish Pharisee and
religious terrorist to be sitting on the riverbank teaching Gentile women about Jesus on a Sabbath afternoon.
Surely this is a sign of the transforming power of the Gospel in a man's life."[12] Respond.

2. "All of us, across the gender barrier, are able to learn and
to communicate God's Word. . . . Women and men are

equally redeemed; women and men are equally given the Spirit; women and men are equally gifted to prophesy."[13] Respond.

3. Do a word search and try to find the number of named women who housed churches. Do you think there is any significance to this?

4. Paul wrote that being single was actually preferable for the kingdom's sake. What is your response to that? Do you think that's what American evangelicalism has taught?

5. "Since Christ can save regardless of one's sex, race, or social class, there is no need to change status in order to improve one's standing before the Lord. Indeed, to assert the necessity of a Christian changing his status [marrying or becoming single] is to imply the insufficiency of Christ for one's present situation and to intimate that Christ is less than Lord over all such worldly conditions and institutions."[14] Respond.

TWELVE

The Worth of Women in the Twenty-First Century

But you are a chosen race, a royal priesthood . . .
that you may proclaim the excellencies of him who
called you out of darkness into his marvelous light.

1 Peter 2:9

Eric opened chapter 1 sharing his experience discovering stereo. You remember how he said that as a youngster he learned that if he turned the balance knob all the way to the right, he would only hear a portion of the music. The same was true if he turned it to the left. He said that listening to only one channel was fascinating at first but that eventually the novelty wore off, and he returned to listening to both channels together. That was the only way he could hear the music as the composer meant for it to be heard.

We know that right about now you might relate to Eric's experience. Perhaps you think that we've turned the knob exclusively to W—and, honestly, you'd be right. We admit that we've been focusing our attention on women and the way that their stories are integral to the story of redemption. We confess that's been our goal and here's our motivation: We think that within conservative Christianity, the knob has been turned to *M* almost exclusively, and we're trying to bring balance to the discussion. Yes, we know that in the broader secular world and even in more liberal churches the opposite is true. The knob has been cranked all the way over to *W* for decades, sometimes with horrendous results, and that the church has felt the need to respond.[1] We're not militating against the desire to uphold biblical truth about women and men.

What we are saying is that, apart from a few notable exceptions, most books that talk about redemption or offer an overview of the Bible major on the work that men have done, the ways God has used them. If women are mentioned, it is only in passing or as ancillary to the story. Even men we personally value shared this perspective. For instance, John Calvin wrote,

> Now Moses shews that the woman was created afterwards, in order that she might be a kind of appendage to the man; and that she was joined to the man on the express condition, that she should be at hand to render obedience to him. (Genesis 2:21.) Since, therefore, God did not create two chiefs of equal power, but added to the man an inferior aid, the Apostle justly reminds us of that order of creation in which the eternal and inviolable appointment of God is strikingly displayed.

And,

> The weakness of the sex renders women more suspicious and timid.[2]

Martin Luther wrote,

> Because of God's work, Adam is approved as superior to Eve, because he had the right of primogeniture. . . . Not only has God's wisdom ordained this, but there was more wisdom and courage in Adam. And by this one sees who is wiser and rightly preferred. But Adam was wiser than Eve. . . . Therefore Adam is approved according to God's

creation and man's experience. These are the two arguments. Paul thus has proved that by divine and human right Adam is the master of the woman. That is, it was not Adam who went astray. Therefore, there was greater wisdom in Adam than in the woman.[3]

As much as I love Calvin and Luther, I (Elyse) have to admit that those words (and others like them in so much of the reformation bibliography) are hard for me to read. I realize that these brothers' words are anachronistic, products of their time. The problem is not so much that this is what they thought. It's that this thinking continues on today, and that if a woman or man seeks to challenge it, they are immediately labeled and dismissed. Perhaps you don't think this continues today, but you'd be wrong. For instance, when Eric posted his article pointing out how important women were in redemption's history[4] he was accused of worshiping the goddess of feminism. We're asking, "Is there a way to honor the *imago dei* in women, to declare their importance and worthiness in the tapestry God is weaving and still be considered orthodox?" or do we have to say that "Women are weak, inferior, lacking in wisdom, suspicious, timid, an appendage to man created only to do his bidding" to be considered orthodox?

We know that some of what we have written may have made some of our readers a little uncomfortable. I remember when I first began to be aware of white privilege—something I was completely blind to—how uncomfortable I felt. It certainly was a painful, yet necessary and good, time of growth in my life. Some of you may have wondered if we are closet (or out-and-out) egalitarians. Perhaps there are also some who have jumped ahead to this last chapter to see what we'll say about women's roles in today's churches and use that as a shibboleth to judge if anything else we have said is worthwhile. In essence, we fear that the other 70,000 words in this book will either be accepted or rejected out of hand if we don't answer the question about women's ordination according to the prevailing rubric. Whether that's fair, or wise, or not is really beside the point.

We accept that *the ordained office of pastor is limited to quali-fied men alone; we believe that husbands are to be the leading servants in their homes and that women and wives are to help pastors and husbands in their calling.*[5] What that means is that in his love and providential rule over the church and in the home, God has called men to be servants who set aside their own rights and comforts in obedience to God to pursue benevolent unity with and the flourishing of other believers—including their wives and sisters in the faith. The husband is to be the lead servant in his family, one who exemplifies what it means to love God and neighbor, following in the footsteps of his Savior, who became a servant to all, washing his disciples' feet and then dying in ignominy. He is to lay down his life and refrain from any domineering or authoritarian action. Likewise, in the church, pastors are to demonstrate what it means to love and shepherd a flock of sheep, as the Good Shepherd did—serving, carrying, protecting, and guiding them. In both the church and the home men are called to be the chief servants, imitating the character of their Savior, remembering the words of the Lord:

> You know that the rulers of the Gentiles lord it over them, and their great ones exercise authority over them. It shall not be so among you. But whoever would be great among you must be your servant, and whoever would be first among you must be your slave, even as the Son of Man came not to be served but to serve, and to give his life as a ransom for many.
>
> Matthew 20:25–28

The term "servant-leadership" is popular in conservative circles. Unfortunately, it puts the emphasis on *leader*, with *servant* taking the modifying role in the phrase.[6] But notice that Jesus (a leader for sure; he is the King!) does not say, "the Son of Man came not to be served but to *lead*." He says he came "to serve," and to do so by dying to save others.

In response to the husband and the pastor's service, women are to strive with all their heart to be strong, faithful, and trustworthy allies in the war against the serpent. They are to seek to develop the gifts they have been given and they are to bring them into the arena where they will fight alongside the godly men God has given them. They are not to check out of the battle and leave everything up to the guys. Rather, they are to step out in faith in every way God is calling them.

We believe that it is right and good—and time—to open as many doors as possible for women and to encourage them to see how integral they are to the mission of the church, and that women should pursue God's call on their life with zeal.

We know that some people might object to the positions we've taken because they view this as a slippery slope; they think that once you go down the road of talking about a woman's worth, you end up working at Planned Parenthood. Some want to avoid this topic altogether and thereby keep themselves safe from the "cult of feminism." In contrast, our opinion is that it is more dangerous to fence the law[7] than it is to speak the truth about the freedom and value that the Bible clearly declares. Whenever we say more than the Bible says or twist it to keep clear of what we fear, we're in jeopardy of obscuring truth. In addition, we wonder if, when we close doors that should be open to women because we're afraid of some precedent it might set, we might inadvertently accomplish the thing we most fear. For instance, when women who are called, gifted, and willing to work for the Lord in the church are made to feel inferior, condescended to, or inconsequential, the goal of keeping them from falling into egalitarianism[8] is actually thwarted. In fact, women are already leaving the faith in droves.[9]

The "Christian Family" Movement

Since the 1980s, Christian publishers have produced materials meant to help Christian women learn how to live godly lives and raise their families in the faith. Some good has come out of those many tomes, but their over-emphasis on being a wife and mother has failed to recognize that the story of the New Testament isn't a story about family ethics. It's about the Son who has been born and who has fulfilled every command to love in our place. It's primarily a call for women and men alike to publish the good news about Christ everywhere God leads us. Dr. Jerram Barrs, a professor at Covenant Seminary, says that this overly narrow focus on women's roles has caused significant damage, leading the Christian community to see women "entirely through the eyes of men reacting to feminist emphases."[10] Ministries have been established and funded on the premise that the most important message of Christianity is that we not succumb to feminism— a byproduct of that message being the importance of marriage and raising a family. We agree that feminism and secularism are to be resisted, but they're not the dominant danger faced by the church. The foremost dangers modern evangelicalism faces are the idolatry of the family, the idolatry of political power, and the self-trust that comes from a message that offers three steps to self-perfection. We're not at risk of losing our morals. We risk losing the Gospel's message—something we encounter every time we speak publicly or interview incoming church members and recognize that our audience is largely illiterate about the doctrine of justification, a truth Martin Luther said was the lynchpin upon which the whole church would rise or fall. If our anecdotal experience is any indication, the majority of the church is in free fall down into the poisonous cesspool that the Reformers so valiantly stood against. Rather than looking to marriage and the family as our primary message, we need to get back to the faith once delivered to the saints:

> The old has passed away; behold, the new has come. All this is from God, who through Christ reconciled us to himself and gave us the ministry of reconciliation; that is, in Christ God was reconciling the world to himself, not counting their trespasses against them,

and entrusting to us the ministry of reconciliation. Therefore, we
are ambassadors for Christ.

2 Corinthians 5:17–20

We believe that the Bible teaches the great dignity and worth of
all people, men and women, and their importance in the story of
redemption. We have sought to reveal and reaffirm the truth that
both genders, female and male, were and are integral to God's
plan of salvation and are to be honored and respected as God's
image-bearers. Women are to see themselves as worthy, not because they've accomplished great things, or because they are married and have well-ordered homes, but rather because they are
created in the image of God, redeemed by the Son, and gifted to
fulfill his commission. They are not to denigrate or degrade themselves, thinking they're inferior as women, nor should they think
they only have value if they have a husband and family. They are
to see themselves as worthy in God's eyes and in light of that, seek
to become wise and strong women who stand, in whatever sphere
of influence they have, as ambassadors called and commissioned
for Christ. That was our goal—and we trust that your heart has
been warmed, encouraged, and informed.

How Might This Work Out in Our Churches?

If men began to see women as co-laborers, as integral to the mission
of the church, how would our churches begin to look? If women
were no longer limited primarily to domestic roles, how might they
be utilized in the local congregation? We know that it's our knee-
jerk reaction to begin by talking about things women aren't called
to do. As complementarians,[11] we recognize those restrictions. But
that's not where we want to start. Rather, let's start here:

So then you [men and women] are no longer strangers and aliens,
but you [women and men] are fellow citizens with the saints and

members of the household of God, built on the foundation of the apostles and prophets, Christ Jesus himself being the cornerstone, in whom the whole structure, being joined together, grows into a holy temple in the Lord [made up of men and women]. In him you [women and men] also are being built together into a dwelling place for God by the Spirit.

Ephesians 2:19–22

In this new kingdom and under our new call, men and women are fellow-citizens. We're members together of God's household—all of us built on the ones who have come before us—Christ being the chief. We are being knit together and are growing together into a holy place where the Lord dwells. That holy temple has to be made up of both women and men—it is incomplete without every one of us. Women, just as men, are integral to the holy temple where God dwells by his Spirit. Paul reinforced this view when he wrote that

in Christ Jesus you are all [male and female] sons of God, through faith. For as many of you as were baptized into Christ have put on Christ. There is neither Jew nor Greek, there is neither slave nor free, there is no male and female, for you are all one in Christ Jesus. And if you are Christ's, then you are Abraham's offspring, heirs according to promise.

Galatians 3:26–29

Please notice how Paul preaches the new covenant truth, "both men and women are here characterized as having the rights of 'sons.'"[12] Notice how gender divisions and wrong attitudes about male (or Jewish or freeman) superiority are abolished by the power of our adoption through Christ.

The Greek word *huioi* ("sons") is a legal term used in adoption and inheritance laws of first-century Rome. As used by Paul here . . . this term refers to the status of all Christians, both men and women, who, having been adopted into God's family, now enjoy all the privileges, obligations, and inheritance rights of God's children.[13]

It's not insignificant that the outward sign that Paul uses to ground his teaching is new covenant baptism and that sign is now open for both genders, women and men. The passage does not teach that gender no longer matters at all. What it does teach is that there is not one gender that is superior to the other when it comes to our relationship to God as "sons" and our relationship to one another in the family of faith.

As a woman who hopes to continue to have an opportunity to speak into the lives of others, I (Elyse) acknowledge that I have sensed within myself a fear that in even pursuing this line of study and writing, I might be placed under suspicion. I don't think I'm being paranoid. When hearing about this book, a friend replied that when she began to ask questions of her leaders about the party line, she was "met with hostile defense and accusations." She was told that she must be an egalitarian who was looking to divide the church and that she had been corrupted and duped by feminist ideology. She wrote wisely,

> This siege/defense mentality is dangerous . . . we can't have conversations about race, gender, or injustice in fruitful ways until we address the *systematic silencing of voices* that ask questions.

Consider those words: *the systematic silencing of voices.* Is that something you have ever experienced? Is it something you've done? I admit that it is something I've seen in myself. I'm willing to admit that there have been times when I closed my ears and my heart to someone who was presenting a differing point of view from my own. I pray that I have repented of this folly and that I would be willing to humble myself and learn from others. The older I get in the faith, the more I am convinced that I'm really not as smart as I thought I was. May God help us all.

In another conversation I had with a pastor, I heard about a conversation he'd had with other brothers, regarding a woman who believed that perhaps ordination should be made open to women. The other pastors were wondering whether she should be disciplined or just branded a heretic out of hand. Again, the prevailing "complementarian" shibboleth was used as the sole litmus test to determine whether a woman even belonged in Christ's church. Upon reading a draft of this, a close friend of Eric's, who is a thoughtful pastor and sharp theologian, replied:

> Just a personal reflection on this: I've personally been guilty of using complementarianism as a litmus test for orthodoxy. It's been under the pretense of expediency. Heresy often hides under orthodox-sounding statements of faith, while egalitarianism is clearly displayed on a pastoral staff directory. This has been sheer laziness on my part. It's not even an accurate test, since there are unorthodox sects that are roughly complementarian and orthodox believers who are egalitarian. It is not how I want to be treated, either. I've heard theological positions, which I happen to hold, lambasted as shameless denial of the Bible's authority—rather than a disagreement over what the Bible teaches. There's a reason it's called theological triage, not exegetical triage. Exegesis shows us the origin of the disagreement but doesn't help us assess its significance for fellowship. But the worst thing I've seen in myself when I've employed this "lazy litmus test" is a tendency to seek unity in a certain kind of church culture, rather than the gospel of Jesus Christ. This is idolatry.[14]

Jared is correct. This is idolatry masked as discernment.

I suppose a case could have been made if the Apostle's Creed included a line that read, "I believe in God the Father Almighty, maker of heaven and earth . . . and in male-only ordination," but alas. That's not to say that we reject a differentiation between male and female authoritative callings in the church and home (as we've said above), it's just that we have to be careful to listen with charity, kindness, and love, believing the best about others, especially those with whom we might disagree. We must get past the place of *silencing* voices that have a different perspective.

One reason that I pray we get past the *silencing* of questioning or dissenting voices is my concern for the young women who are just now finding their place in the church. We've got to open a conversation with them, we must welcome their questions, respect their disagreements, and open the door as wide as possible for them to find places of ministry according to their calling. There are many ways they can serve, and we must let them. Of course, some women will be satisfied and love to be homemakers and won't have a desire to serve more broadly. And that's a great thing (if they're remembering Christ's commission). But there are others, either because they aren't married or because that's not their calling, we will lose if we don't welcome them and their gifts in any of the many ways their Lord wants to use them.

Worthy Women Today

Which brings us now to our discussion of worthy women whose stories we don't read in the Scriptures. Surely entire books could be written about female ambassadors, women who gave it all on the mission field or on the blood-soaked sand in the coliseum, who lived hard lives of service for the sake of the kingdom. Standing among these women is Perpetua, a young mother who lived in Carthage around AD 200. She had become a believer and was preparing, along with her servant Felicitas, to be baptized when they were arrested and put on trial for failing to offer tribute to the Emperor, Septimius Severus. Perpetua's unbelieving father, a nobleman, came to her jail cell and begged her to denounce Christianity, offer the tribute to the Emperor, and live—if not for his sake, for the sake of her young son, whom she was still breastfeeding. I can't imagine the terror that filled her soul. In the end though, she said that she could no more deny her faith than say that reality didn't exist. So, she was cruelly executed before bloodthirsty crowds in the arena.[15] And though her voice was silenced that day, she still testifies that Jesus comes before everyone else, even family, as he said,

> If anyone comes to me and does not hate his own father and mother and wife and children and brothers and sisters, yes, and even his own life, he cannot be my disciple.

Luke 14:26

I (Elyse) wasn't raised in a believing home. My father was a non-practicing Jew and my mother was a lapsed Catholic. They divorced before my fifth birthday. As a result, I really had no relationship with my father for much of my childhood, but in my early twenties, I finally reconnected with him. I was so happy: At long last, I had a dad! But then Jesus saved me, and I knew I had decisions to make. I knew that my following Jesus might end my relationship with my dad, so I did what I've since told people never to do: I opened my Bible and stuck my finger on a verse and hoped for direction. In his mercy, I didn't read "When Eber had lived 34 years, he fathered Peleg" (Genesis 11:16). Rather my eye fell on the verse above and I knew I had to be willing to leave my father, the one relationship I had longed for my entire life, in order to demonstrate faithfulness to my Husband. And so I called him, told him that I had converted and that I would be leaving college to go to Bible school. After yelling at me, he hung up. And that was the end of my relationship with him until many decades later when we reconnected again—about five years before his death.

I'm not telling you that story because I fashion myself a modern-day Perpetua. I certainly didn't sacrifice what she did. But I am telling you my story because I want you to begin to think about all the ways in which the Lord has already shown you how your relationship with him is preeminent and how the seemingly insignificant or ordinary choices you make every day are a fulfillment of his high call on your life. As they have from the very beginning, women remain integral to God's plan of redemption.

Women like Perpetua, you, and I, have been refusing the siren's call to live for ourselves, and have instead laid it all on the line, sometimes unto death, for Jesus. Women like Florence Nightingale, who instituted modern nursing; Rosa Parks, who bravely pushed the civil rights movement forward; Evangeline Corey Booth, who oversaw the establishment and growth of the Salvation Army; Lottie Moon, whose missionary work in China laid the foundation for today's Baptist missionary support; Fanny Crosby, a blind woman who wrote more than 9,000 hymns, many of which we still sing today; Sojourner Truth, a former slave who became an abolitionist and women's rights advocate; Amy Carmichael, a missionary to India who helped save children out of temple prostitution; Corrie ten Boom, a woman who hid Jews from the Nazis and spent years in a woman's labor camp and gave testimony to Christ's love; and author Harriet Beecher Stowe, who through her book, *Uncle Tom's Cabin*, changed the way that Americans looked at slavery. Each of these women was a believer, some single, others married; they and millions of other worthy women like them have served their King and been ambassadors for him in every land.[16] And countless more are serving him right now, are vital to the health of the church, and necessary to the message of the Good News. And they're doing it everywhere.

Entire books could also be written about women who have quietly stayed faithful through years of loneliness and heartache, as they experienced the sorrow that comes from marriage, singleness, or parenting in a broken world. The church is filled with valiant women who get up and serve again in faith every day whether that's in a boardroom, on an airliner, behind the barista bar, or in their kitchen with a dripping faucet and a colicky infant. As I write this, I've just returned from a visit to my primary care physician. She and her nurse are both Christians, and I'm thankful for the fellowship I have with them. The world is filled with intelligent, wise, courageous, and self-sacrificing women who have been loved by their Savior, who love him in return, and who serve him in as many vocations as there are women. Their stories will surely adorn the walls of the New Jerusalem. They are people of whom the world is not worthy (see Hebrews 11:38), and I'm blessed to be one of them.

Where Are We Headed Now?

So, where are we headed as a church, as believers in the twenty-first century? Of course, that's hard to know. On one hand, I see loads of young women who do seek to make his Word known and cleverly use the internet to make that happen. I'm really encouraged by them and I love seeing how they are calling their sisters into deep Bible study. I'm encouraged that the publishing door is open to them and that women are buying their books and watching their videos. These are women who are tired of silliness and fluff and who know that what we need to hear is truth. I am encouraged because everywhere I go, I see women who are in the fight, whether they're like my friend's daughter, who is a spokesman for Students for Life, or Rachael Denhollander, who almost single-handedly stood against wicked perversion and brought down power structures in elite gymnastics. I'm proud of all these women. I'm proud to call them "sister." They're all involved in nurturing life in the name of the King, and the world would be a much darker place without them.

I'm also encouraged because men are beginning to see that the traditional ways some have employed of denigrating, objectifying, and dismissing women's concerns are beginning to change. In part due to the #MeToo and #ChurchToo movements, men are starting to see that the neglect and abuse of women is sinful, and that God abhors it. I'm thankful that some men who have consistently dismissed women's concerns and even abuse are now facing their folly. I'm also thankful that there are groups of pastors and counselors who are standing up for women who have been in abusive relationships, and who, rather than disciplining the wife for "not being submissive enough," are now going toe-to-toe with their husbands and calling them to repentance. These are good signs, and I'm glad.

I'm hoping that the following testimonies from several women may soon become unheard of rather than common in the church:

One day while cleaning the baseboards in her guest bathroom, a woman found a videocamera that her husband had installed to film women who were coming to their home for Bible study and game nights. After confronting her husband, she called an elder. The elder came to their home, and her husband admitted his sin saying, "I was curious about other women." He had also admitted to viewing pornography on the internet.

After questioning from the elder, the wife admitted that their physical relationship hadn't been the best but said that she had never refused him because she knew that would be wrong. The elder told her she needed to "take one for the team," meaning that she was to be more sexually active. That particular elder may have met with her husband once or twice more after that, but nothing was ever done. She wondered whether that was all that was going to come of it, and the elders assured her that they would deal with it. They never did. She thought it would have been a disciplinable offense (ignoring the fact that it's a crime) to do these things, but evidently they didn't agree. So she persevered.

A few years later, the wife found another camera, this time in the back of her husband's truck. It had video on it that her husband had taken up women's skirts at the grocery store. At that point she decided that neither she nor her children were safe and she had learned the hard way that her elders wouldn't take any action to protect or shepherd her, even though she had attended that church for twenty years, so she left the home and eventually divorced her husband.

Later on, a female friend of hers who had been involved in leadership had asked one of the elders if that sort of behavior on the part of the husband didn't constitute adultery. He said that it did not because the physical act of sexual intercourse did not occur.

Another woman met her future husband while he was enrolled in a well-known evangelical seminary. Thinking that he was a godly man, she married him and sought to build a Christian home. After seminary, he was employed at the church where his father was the senior pastor.

Soon she began noticing his habitual lying and suspected that he was also being unfaithful. She went to her pastor (her father-in-law) who, after hearing her concerns said, "Abraham lied. Sarah still obeyed. Are you even a Christian?"

Later on it was revealed that her husband was not only a serial adulterer but also abused her physically. When she confronted him and sought the help of the elders she was told to memorize 1 Corinthians 13:4–7, and her faith in Christ was questioned once again. She eventually divorced him. Her ex-husband remains a member in good standing at the church while she is denigrated as an unforgiving unbeliever.

Still another woman shares her experience:

During my counseling with my pastor, I had absolute blind trust in him and his guidance. So much so that many of the low-lying feelings I had in response to his counsel took a back seat to the feelings I had that he was wiser and better than me. Looking back, I see that I often felt like the abuse I lived with was far less important to my pastor than my fulfillment of my role as the believing spouse and the implication that through my endurance our household was sanctified and my husband could be saved.

I knew Scripture and trusted that my pastor's application of God's Word was right, but what was missing was any acknowledgement or affirmation that what was going on was abuse and that it shouldn't be tolerated. It absolutely perpetuated the feelings I already had, that I did not matter. These feelings profoundly influenced my perception of how God felt toward me. Years later, I am grateful that my heart and behavior were called into account, I was definitely sinning in many areas of my heart within my marriage, but it makes me so sad to look back on how the lack of compassionate shepherding hurt me, and distanced me from God.

When a violation of my trust occurred and a supposed friend shared with my pastor that my husband insisted I sleep in another room, my pastor suggested that stepping down from Women's Ministry would "allow me more time to focus on my marriage." I was completely crushed by that. My involvement in women's ministry was something I cared about and was one way that I could stay connected to other women and feel a sense of value. Because I didn't trust myself to identify what was happening to me as abuse, and because the people counseling me didn't call it that, the loss of involvement was just another thing I had to endure, because it was what I wrongly believed I deserved. It felt like punishment, which was a very familiar feeling for me.

One of the most devastating blows I received came when, years later, I learned that my pastor and the woman who was counseling me with him were having an affair the whole time. So, I was being called to endure an abusive situation by being a good Christian wife, while my two counselors were cheating on their spouses. What I needed so desperately was a shepherd. It was right that my role as a Christian wife be a topic addressed in counseling. What was not right was the lack of true care that a shepherd has for his sheep, the protection and the valuing. That is not what I got. Telling me how to live out my faith in the face of abuse wasn't caring for my heart. I don't think that the church has served women in my position well. In addition, my former pastor has never asked for my forgiveness for his deception.

Disappointment Upon Disappointment:
When the God an Abuse Victim Worships Is Not Reflected in the Church She Attends

By Chelsey Gordon[17]

Acting as assistant to Chris Moles[18] allows me the opportunity to regularly speak to women and hear their stories not only of marital abuse, but also (equally tragic) stories of churches whose responses to both victims and perpetrators of abuse resulted in additional hurt and harm. No matter how many times I am privileged to participate in conversations like these, the contrast between what I know of God and His loving-kindness toward women and the way many churches bearing His name handle cases of abuse never ceases to astound me. Reflecting on the conversations I've had with victims, I believe there are two primary ways in which this contrast is most glaring.

Provision and Protection

God's provision and protection of women throughout Scripture is primarily unconditional and rooted in his gracious, merciful love for sinful, broken people as a whole. Quite differently, we often see churches establishing strict limits and conditions around their potential support of abuse victims. Many churches wash their hands altogether of their biblical responsibilities to provide protection and provision to a victim simply because the church's leadership disagrees with the means she may use to resist her husband's abuse. Please realize, in the cases we see, women are not retaliating with physical violence, slander, manipulation, or any other number of obviously sinful responses (though their husbands are likely employing these very same tactics with little to no recourse from these very same churches). Instead, these women are choosing to pursue avenues of help and safety such as seeking outside counselors or advocates educated in the dynamics and impacts of abuse, fleeing the home or contacting police without the express "permission" of their pastors, or filing for divorce in light of their husband's continued blatant (and frequently years-long) unrepentance. What's more, these women typically only seek out these additional care paths after months and sometimes even years of patiently attempting to respond to their abuser according to the strict dictates of their church's leadership.

Value and Honor

The Old and New Testaments both offer examples of God bestowing on women value and honor uncommon to that period of history. We see this in the creation narrative, as God fashions the first man and woman, each bearing His image equally. We see this when the angel of the Lord appears and speaks to a discarded Hagar, bringing not further shame and humiliation but dignity and care. We see this in God providing the prostitute Rahab with safety and redemptive inclusion in the royal line of Israel. We see this in Jesus and the apostles laboring in fellowship alongside women as essential assets and partners in Gospel ministry. Sadly, this kind of value and honor is not often bestowed on the victims we speak with. Instead, many church leaders (primarily men) treat these women as simple and spiritually inferior at best, and suspicious and scheming at worst. This is especially devastating for women who have served their churches and supported their pastor's leadership faithfully over the years (unlike many of their abusive husbands). What these women once thought was a mutually honoring relationship with their pastor and church can quickly turn sour when a woman approaches them for help (or worse, by doing so she exposes their inadequacies) in the area of abuse intervention.

The saddest irony of all is that, for many of these women, their initial expectation was that their church *would* provide the help and hope they longed for, and they would then have had no need to pursue outside resources. They expected their churches to be a refuge of safety and security. They expected their churches to respond with righteous indignation to the abuse taking place, not their cries for help or means of biblical resistance. For these women, their disappointment in and disenchantment with the church is deep. Based on what they knew about God from Scripture, they expected His under-shepherds to provide and protect them as sisters worthy of value and honor just as He always has done. But sadly, this is not the experience of many women. One of the most heartbreaking sentiments victims have repeatedly voiced to me is that they are well aware of this disparity.

Realizing this, they remind themselves regularly, "The God I love and worship is not accurately reflected in the church I attend, therefore I must fight to put my faith in Him and not His fallible people." While I admire these women and their commitment to love, trust, and fear God above all else, it shouldn't have to be this way. These women shouldn't have to tend to wounds inflicted not only by their abusive husbands but by their churches as well. These women shouldn't have to grieve the Godlessness of their husbands as well as the Godlessness their churches. These women shouldn't experience more God-like care and compassion in the company of nonbelievers than in the presence of His people, the church.

Speaking with these women brings many occasions for tears as I grieve with them not only the loss of marriage relationships, but also the church relationships dashed in the wake of abuse. But along with that grief comes rejoicing, because the God these women have chosen to put their faith in will not disappoint them. He has always been and will always be their Protector, Provider, and Bestower of value and honor. Time and again, as I speak with these women navigating the deep, dark waters of abuse, I am astounded by the humble strength that comes as a result of being anchored to Him. While their churches might wrongly view them as rebellious or far from God, these women of faith are actually intimately and desperately dependent upon Him to be who He says He is because all other lifelines have long since gone away.

I'm glad that the 1950s' idolized caricature of a woman of worth being June Cleaver, with her crisply ironed dress and string of pearls, has been seen for the stifling superficiality that it was. What I mean is that the days of telling women of faith that the only options open to them are marriage and childbearing are hopefully over. Please don't misunderstand: I think I've already made it clear that for women who are so gifted and so inclined, marriage and family are not second best. It's a great blessing. I have been married for four decades and have three children and six grandchildren. My family is one of the dearest blessings in my life, and I am thankful. But there are now other opportunities open for women to pursue in the name of Christ and as ambassadors for him. I'm thankful that I have been not only given the opportunity but have also been encouraged by my sweet husband to seek out and pursue God's plan for my life. Because of his support I've pursued a master's degree, written two dozen books, and spoken to thousands of women around the world about Jesus. I am blessed, and he has been one of God's sweetest gifts to me.

I'm also thankful for the pastors, including my co-author, Eric, who are not threatened by women who love theology and have a voice. I see these men on social media, encouraging and standing with women who are longing for their voices to be heard. I know they take some heat from other guys who assume that what it means to be a manly pastor is that you only listen to and encourage other men. I'm also really thankful for the many men in my life, within my family and without, who actually read books written by women and assume that they have something important to say. This past weekend I was blessed to hear my son preach and to know that a quote he read, written by a woman, he found in a book of mine. I know that there are now many pastors who are seeking to speak with women in their congregations by asking them their opinion and requesting help with their sermons, especially their illustrations. They realize that the primary demographic within their congregations are women and that they need to preach the truth in such a way as to speak to them also. Again, I am aware that this is happening all around the world and I'm so glad.

As Mary McDermott Shideler quoted in her introduction to Dorothy Sayers' *Are Women Human*,

> As we cannot afford to squander our natural resources of minerals, food, and beauty, so we cannot afford to discard any human resources of brains, skills, and initiative, even though it is women who possess them.[19]

I wonder where the church would be if women were allowed to work according to their gifting and if their skill, intelligence, wisdom, and piety were taken as seriously as men's. Surely if a business had hired a staff of 100 people but only allowed 40 of them to actually work, they wouldn't be in business for very long. Perhaps that is one reason for the weakness of the twenty-first-century evangelical church.

What Can Women Do in the Church?

If women are, as we've proposed, worthy and integral to the success of Christ's kingdom, as strong helpers in the battle, then what kinds of ministries can they do in the church? How would they have helped in the situations we have described above? We've seen ancient women of faith do myriad tasks, from making a home, to using their job to turn their home into a church. We've seen them deliver and read documents to house churches, correct a man's theology, co-labor with the apostles, function in the deaconate, and pray and prophesy publicly. Certainly, women today who have the opportunity for education and the entire corpus of Scripture to explore, should be allowed and encouraged to do everything seen in the New Testament churches.

> All of us, all believers, female and male, are called to instruct, to encourage, to comfort, and to edify one another, for we all are given the Spirit of prophecy. Christ lavishes his love on us all, for he is the bridegroom who cares for and cherishes his church.[20]

Perhaps in your church it might be a good idea to identify wise, mature women who can meet with and guide other women as counselors. At the very least, there should be women on staff who will meet with women who have concerns and who will be listened to by the pastoral staff. Given the prevalence of sexual abuse in the church, male leaders should not expect or require that women come to them. One of the main reasons that women are leaving their church is that "fewer than half of them indicate receiving any emotional support from people at their church. . . . Nearly half of women (43%) say they do not feel any emotional support at all from church."[21] I wonder whether women would say they were emotionally supported at church if they knew there were godly, loving, wise, and strong women on staff they could talk to. As one woman who was in a decades-long abusive marriage and sought counseling from her pastor told me,

I wonder if most pastors even know how to recognize abuse when they see it. You had to be completely checked out to miss it in my case. It was so obvious in how I saw myself and my relationship with God. The effects of abuse touched every area of my life. I thought I wasn't worth anything.

I assume that many men have no idea how difficult it is for a woman to talk about abuse and how, if there are no women in the room representing and comforting them, it is overwhelming and painful. I recently heard that a professor in a college had asked his students to think about their most intense sexual experience and then think about sharing it with a fellow student and how uncomfortable that would be. Then he asked them to imagine how hard it is to talk about rape[22]—and particularly with men they don't know or who are in positions of authority. Sadly, in these cases, secular law enforcement have become more righteous in caring for women than the church. No woman in any church should ever be forced to talk to men about anything sexual in nature—at the very least without other women in the room representing, believing, and comforting them.

I have personally listened as men dismissed a woman's concerns about sexual advances, who referred to women who reported feeling uncomfortable by a pastor's advances as flirts, and as a respondent to the #MeToo movement myself, I can testify to the pain of having to admit that something like that abuse or rape actually happened to you. To say it in front of a group of men who may or may not try to protect other men is abusive in itself. Even if you don't think that women should be deacons, you still need to grapple with the needs of women and the discomfort most women experience in opening up the most private parts of their lives before men and trusting them.

Aside from these difficult situations, it would also be good for male leaders to listen to the opinions of wise women who probably know the state of the church (at least among the women) better than they do. Asking women their opinion about things as mundane as carpet color or the marketing of a new ministry would undoubtedly be helpful. Women can and should be speaking into the leadership of the church on a regular basis. They have gifts that the whole church needs,

> These women are not agitating for control of the church. They are concerned about their stewardship to Christ, mindful of the magnitude of our mission and of how serious a matter it is to Jesus when one of his followers buries his or her talents in the ground.[23]

Sisters and Mothers

In teaching his dear son in the faith how to faithfully pastor, Paul wrote,

> Do not rebuke an older man but encourage him as you would a father, younger men as brothers, older women as mothers, younger women as sisters, in all purity.

> 1 Timothy 5:1–2

Timothy was to encourage the women in his church as he would his mother. He was to welcome their counsel, honor them, and be thankful for them, and not look at them as a nuisance. He was to cherish the older women in his church and look at them as a treasure trove of wisdom and faith, not see them as inferior. He was to care for them and protect them, especially if they were widows who were alone. Those women with gray hair who might talk too much or require special care were probably the best prayer warriors in his congregation. He needed them. They had lived a life of faith that he had yet to even imagine, and they knew what it was to bombard heaven with their needs and the needs of others.

Further, he was to encourage the younger women as he would his sisters. As the mom of two sons and one daughter, I've enjoyed watching how my daughter's brothers care for her and stick up for her. Sure, they tease each other, and they certainly had their fights as children, but now their sister better not be messed with. They love and cherish and protect her. That's how Timothy was to view the younger women in his congregation. He was to look at them as dear family members, those who were called and gifted by Christ to minister to and with him.

Dear brothers and sisters: From the very beginning of the family of faith, women have been Satan's target. The ancient dragon in Revelation 12 sought to kill her and her offspring. Failing that, he has since stirred up misogyny, persecution, pornography, prostitution, sex-slavery, hyper-patriarchy, and feminism. Each of these attacks and so many more are meant to silence the voices of women. But Paul's voice speaks on:

> So then you [men and women] are no longer strangers and aliens, but you [women and men] are fellow citizens with the saints and members of the household of God, built on the foundation of the apostles and prophets, Christ Jesus himself being the cornerstone, in whom the whole structure, being joined together, grows into a holy temple in the Lord [made up of men and women]. In him you [women and men] also are being built together into a dwelling place for God by the Spirit.
>
> Ephesians 2:19–22

We are fellow citizens. We are all members of God's house. We are growing together into a holy temple, a dwelling place for God by the Spirit. All of us.

––––––– DISCOVERING A WOMAN'S WORTH –––––––

1. Do you think the voice of the church has been turned toward *M* or *W*? Do you think there are any consequences of that?

2. Have you ever read anything in the church's writings that has made you think women are inferior?

3. Do you think that agreement with complementarian doctrine is a shibboleth? Do you think that's a good thing?

4. Have you ever questioned your leaders about the roles women are allowed to fill in your church? What was their response?

5. Summarize what you have learned in this chapter in four or five sentences.

DIGGING DEEPER

1. Read over your chapter summaries and then summarize what you have learned in this book in four or five sentences.

2. What truths did you learn that were most beneficial?

3. How will you seek to implement these truths in your life?

4. What role do you think you're gifted to play in "proclaiming the excellencies" of Jesus?

A Call to Hope-Driven, Courageous, Compassionate Conviction

Come, I will show you the Bride, the wife of the Lamb.
Revelation 21:9

Outside our picture window, the Iowa landscape is white, the ground and rooftops covered in a crust of snow and ice under a cloudy sky. The barren trees sway in a wind that brings the wind chill a few degrees below zero. The air hurts your face. It is, however, noticeably warmer than a few weeks ago when the polar vortex brought our wind chill to nearly fifty degrees below zero. When this project began last summer, Elyse messaged me, complaining about the high temperatures and wildfires in California—a "feels like" temperature difference of nearly 150 degrees. Sometimes, in the midst of such extremes, it seems like the perfect day will never come.

We inhabit similar climates when it comes to the value of women. There are dangers on every side, with extremes that are painfully uncomfortable, if not hostile to life itself. Some oppose the simple biblical teaching that men and women are, in some ways, different. It is questioned whether one's sex is a permanent, God-assigned state, or whether it can be reassigned with surgery. Others use the Bible as a weapon against women, promoting demonic lies that characterize women as unintelligent, inherently dangerous, and inferior to men. Some reduce the value of women to their body types and sexual performance. Others demean the bearing and nursing of children. The onslaught against the value of women comes from every direction, in all extremes.

When we face extreme weather, we generally face it one system at a time. It is bitterly cold, or it is insufferably hot. But it is not freezing and scorching *at the same time*. Even then, we have thermostats to control heating and cooling systems. We watch (and complain about) the weather from the comfort of our climate-controlled homes. We find relief. Not so with the devaluing of women.

Threats to the value of women exist in our homes, churches, workplaces, schools, government, entertainment, music, sports—they grow in the soil of our sinful hearts. It feels inescapable. Neither do we have the luxury of facing hot or cold separately. Opposition to the Bible's value of women comes from all extremes simultaneously. We walk through flood and drought, firestorm and blizzard at once and all the time.

On more than one occasion while writing this book, Elyse and I have said to each other, "We're gonna take hits from all sides on this." There will be those who misunderstand what we're saying and condemn us for it. There will be those who understand what we're saying and criticize us for it. It will come from the secular culture and the church—and it will come all at once. Perhaps you feel like that as you try to walk the tightrope of sex, gender, faith, and culture. How should we then live?

We must live with hope-driven, courageous, compassionate conviction. In this conclusion, we will unpack each word of that statement.

Christian Conviction

In 1521 at the Diet of Worms, Martin Luther's opponents demanded that he recant his writings. The Reformer concluded with his famous declaration:

> If, then, I am not convinced by testimonies of Scripture or by clear rational arguments—for I do not believe in the pope or in councils alone, since it has been established that they have often erred and contradicted each other—I am bound by the Bible texts that I have quoted. And as long as my conscience is captive to the Word of God, I cannot nor do I want to retract anything when things become doubtful. Salvation will be threatened if you go against your conscience. May God help me. Amen.[1]

Luther reminds us that—whether it be the doctrine of justification or the value of women—our conscience must be captive to the Word of God. The Jews in Berea were praised for being "more noble" than their counterparts in Thessalonica, for "they received the word with all eagerness, examining the Scriptures daily to see if these things were so" (Acts 17:11). Our highest hope for you, our readers, is that you examine the Scriptures to determine the truth of what we have written about women. Develop your conviction about God's world and the image of God from the Word of God. Then, having done so, live according to your conscience under the Lordship of Christ. For, "we must obey God rather than people" (Acts 5:29 CSB).

Such a stance need not frighten us, for we know that "all Scripture is breathed out by God and profitable for teaching, for reproof, for correction, and for training in righteousness, that the man of God may be complete, equipped for every good work" (2 Timothy 3:16–17). Whatever God teaches, he teaches for our good.

Christian Courage

Faithfulness to our Christian convictions requires courage on several fronts.

Christian faithfulness requires the courage to confess our errors. In chapter 8 we saw the extent to which misogyny, chauvinism, and sexism polluted the waters of first-century Judaism. As we look back at the first-century culture, we should thank God for the effect the Gospel has had over the past two thousand years. We see the results in our local churches every Sunday morning.

Praise God that no one would rather burn the Bible than give it to a woman. Praise God for local, regional, and national women's ministries that put the study of the Scripture front and center. Praise God that women are not hidden behind screens or sent away to separate chambers in our church buildings, but are present, seen, and heard.

Nevertheless, progress does not equal perfection. Solomon reminds us, "What has been is what will be, and what has been done is what will be done, and there is nothing new under the sun" (Ecclesiastes 1:9). The sinful flesh we fight in ourselves today is no different than the human nature that blinded Judaism in the first century. The fact that we live in a different culture, context, and century in no way means that we are not susceptible to the same sins. Let us be on guard.

It may be that, in the course of this book, God convicted you of thoughts, words, and deeds (done or undone) that have demeaned and harmed women. Resist the temptation to justify yourself and to excuse sin, whether through appeal to cultural norms, ignorance, or misunderstanding. Christ owned all our sin on the cross. Therefore, we can own all our sin in repentance and faith. The cross speaks a more accurate and complete condemnation of our sinfulness than we could ever imagine. The resurrection gives us a complete and final declaration of righteousness. Our unity with Christ provides us with the confidence to confess with Paul:

"Christ Jesus came into the world to save sinners, of whom I am the foremost" (1 Timothy 1:15).

Christian faithfulness requires courage in the face of hostility in the church. In seminary, a (conservative, complementarian) professor recounted an anecdote originating with a moderate (female) Baptist pastor. The children at her church were "playing church" in the childcare room. As they picked roles, one of the boys expressed his desire to play the pastor. He was denied because "Boys can't be pastors. Only girls can." These children believed this, not because they were taught it from the Bible, but because a female pastor was all that they had ever seen.

That story illustrates the unfortunate truth that Christians often believe what they believe not because it developed from a rigorous study of the Bible, but because it is all they've ever seen or been told. They may have no scriptural reasons to object to a woman praying aloud during a public worship service. (In fact, Scripture provides examples of precisely that!) Nevertheless, because they have only seen male deacons praying in the service, they believe that it is the biblical pattern.

Furthermore, it may be that every example of female involvement in the church they have witnessed or heard about has been in the context of a local church that denies Christian orthodoxy. This leads them to the (unjustified) conclusion that the involvement of women is inherently tied to the denial of the Gospel. In such cases, asking honest questions and raising genuine concerns may be met with suspicion. Worse yet, it may be interpreted, dismissed, and accused as liberalism, egalitarianism, divisive behavior, or a lack of submission to church leadership. Such unfortunate responses only encourage women to wonder in silence, cautioned by their sisters about being misperceived or condemned.

Opposing demeaning speech, asking for clear statements on gender, calling for consistency in the application of principles, and requesting the inclusion of women to the fullest extent possible is neither insubordination nor divisive behavior. Done in good faith and humility, such are the calling of a Christian. The daughters of Zelophehad were not sinning (nor were they rebuked) when they went to Moses and said, "Give to us a possession among our father's brothers" (Numbers 27:4). Rather, the Lord told Moses, "The daughters of Zelophehad are right" (Numbers 27:7). No woman (or man) should, in any context, feel ashamed to ask that women receive the respect, dignity, value, and inclusion that is rightly theirs as human beings and, especially, as members of Christ's kingdom.

Nevertheless, the call to value women will not always be met with approval. Merely speaking of and highlighting the value of women can raise an eyebrow of suspicion in the church. Rachael Denhollander serves as a heroic example. In 2016 Denhollander reported USA Gymnastics doctor Larry Nassar for sexual abuse.[2] Christians lauded her victim impact statement as a model of courage and grace, which it was. However, it contained a troubling statement. She said:

> My advocacy for sexual assault victims, something I cherished, cost me my church and our closest friends three weeks before I filed my police report. I was left alone and isolated. And far worse, it was impacted because when I came out, my sexual assault was wielded like a weapon against me.[3]

In a follow-up interview with *Christianity Today*, she explained how advocacy cost her her church:

> The reason I lost my church was not specifically because I spoke up. It was because we were advocating for other victims of sexual assault within the evangelical community, crimes which had been perpetrated by people in the church and whose abuse had been enabled, very clearly, by prominent leaders in the evangelical community. That is not a message that evangelical leaders want to hear. . . . It would cost to take a stand against these very prominent leaders, despite the fact that the situation we were dealing with is widely recognized as one of the worst, if not *the* worst, instances of evangelical cover-up of sexual abuse. Because I had

taken that position, and because we were not in agreement with our church's support of this organization and these leaders, it cost us dearly.

When I did come forward as an abuse victim, this part of my past was wielded like a weapon by some of the elders to further discredit my concern, essentially saying that I was imposing my own perspective or that my judgment was too clouded. One of them accused me of sitting around reading angry blog posts all day, which is not the way I do research. . . .

. . . rather than engaging with the mountains of evidence that I brought, because this situation was one of the most well-documented cases of institutional cover-up I have ever seen, ever, there was a complete refusal to engage with the evidence.[4]

It took courage on Rachael's part to take on both a corrupt system in the world and within the church. She lost her church.[5]

As we finished the first draft of this book, the *Houston Chronicle* published a three-part series on sexual abuse in the Southern Baptist Convention over the past twenty years. The report found that "since 1998, roughly 380 Southern Baptist church leaders and volunteers have faced allegations of sexual misconduct," including "220 offenders [who] have been convicted or took plea deals" and "left behind more than 700 victims."[6] This went on despite a decade of advocates asking for preventative solutions.[7] To raise questions and call for change brings with it the risk of conflict and the loss of friends.

Brothers and sisters, be courageous. Our calling is not to preserve our reputations, to please those who hold more tightly to tradition than to Scripture, or to maintain our status among the "in crowd" of influential Christians. God doesn't need you to be accepted by the "inner ring."[8] He's already received you by grace through faith in Jesus Christ. Rest in that.

You are not required to please people. The Apostle Paul writes in 1 Corinthians 4:2–5 that "it is required of stewards that they be found faithful." Such a perspective frees him from the fear of human judgment. "But with me it is a very small thing that I should be judged by you or by any human court. In fact, I do not even judge myself. For I am not aware of anything against myself, but I am not thereby acquitted. It is the Lord who judges me. Therefore do not pronounce judgment before the time, before the Lord comes, who will bring to light the things now hidden in darkness and will disclose the purposes of the heart. Then each one will receive his commendation from God." Be faithful to God's Word. Do not fear the judgment or suspicion of humans. God is your judge. The only commendation that matters comes from him.

Christian faithfulness requires courage in the face of hostility in the world. We live in a culture that is *very* confused about gender. And so, our beliefs about gender—particularly those relating to marriage, sexuality, and church offices—are highly offensive.

Nevertheless, we cannot deny such things. We are not embarrassed by such things. We see them in the Scriptures. Our Lord's Commission is to make disciples, "teaching them to observe all that I have commanded you" (Matthew 28:20). Those commands are recorded in the Gospels and unpacked in the writings of the New Testament. So, we teach them, even as we obey them. We cannot deny them. That said, we offer these cautions, which flow from Jesus' example and teaching:

We are not allowed to over-offend our culture. We must strive to offend our culture no more than the Bible actually does when accurately interpreted and communicated. If they would be offended that we restrict marriage to the union of one man and one woman—then, so be it. But let them not be offended because we encourage women to suffer abuse at the hands of sinful husbands. If they would be offended that the office of pastor is reserved for men—then, so be it. But let them not be offended because we exclude women from areas of service from which the Lord does not exclude them.

We are not allowed to over-guard our doctrine. One of the things Jesus battled was the rabbinical practice of "fencing the

Law" mentioned in chapter 12. "In an attempt to make sure the command proper was never violated, the rabbis created secondary, rigid rules which, if followed, would theoretically prevent a person from ever violating the biblical command itself."[9] This happens today when we treat gender issues like the children's book *If You Give a Mouse a Cookie,* which humorously outlines what the mouse will ask for next—one thing necessarily leads to another, a slippery slope of sorts. The New Testament never argues this way (nor does the Old). Yet we find some contemporary, conservative, complementarian churches prohibiting women from serving in ways the Bible does not forbid in well-intentioned efforts to fence the teaching of the new covenant. We have no more right to add to the new covenant teachings and restrictions than an Israelite had to add to the Mosaic Law.

If we would build a wall around anything, let us build a wall around the offense. Let us build a wall of respectful speech about women (both in public and behind closed doors), such that they are never torn down, dismissed, demeaned, or stereotyped. Let us build a wall of serious Bible study and theological discussion amongst men and women, in which no woman ever is made to feel that she cannot understand because of her sex. Let us build a wall of healthy touch, touch that does not approach the female body as little more than a stumbling-block or an object to be used for gratification, but as part of what it means to be made in the image of God. Let us build a wall of humility in which a brother welcomes a sister to share with him her wisdom, observations, and correction as they walk together as a family in service together for the Gospel of Jesus Christ. Let us build a wall of friendship between men and women that does not see women as snares or seductresses, but in all purity treats older women as mothers and younger women as sisters. Let us build a wall of husbands who genuinely love their wives as Christ loved the church, serving their wives in humility and never, *never* giving them the slightest reason to suspect unfaithfulness. Let us build a wall of cooperation in the Great Commission, welcoming and including women in the service of the church and the ministry of the Gospel in each and every way to which the new covenant calls them.

Build those walls. Build them tall and strong and visible to all the world so that a critic must first go over, under, around, and through them before ever getting to what may be offensive. So that any honest detractor from our doctrine must be forced to admit—"I do not agree with where they land on gender, but, oh my, how they love and honor women!" Brothers and sisters, this is how our Lord lived—and when he said "Follow me," what he really meant is *"Follow me."*

Christian Compassion

Christian conviction requires courage. Courage is not raw and angry aggression. It is a confident conviction tempered with abundant, Christlike compassion.

Christian faithfulness requires compassion toward hurting women. True Christianity has been good for women. But there is no getting around the fact that much harm has been done to women in the name of "Christianity." This is true in history. This is true today. There are women in our churches, workplaces, schools, and neighborhoods who have been demeaned and insulted, overlooked and discriminated against, molested and raped, verbally and physically assaulted—all at the hands of men (and women) who call themselves "Christians."

These wounds are real. They are deep. They are not quickly healed. Their experiences have produced a justified suspicion of the church, particularly of men in positions of authority, especially spiritual authority.

This means, particularly for church leadership, that some of our actions will be misunderstood and misinterpreted. Women may see in our actions and hear in our words things that we do not intend. We must be patient with such things. Defensiveness and dismissiveness have no place in a shepherd of God's flock. Compassion is our calling toward wounded sheep.

Likewise, those who have suffered the results of misogynistic sin may be growing fed up with the church, leading to impatience. They may demand that everything is set right, and *right now*. What may be wisdom and patience in steering a flock, they interpret as weakness, hypocrisy, fear, and evidence that you do not care about women. Such interpretations of faithful shepherding are wrong—but they are also understandable. Again, harsh responses, theological suspicion, accusations of divisiveness and insubordination are not the first responses of a faithful shepherd. They help no one.

We must have compassion on the wounded, patiently demonstrating care, faithfulness, and safety—even as the Good Shepherd patiently and repeatedly shows his goodness to frightened and injured lambs.

Christian faithfulness requires compassion toward men (and women) struggling to figure things out. Perhaps you are one of the women (or men) wounded in the name of "Christianity." Our wounds make it easy to be suspicious, uncharitable, dismissive, and cynical. In pride, we may boast of how clearly we see things, forgetting how often our vision has been clouded. We forget how patient our Savior has been (and is!) with us as we follow him in fits and starts.

Remember the love of God.

> God shows his love for us in that while we were still sinners, Christ died for us.
>
> Romans 5:8

> Beloved, if God so loved us, we also ought to love one another.
>
> 1 John 4:11

> Love is patient, love is kind. Love does not envy, is not boastful, is not arrogant, is not rude, is not self-seeking, is not irritable, and does not keep a record of wrongs. Love finds no joy in unrighteousness but rejoices in the truth. It bears all things, believes all

things, hopes all things, endures all things. Love never ends. But as for prophecies, they will come to an end; as for tongues, they will cease; as for knowledge, it will come to an end.

1 Corinthians 13:4–8 csb

Walking together in cynicism, bearing grudges, and believing the worst of each other helps no one. "Help the weak, be patient with them all. See that no one repays anyone evil for evil, but always seek to do good to one another and to everyone" (1 Thessalonians 5:14–15).

As your fellow believers—church members and leaders—wrestle with hard questions, search the Bible, and consider how to faithfully live together as a family of believers; do not view them as enemies. View them as God does—as *family*. You share the same blood—that of Christ—and the same future. View them as necessary allies, gifts of grace, given by God for your good. You need this Spirit-filled family to sharpen, challenge, and shape you, just as much as they need you.

Christian faithfulness requires compassion toward Christians who disagree with us. We realize that as sincere Christians go to the Bible to develop their doctrine, we often come away with *different, yet Christian* convictions. This is why we have paedobaptists and credobaptists.[10] This is why we have congregationalist and elder-ruled churches. This is why we have Christians who serve in the armed forces and those who are conscientious objectors to war. This is why we have complementarians and egalitarians. People who love Jesus, believe the Gospel, and submit to the authority of Scripture, come away from the Bible with differing but sincere convictions.

We must not shy away from discussion and debate about what the Bible teaches. But we must bear in mind that we hold our differing convictions as members of a larger family. Let us not turn genuine brothers and sisters in the faith into enemies, but remember to show compassion in each disagreement. We are part of a bigger realm, the kingdom of God, in which brothers and sisters disagree as we wait together for our King to come and make us (and our doctrine) perfect.

We are complementarians by biblical conviction. We are not ashamed of this conviction. Nevertheless, we wish to emphasize that we are *with* and *not against* egalitarian brothers and sisters in the faith; we join them in defending and upholding the worth of women, even as we delight to link arms with them in declaring the one true Gospel. Christian conviction should compel Christian *unity*, not excuse Christian division. We should strive to stand and serve together to as great an extent as possible with all who confess Jesus Christ as the Son of God who died for our sins and rose from the dead. If we believe the same Gospel, credobaptists and paedobaptists, congregationalist and elder-ruled, continuationists and cessationists, complementarians and egalitarians ought to be together for the Gospel.

Christian faithfulness requires compassion toward a confused and hostile world. There will be those in the world who hate you, oppose you, mistreat you, and say false things about you. It will happen when you speak on matters of gender and sex because you say what Jesus says in his Word. It is a blessing to be so associated with Christ (Luke 6:22). In light of this abuse, he calls us to love. "But I say to you who hear, Love your enemies, do good to those who hate you, bless those who curse you, pray for those who abuse you" (Luke 6:27–28). Remember who you were and what God did.

> For we ourselves were once foolish, disobedient, led astray, slaves to various passions and pleasures, passing our days in malice and envy, hated by others and hating one another. But when the goodness and loving kindness of God our Savior appeared, he saved us, not because of works done by us in righteousness, but according to his own mercy, by the washing of regeneration and renewal of the Holy Spirit, whom he poured out on us richly through Jesus Christ our Savior, so that being justified by his grace we might become heirs according to the hope of eternal life.
>
> Titus 3:3–7

We have no right to respond with any less grace than that shown to us by God in Christ.

Christian Hope

The conviction, courage, and compassion described above is a tall order. It sounds impossible. In fact, left to ourselves, it is impossible. Faithful obedience, compassion, courage—these are not produced by gritting our teeth and trying harder. There is only one source for such sanctification, transformation, and patient endurance—"the gospel is the power of God for salvation" (Romans 1:16). The Gospel trains and empowers us in transformed living.

> For the grace of God has appeared, bringing salvation for all people, training us to renounce ungodliness and worldly passions, and to live self-controlled, upright, and godly lives in the present age, waiting for our blessed hope, the appearing of the glory of our great God and Savior Jesus Christ, who gave himself for us to redeem us from all lawlessness and to purify for himself a people for his own possession who are zealous for good works.
>
> Titus 2:11–14

As we find our identity in Christ, see ourselves crucified and raised with him, we begin to live like him. But such grace-based living in the present is not done merely by looking back. It also happens by looking forward. Did you catch the middle part of that passage? "*Waiting* for our blessed hope, the appearing of the glory of our great God and Savior Jesus." Our training in how to live now is characterized by *waiting* for what is to come.

What are we waiting for? "Our blessed hope." In the Bible, hope is not wishful thinking, a desire for something that may or may not happen. Hope is a future certainty. It is what we are confident *will* happen because God has declared it to be so.

What are we hoping for? Our "blessed hope" is "the appearing of the glory of our great God and Savior Jesus Christ." One day, just as Jesus ascended bodily into heaven, he will reappear—glorious and imperishable (1 Corinthians 15). Looking forward to Christ's return equips us for life now. "Therefore, preparing your minds for action, and being sober-minded, set your hope fully on the grace that will be brought to you at the revelation of Jesus Christ" (1 Peter 1:13).

Why are we hoping for Christ's return? What will happen on that day? For starters, we love Christ, and we want to be with him. Moreover, we love Christ, and we want to be like him. And when he appears, not only will we have him, but we will be like him. "Beloved, we are God's children now, and what we will be has not yet appeared; but we know that when he appears *we shall be like him, because we shall see him as he is*" (1 John 3:2, emphasis added). This is Christ's goal, to make us like him; he "gave himself for us to redeem us from all lawlessness and to purify for himself a people for his own possession who are zealous for good works."

Creation will end with a glorious and perfect resurrection. Everything will be born again. In fact, Jesus calls the new world "the regeneration" (Matthew 19:28 KJV)—the same word used to describe the renewal that the Holy Spirit works in us when we trust Jesus (Titus 3:5). But what will become of gender—of male and female?

Some argue that there will be no male and female in the resurrection. They take this from Jesus' statement, "For in the resurrection they neither marry nor are given in marriage, but are like angels in heaven" (Matthew 22:30; see also Mark 12:25; Luke 20:34–35). They take this to mean that our bodies will not be resurrected male and female. This reads too much into the passage. For one, angels always appear as male beings—they have a sex! But Jesus does not say that humans will be resurrected neither male nor female. He says that they "neither marry nor are given in marriage." Since Jesus was raised as a man in continuity with the male body he lived and died in—and since we will experience the same type of resurrection (1 Corinthians 15)—it is reasonable to assume that we will be raised male and female in continuity with the earthly bodies that we have now.

Why will there be no marriage in heaven? If you're asking that, you're asking the wrong question. We will "neither marry nor are given in marriage." This is because death is destroyed and the multitude of God's people have received their standing as God's children (Luke 20:36). It is also because *we will be married*. Yes, there is marriage in the new heavens and the new earth—a glorious marriage between a glorious Bridegroom and a glorious bride.

The Bible concludes with a picture of a glorious man—Jesus—and a glorious woman, the bride of Christ. In the last chapters of the last book of the Bible, the Apostle John records an invitation from an angel: "Come, I will show you the Bride, the wife of the Lamb" (Revelation 21:9). The angel points him to a new Jerusalem, coming down from heaven, symbolic of the people of God who dwell there. Consider this description of "the Bride, the wife of the Lamb":

> Then I saw a new heaven and a new earth, for the first heaven and the first earth had passed away, and the sea was no more. And I saw the holy city, new Jerusalem, coming down out of heaven from God, prepared as a bride adorned for her husband. And I heard a loud voice from the throne saying, "Behold, the dwelling place of God is with man. He will dwell with them, and they will be his people, and God himself will be with them as their God. He will wipe away every tear from their eyes, and death shall be no more, neither shall there be mourning, nor crying, nor pain anymore, for the former things have passed away."
>
> And he who was seated on the throne said, "Behold, I am making all things new." Also he said, "Write this down, for these words are trustworthy and true." And he said to me, "It is done! I am the Alpha and the Omega, the beginning and the end. To the thirsty I will give from the spring of the water of life without payment. The one who conquers will have this heritage, and I will be his God and he will be my son. But as for the cowardly, the faithless, the detestable, as for murderers, the sexually immoral, sorcerers, idolaters, and all liars, their portion will be in the lake that burns with fire and sulfur, which is the second death."
>
> Revelation 21:1–8

This is our blessed hope—the great reversal of the Fall, the establishment of a new and better Garden of Eden. The strength to face the extremes and the frustration of our present world comes through the confidence that a better world is certain.

In *The Lord of the Rings: Return of the King*, Sam asked Gandalf, "Is everything sad going to come untrue? What's happened to the world?" to which Gandalf replied, "A great Shadow has departed."[11] The return of Christ will be everything Sam hoped for—everything sad is going to come untrue.

Some of you read this book with great sadness. What happened to you as a woman (or to a woman you love)—or what you see happen to women and girls across the globe—is a great shadow, a darkness that seems to have overcome the light. You wonder if you will ever heal. You wonder if justice will ever arrive. You wonder if all can be made right in this world. The answer to those questions is a resounding yes.

One day, the Lamb will return for his bride. She shall be made perfect. He will dwell with her in a perfect world, a new heavens and new earth. There the sting of every misogynistic remark, every act of discrimination, every sexist joke, every molestation, every rape, every act of exclusion, every strike of the fist, every abusive word—*all of it*—will be wiped away. Every tear dried. Every bruise healed. Every wrong righted. Every death undone. All the sadness made untrue. The perpetrators of such wickedness against the bride—those who would not surrender to the reign of the King—he will cast out, giving them full justice for their wicked deeds. The walls of the city shall be strong, such that no one may enter to do her harm again. He will satisfy her longings, freely and fully, serving her at his banqueting table. He will give her himself. The King shall dwell with his bride. They will reign together in his kingdom without end. It will be a storybook wedding. And they will live happily ever after.

This is the final scene in the story of woman, the final display of her value—the glorification of the bride to live and reign with the Bridegroom, Jesus. This is our blessed hope, as certain and sure as the rising of the sun. It is given freely to all who thirst for it, to all who come to Jesus.

Friend, will you join us in this kingdom? You are most certainly invited to join us. "The Spirit and the Bride say, 'Come'" (Revelation 22:17).

Ladies First

In order to help you remember what we've written about the importance of women in redemption's history, the following list includes many biblical examples of women premiering in the way of faith. We hope that this list will encourage women who wonder if God can ever use them. We also hope that it will instruct others who have (either intentionally or unintentionally) assumed that women are ancillary in God's kingdom or that God only uses men.

- A woman's absence is the first thing declared "not good" in creation (Genesis 2:18).
- The first recorded song in human history is the man rejoicing over the woman (Genesis 2:23).
- The woman is first to be named as being at enmity with the serpent (Genesis 3:15).
- A woman will give birth to the serpent-crushing seed—the Messiah (Genesis 3:15).

- The first recorded words of faith were spoken by Eve (Genesis 4:1).

- A woman, Eve, is the first person recorded to speak the name "Yahweh" (Genesis 4:1).

- The first man said to have found favor in the eyes of the Lord (Noah, Genesis 6:8) is followed by the first woman specifically said to have found favor with God, Mary (Luke 1:30). Noah saved humanity through the ark he built. Mary delivered humanity's salvation through the Son built in her body.

- The first recorded appearance of the Angel of the Lord is to Hagar (Genesis 16:7).

- The first character in the Old Testament to confer a name on God, "The God Who Sees," is a woman—Hagar (Genesis 16:13).

- The first declaration of the Lord's ability to do the impossible is spoken in regard to what he will do through a barren woman who formerly worshiped the moon (Genesis 18:14).

- The first (and only) time Abraham is recorded as weeping is at the death of his wife, Sarah (Genesis 23:2).

- The first declaration of unconditional election is made to Rebekah, (Genesis 25:22–23; Romans 9:10–12). She is also the first to "inquire of the Lord."

- A woman, Miriam, is the first person recorded to dance in worship (Exodus 15:20–21).

- The daughters of Zelophehad were the first people God declares as "right" in their request and judgment (Numbers 27:7).

- A woman, Hannah, is the first person recorded to speak the divine title "Yahweh of Hosts" (1 Samuel 1:11).

- Hannah is also the first person to mention the Messiah in her song. "The adversaries of the Lord shall be broken to pieces . . . he will give strength to his king and exalt the horn of his anointed" (1 Samuel 2:10). This "anointed" one is the Messiah.

- At the anointing of the first king in the Old Testament, Saul, women give directions and instructions to him on how to find Samuel (1 Samuel 9:11–12).
- The faith of a woman, Rahab, was crucial in the conquering of the first city in the Promised Land (Joshua 2); her family was the only Gentile family saved in Jericho (Joshua 6:23–25). Her direct descendant would be the Messiah (Matthew 1:5).
- The first New Testament declaration of the Lord's ability to do the impossible is in regard to what he will do through a young virgin (Luke 1:37).
- Women, Mary and Elizabeth, are the first to believe that Jesus and his forerunner, John the Baptist, would be conceived (Luke 1:5–38). They are also the first to speak aloud of it.
- A woman, Elizabeth, and her child (in utero) are the first recorded people to recognize the Messiah's arrival. She is the first to speak of it (Luke 1:39–45).
- A woman, Mary, composes the first hymn of the new covenant age (Luke 1:46–55).
- A woman, Anna, is the first to speak publicly and broadly of the arrival of Jesus (Luke 2:36–38). See note in chapter 8.
- A woman, Mary the mother of Jesus, is the first to expect and request a miraculous sign in his public ministry (John 2:1–11).
- A woman, the Samaritan at the well, is the first recorded Gentile to whom Jesus reveals himself as the Messiah. She is also the first to tell a non-Jewish community about him (John 4:4–42).

- Only women are said to give general, regular financial provision (out of their own means) to Jesus and the Twelve (Luke 8:3).
- No individual woman is ever recorded in the Gospels as acting as an enemy of Jesus.
- A woman, the wife of Pontius Pilate, is the first person to declare Jesus' righteousness during his trial (Matthew 27:19).
- Women were the last to stay with Jesus at the cross, along with one disciple, John (John 19:25).
- A woman, the mother of Jesus, is the final person Jesus directly ministered to before his death (John 19:26–27).
- Women were first to go to the grave after the Sabbath (Matthew 28:1; Mark 16:1–2).
- Women were the first believing people tasked with proclaiming news of the resurrection (Matthew 28:6–7; Mark 16:6–7). The guards at the tomb told of his resurrection but they were not doing so in faith.
- Women were the first to see and enter the empty tomb (Matthew 28:6, 8; Mark 16:4–5).
- Women are the first to see the resurrected Lord, and also the first to touch his resurrected body (Matthew 28:9; John 20:14).
- A woman, Mary Magdalene, is the first to hear the resurrected Lord's voice. The first name he utters is a woman's (John 20:14–18).
- Women were the first to worship the Risen Lord (Matthew 28:9).
- Women were the first to meet unbelief when heralding the resurrection of Jesus (Luke 24:10–11).
- The mistreatment and neglect of women (widows) was the impetus for appointing the first deacons (Acts 6:1–6).

- A woman, Lydia, was the first in Europe to believe the Gospel and be baptized (Acts 16:15). God uses a strong helper (*ezer*), Lydia, to supply the help that the Macedonian man begged for in Paul's vision. Together Paul and Lydia form a blessed alliance that will meet his need. His urgent pleas for help were answered by a male and female team.

- A woman, Lydia, was the first in Europe to provide hospitality for the apostles on their mission (Acts 16:40). In fact, of the six churches that met in the homes of named people in the New Testament, three met in single women's homes, two in the homes of married women, and one in the home of a man. Hosting a church in one's home meant more than furnishing coffee and cookies. It meant that these women (and man) were legally responsible for their guests and might have to post bond to ensure their good behavior (Acts 17:9).

- Of Paul's four greetings that include specific names, a woman's name is listed first in three of them (Romans 16:1, 3; Colossians 4:15; 2 Timothy 4:19).

- A feminine voice—that of the bride—is the last to be quoted in the Bible (Revelation 22:17).

What Women Wish Their Pastors Knew

A Word to Our Ordained Brothers

While both of us agree that the office of pastor is to be filled only by called and ordained men, we also recognize that differences exist among sincere Christians as to which church offices are restricted to qualified men. Even so, we hope that all can agree that women have been gifted with significant wisdom, insight, zeal, and faithfulness that is meant to augment and encourage these men and others. As someone who has gladly attended church and listened to sermons delivered by beloved pastors weekly since 1971, I (Elyse) have heard well-nigh 3,000 sermons in my life. Some of them have been really wonderful and others . . . well . . . not so much. That doesn't count all the cassette tapes (yes, I know that's ancient!) I've heard, nor any of the sermon podcasts I enjoy every week. The Lord has been so kind to me in giving me this wealth of teaching. I've been so blessed.

Having said all of the above, and having said it in utter sincerity and gratitude, I have to say that there are certainly things I wished these pastors and leaders knew about how to communicate to a woman and also how women long to be included in the broader ministry of your church. What you'll read here are words spoken in respect and in faith that somehow the women who will come after me living lives of faith will do so hearing sermons that speak to them in the same way that they speak to their brothers and finding open doors to give their lives in service to the Savior they love.

Let me make a few things clear first:

My primary hope is that you'll preach the Gospel. That seems obvious, I know, but still. We all need to hear the good news of the life, death, resurrection, ascension, reign, and return of the King. We need to hear that we are forgiven, counted righteous, and empowered to strive to love our neighbor. We need to hear that every single Sunday. Words fail me to express the great need women have of hearing good news, especially that they are forgiven. They spend all day, every day, hearing about all the ways they're failing and how those failures are liable to ruin those they love most. Please, please tell them that "he remembers their sins no more," and that they're already counted completely perfect in him. I've said that in front of thousands of women and watched them break down in sobs. So, if all you hear from me in this short appendix is that, well, that's good.

Preach the text. I'm not saying you should stop doing that to talk about other issues, like what women might need/want to hear. I am saying that in the process of preaching the text, be sure that any areas of the text that might be confusing or even denigrating to women are not assumed, avoided, glossed over, or viewed from a patriarchal perspective. For instance, when preaching about David and Bathsheba, don't use the word *affair*. What happened to Bathsheba wasn't a consensual romance. It was, at the very least, sexual assault by someone in a position of power, and most probably rape, as Bathsheba would have had no ability to give her consent. So, when you refer to David, you can call him what he is, "a man who abused his power to abuse a woman sexually," and then talk about God's forgiveness and mercy for even men and women who abuse others. This might be a good time to preach Christ and say something like, "David used his power to abuse a woman and tear her home apart, but because of the righteousness of Christ, he's also called a man after God's own heart." How powerful would that be? It would speak to men who have committed sexual sin and abused power (they are in your church, whether you realize it or not), while at the same time reassuring women that you know that what David did was heinous and that in your church abuse of women won't be tolerated or glossed over, and that women won't automatically be blamed when sexual impropriety occurs.[1]

What follows are some responses from godly women (who will remain anonymous) to my question of what they wished pastors/male leaders in church understood about women. I've paraphrased their answers to protect their identities.

What do you wish your pastor/male leaders knew about women?

- That I am not a feminist just because I want to talk about women's issues and valuing women.
- That they knew how to preach to women: i.e., anticipate questions different women might have about a text, use illustrations that both genders and various life stages can appreciate, think of applications that connect with women as well as men.
- That there are many women in their congregations who are post-abortive or struggle with feelings of same-sex attraction; that they need your understanding and empathy.
- That they would value older women and train and encourage them to teach younger ones.
- That I'm not out for their job.

- That I am not like their wife.
- That my opinion is valuable and that, as a faithful member of his church, I would like to have input on key church conversations.
- That I truly see them as brothers—especially that I don't see them as potential conquests.
- That their presence is welcome and helpful at "women's" events at the church. I find that so many pastors stay away. But this is half of their congregation! A pastor who attends a women's event demonstrates that the women are important to him and that he sees himself as their shepherd. A shepherd should be very interested and engaged with any person who is coming in to teach half of their congregation. This doesn't mean he has to be in charge or stay the whole time. But a pastor is wise to show his face and mill around with the women at a women's event and not make a stupid joke about estrogen or feeling weird, but rather just love on his congregation that is gathered there.
- That they would welcome women who could wisely speak into their lives without being so afraid of sexual sin. Obviously, parameters must be in place. But women have a different perspective, one that must be valued.
- That they would not be afraid of the strength of a woman. Her strengths can be used in all aspects of the church, including leadership. That they not fear that women will take over and try to control things if they acknowledge and value their strength and wisdom.
- That they would consider women in planning events or even use of facilities. For instance, once a church I was attending was planning a new church campus and as I looked at the renderings, I wondered if any woman had been asked for her opinion. So, it might be better when revealing plans to mention that a group of women and men had significant input.

- That they would consider asking women to help in the planning and implementation of events.

- That women should be paid for the work they do. Sometimes pastors only consider paying a man because he might have a family to provide for. Remember that Paul encouraged the church at Rome to provide for Phoebe, setting the example of women being compensated when on official church business. It's wrong to create paid positions for men and take women for granted, expecting them to volunteer, especially for a leadership role in church. Would it be too much to ask that they consider paying a woman as much as they would pay a man if he were doing the same job?

- That they would know that married women are longing for them to speak to their husband with specific challenges during a message. Also, that they would confess their sin publicly so that the husbands would know that confession of sin is manly. I love when the pastors pour into men and challenge them to be godly, involved husbands and fathers. I don't know a wife who is not beaming when a pastor turns his attention to the men with specific challenges during a message. This makes us feel loved and safe, as if the leaders want us to be cared for and want to hold the men accountable.

- That some men take teaching about headship/submission too far and are demanding and abusive of their wives. That if they're going to teach on these things, and they should, they need to make very clear what they are and are not saying and that men are not allowed to bully, denigrate, or abuse their wives; nor are they allowed to demand sex at any time.

- That pornography injures both men and women and if a husband gives himself over to it, it is not his wife's fault; that when a wife discovers her husband is viewing pornography, she feels the same sense of betrayal as if he had an affair; that the wife needs to be protected and built up as she struggles to walk through his unfaithfulness; and that she needs to be supported if she decides that this sin makes it impossible for her to trust him again. Pastors need to understand that adultery is not limited to actual sexual intercourse. Habitual use of pornography is a breaking of the covenant vows of marriage for a man— just like it would be for a woman.

- That single (or divorced) women feel invisible and need to feel loved, rather than tolerated. I don't know the answer for this, but they are desperate for the church to help them. Perhaps pastors could make sure they mention them (without always assuming that they're discontented or dying to be married) whenever appropriate and that they avoid celebrating mothers exclusively. When they talk about workers in the church, make sure that they point out singles too. Also, when they talk about how the church has met its financial goals, they can be thankful for the women who work and provide for the needs of the church. Remember that Lydia did this for Paul and he was openly grateful to her and the church that met in her home.

- That they wouldn't plan events that would automatically exclude women who work. For instance, if the primary weekly Bible study is on Wednesday mornings, working women will likely assume that the decision-makers (pastors and elders) don't care if they attend or not. Perhaps a study group that meets once a week at night or even a group that meets online for those who cannot make it to the church campus can still study with their sisters.

- That they wouldn't assume that every woman even wants children.

- That they wouldn't assume that every woman loves shopping. Some of us love studying and digging deeply in Scripture.

- We love courtesy but hate condescension.
- I do need to understand my roles as a woman in the home and in the church, but I don't need to have that role pressed into any other sphere of public life.
- That they would rarely meet with a husband and wife for counseling without another woman in the room. Even a strong wife will appreciate the comfort and protection that a female ear in that room will bring. Then, even if the woman counselor has to confront the wife, it's better than being ganged up on by two men, which is how women feel. It will also be more difficult to ignore, put down to male prejudice, or misunderstand words spoken by another woman rather than by men, especially if those men have friendships with each other outside of the counseling room.
- That they need to have female ministry staff (paid or unpaid depending on the financial strength of the church) who are available to meet with women to discuss anything that women want to talk about including (but not limited to) past or present sexual abuse, physical or emotional abuse, inappropriate speech/actions from another man in the church.

On this topic another woman wrote,

- A huge portion of women have personally endured inappropriate sexual comments, physical sexual assault (to varying degrees), men who have used them and/or made them extremely uncomfortable, or worse. While some of them will share this and pursue counseling, most will never speak of it again. They will take it to Jesus alone. The hurts are maybe decades old—their own husbands might not know all the details. The more I talk to women in the church, the more I think these are prevalent realities. For many, many reasons (some healthy, some not) women won't share them, but that doesn't mean they aren't affected by them. Be aware that your preaching and teaching and shepherding can trigger some of those wounds. A specific remedy: Just know it exists. That doesn't mean you can't say anything hard or develop close relationships or friendships with women, but know that everyone has a story. Another specific remedy: Give women avenues to share their stories and receive counseling and prayer as desired. Some who want to speak aren't even sure who to tell and how they can be shepherded. Have you identified the women leaders in your church?

[Perhaps your congregation could contact GRACE ministries (https://www.netgrace.org) to obtain training in how to respond to and prevent sexual abuse of children and to minister to adult survivors, remembering that more than 20 percent of women have experienced sexual violence including rape.[2] Also the Southern Baptist Convention has produced a video series and handbook, *Becoming a Church That Cares Well*, to equip churches to care well for the abused, available online free at https://www.churchcares.com.]

- That they would take seriously a woman's report of sexual harassment and not brush it off as a woman's touchiness or silliness. At the very least, pastors should avail themselves and their staff of their state's sexual harassment laws and training. A public document that makes it clear that any report of workplace harassment will be handled with seriousness, timeliness, and detailed investigation, is necessary. A document like this, added to the church's statement of faith or bylaws, will assure the female members of the staff and the lay women in the congregation (as well as warn any would-be perpetrators) that this kind of behavior will not be tolerated, no matter who does it.
- That they would promote women's events with the same enthusiasm as the men's. That they would be sure that there are men available to help when women are having an

event, i.e., with the sound. That they would value women's ministries as much as they value the men's.

- That they would not misinterpret caustic responses from a woman by automatically labeling them "rebellious" or "stiff-necked," without understanding that this kind of a response usually stems from a heart deeply wounded by a man. What would it mean for male leaders to meet such a woman with an internal prayer—"Lord, how has she been wounded and how do I minister your grace to her?"
- That they not view me as a deceptress or someone who wants to have sex with them. Honestly, it's the last thing on my mind.
- Encourage your women to pursue education and training, and when they do, defend their decision. Speak to male leadership so that the women aren't seen as a threat, but as co-ministers of the Good News of salvation and truth. If a woman is getting training in order to serve the church, offer to help her with the costs.
- I need to hear that I am a co-laborer with Christ and with my fellow Christians, male and female.
- I need strong comfort in this sad world and encouragement for the one to come.

Some Simple Suggestions

Perhaps pastors should have a group of women and men (single, married, with family/career) that they could call on for feedback— perhaps they could tell them the passage for the week and have them read it, give brief responses/pose questions about portions they struggle with; or they could ask certain wise women in the congregation whether/how the sermon ministered to them in the week after.

Of course, some pastors might say that they don't have time. We get this. But perhaps this could be set up by email. Remember that the women you will ask are as busy as you are. Just tell them you'll only want a little feedback on occasion.

Other pastors might say that they don't even ask men for feedback, so they might wonder why they should ask women for their perspective. We understand that concern, but would respond that they probably use commentaries/books/articles/blogs written by men in their preparation, and that they have probably heard other men's take on the passage through sermons they've listened to, so they actually are already hearing from men and without knowing it undoubtedly already have a predisposition to read it from almost an exclusively male perspective.

Remember That the Women in Your Congregation Love You and Understand More Than You Might Think

As one woman wrote,

> Many women (moms in particular) can empathize with the unseen, sacrificial, unglamorous work of shepherding. While we're not the head of the family flock or front and center on Sundays, we have more in common than you think. We care for the sick in our homes, sometimes even crying with them and feeling discouraged at the effects of the fall. We run the long game in relationships with people who take from us while we patiently give our heart, wisdom, and presence, even when it's not received with gratitude. We minister the Word to disobedient, never-happy sinners who don't seem to understand our care and direction. Of course, some of our specific responsibilities are different—but you're not alone. Many of your daughters, sisters, and mothers in the body are praying for you and can imagine what your ministry costs. They are grateful for you. You are necessary allies in the kingdom.

Please also remember that

> many women wish pastors knew that we are thinkers and need the life of the mind cultivated as much as men do. I wish they would

265

explore the commonalities between men and women with the same eagerness that they meditate on our differences. Too often men and women are viewed as being from different planets instead of from the same garden, made in the same image. If C.S. Lewis is right about friendship beginning at the moment one person looks at another and says, "You, too? I thought I was the only one," then it is crucial for men and women to understand similarities as well as differences. Otherwise, we may never begin to develop mutual respect.

Our guess is that this appendix may have made some of you uncomfortable. Please believe us when we say that it is not our goal to usurp authority or denigrate male leadership in the church. Please know that we want what you do: that God's kingdom would come and his will would be done on earth as it is in heaven. Like you, we long for the day when the church is whole and holy and that both women and men find their gifts valued and utilized. We pray that this short appendix may have been of some help.

31 Things (Good) Pastors Want Women to Know

I (Eric) asked several pastor friends to tell me what they want the women to know about how they feel about and relate to the women in their church. Below is a list of their answers—along with several of my own.

Instead of including an explanation for each point, I offer them here as a list of statements for personal meditation, church examination, and pastoral conversations. I've provided a few notes about that at the end.

1. We haven't said all we want and need to say.
2. We value you.
3. We love you.
4. We like you.
5. We want *you* the individual, not a cliché or stereotype of womanhood.

6. We affirm you.

7. We respect you.

8. We need you.

9. We hear you.

10. We lose without you.

11. We trust you.

12. We fail you.

13. We try on after we fail.

14. We want you to feel safe and valued in the church and by us.

15. We want you to be comfortable around us.

16. We want to be comfortable around you.

17. We know that some pastors aren't safe—and we respect your caution.

18. We welcome you to bring an advocate or safe person when you talk to us.

19. We do not want to have sex with you.

20. We find navigating varied cultures and expectations a confusing task.

21. We find consistent, culturally-appropriate application of the Bible a confusing task.

22. We're jerks sometimes, but it's not because you're a woman.

23. We welcome your correction.

24. We can't read your minds; we need your words.

25. We're scared sometimes—of culture, change, conflict—but not of you as women.

26. We need your friendship.

27. We need your patience.

28. We need your grace.

29. We are blessed by you.

30. We remember you.
31. We thank God for you.

I know, sisters, that if these things do not ring true about your pastor, this appendix could spark frustration, bitterness, or complaining. Resist those temptations. Instead, consider turning this appendix into a prayer list for your pastor. If you have a good relationship with your pastor, perhaps you buy him a copy of this book, ask him to read it, and then tell him you'd like to share with him the ways he really encourages you as a pastor, along with a few ways he could continue to grow in this.

Pastors, would you consider spending one month meditating on and applying this list? Perhaps you could take one point a day and ask these questions:

- Is this true of me? Why or why not?
- Would the women in my church find this a believable statement coming from me? Why or why not?
- What can I do to express this to the women in my church
  - immediately (today!)?
  - next Sunday?
  - over the long-term life of our congregation?
- What woman could I have a conversation with about this today?

Or—if you're really brave—send this list to some women in the church and ask

- Which of these would you say is true of me?
- For those that seem true:
  - What have I done to help you see and feel this?
  - How can I continue to encourage you in this way?
- For those that do *not* seem true:

- What makes you think that this is not true?
- How can I do better?

Let's do better at communicating our love and appreciation for one another—just as our Father looks on us with pleasure through the finished work of Jesus and proclaims his delight in us.

Sample Letter from Pastor to Initiate Conversations

Here is an adaptation of an email I (Eric) sent to a few groups of women in our congregation:

> I've been meaning to ask you about a few ideas I've had for connecting with Grand Avenue Baptist Church women in general. I want the women of GABC to know that I value them, their presence, their gifts and ministry, their lives and spiritual well-being. I also want them to know that I'm not scared of women—their intelligence, strength, gifting, feedback, criticisms, questions, or friendship. In fact, I desire and value all those things. (But I want to pursue those in a way that doesn't make women feel uncomfortable or make me look like a creep!) So, I thought I'd throw out a few thoughts and would love to hear your thoughts or suggestions.
>
> 1) Women's Lunch — A few years ago, I worked my way through all the men in the church doing one-on-one lunches. That morphed into men's lunches with five to six men a week.

I've always wanted to do something like that with groups of women. No real agenda, other than to hear what's happening in their lives and be available as a pastor for general conversation and encouragement. I know I'd really enjoy it.

Would that be a good idea? If so, what's the best way to facilitate it?

2) Women's Events — I'd be delighted to show up at women's events, just to say/show that I love the women in our church and value what's happening. How do I do that in a way that is helpful and not distracting? (In a previous church, I'd occasionally drop in and could tell it changed the dynamics. While some appreciated it, I'd also hear others viewed it as me "checking up on the women" in a negative way.)

3) Women's Input in Teaching — I've been trying (as much as I know how) to include women's voices in the life of GABC (reading liturgy and Scripture in the service; I have women help write the liturgy and pick songs; I try to include women in ministry lunches and special event planning, try to strike up conversations with women, etc.). I'd love to include women's perspectives when I teach. (As I mentioned, if I were preaching weekly, I would have a standard weekly meeting of a cross-section of the body to hear perspectives on the text and its application. But that's not where I'm at now.) Any thoughts on women who would be good to ask for such feedback and how to go about it? Any advice on how to go about that?

4) Physical Touch, "Billy Graham Rule," etc. — We had a really good conversation yesterday on things like hugs and the "Billy Graham rule" and church culture between men and women.

I love hugs (except when people are creepy!) and come from a background of a family, high school and college friends, seminary, and church that all hugged. In general, I am an affectionate person (though church controversy and trauma have had a really negative effect on that). When I came here, I didn't get hugs and so assumed

272

the culture wasn't a hugging one. And, honestly, I feel really, really uncomfortable initiating a hug when I read about these abuser pastors and the way they treat women. Those reports, knowing how some church circles view male/female friendships and being in a position of authority, make me really nervous about initiating anything! (UGH!)

I also am not an adherent to the so-called "Billy Graham rule." I've met women one-on-one for coffee to do counseling or pastoral care, I give a widow rides in my car, etc. It's transparent (on my schedule, Jenny knows, etc.) and I adhere to fairly common sense precautions, I think. I fear rules that make women out to be little more than temptresses and temptations. (I think that putting fences around them as such only leads to regarding them as such.)

All that is to say: I view the women in my church as my mothers and sisters, not as objects or snares. I want to treat them with relational affection appropriate to a close family member. So my question is: As GABC women, what do you think our culture needs? What's the best way to cultivate that culture? And how should I act or not act as a pastor?

5) General Availability to the Women's Ministry and Leadership Team — If I could ever be useful to you or your leadership team to converse and bounce ideas off of, I'm happy to serve (and attend meetings). I'd also love to speak or answer questions at women's events if that would ever be helpful.

APPENDIX 5

An Open Letter to Rachael Denhollander on #SBCtoo

On February 11, 2019, in response to a series in the *Houston Chronicle* on sexual abuse in the Southern Baptist Convention, Rachael Denhollander tweeted a sincere question to pastors. She asked where they were the previous ten years when so many were calling for reform. As a pastor in the Southern Baptist Convention, Eric published this public answer to her public question.[1] We include it here both to tell the story of how Eric grew in his value of women—particularly abuse survivors—and as an example of how pastors might publicly repent of wrong attitudes and inaction.

Dear Rachael,

This past week, the *Houston Chronicle* published a three-part series on sexual abuse in the Southern Baptist Convention.[2]

In response, you asked: *"Pastors, where were you? When we were pleading for you to speak up against your peers or the leaders your support props up, where were you?"*[3]

I want (and need) to answer your question.

Ten years ago, I was thirty-two years old, almost three years into pastoring my second church. We were recovering from some heart-breaking and regrettable division while walking into new conflicts. I was in the throes of life-paralyzing depression, not knowing how to handle what was happening.

My heart and mind were (as they so often are now) a jumble of conflicting desires and aspirations. On the one hand, I sincerely desired to glorify God, preach the Gospel, and shepherd a healthy church. On the other hand, my heart nurtured ambitions of personal glory, wishing to be known for my preaching and be influential within reformed evangelical circles. To go back and separate my decisions—the righteous from the unrighteous—is like trying to untie the Gordian Knot. That can only be remedied by the sword of the Gospel.

I idolized pastors and theologians within my tribe (a struggle that long-preceded pastoring). I had attended the inaugural Together for the Gospel (T4G) conference in 2006 (and every conference afterward until 2018). To me, these men (including CJ) represented the pinnacle of evangelical leadership, the ultimate "inner ring." What they said was received with little discrimination on my part. Their recommendations—whether of books, doctrine, practice, or people—carried great weight.

I found my way into networks and friendships within these tribes. It felt good to be connected. I felt important. I met and became friends with remarkable pastors—men who I love, respect, and admire to this day. Those partnerships did me spiritual good. They helped me learn to pastor better. They provided a support base through difficult times. I cannot overstate how helpful they were to me.

Nevertheless, at the same time, my sinful flesh perverted these relationships. An undiscerning loyalty grew in my heart. I refused to listen to concerns that might conflict with what these men said or did. Fear of losing these relationships kept me from listening to hard questions and pursuing good answers.

When Wade Burleson raised concerns about sexual abuse within the Southern Baptist Convention, I read them but did nothing.

Why? Because I did not hear anything about it from the Southern Baptist leaders I trusted (such as Al Mohler, Founders Ministries, 9marks, and others). (I am not here implicating these leaders. They may have spoken, and I simply did not hear it. I am condemning only myself. What they did or did not do is immaterial to my responsibility to listen, investigate, and act as a pastor of a church in cooperation with the Southern Baptist Convention.)

At one point, a church member (and friend) asked of my awareness of concerns about sexual abuse cover-ups within Sovereign Grace Ministries (now Sovereign Grace Churches) and CJ Mahaney (one of the co-founders of T4G). He mentioned that evidence had been posted online that seemed worth considering. Though I was aware of such posts, I brushed them (and him) aside. I assured him that Al Mohler and Mark Dever would not be such close friends with CJ and partner with him in T4G if there were any warrant at all to the concerns. Based entirely on the implications of their on-going partnership and silence in the face of concerns, I refused to investigate for myself. This was sinful on my part. (On recalling this conversation, I contacted my friend and asked his forgiveness. I failed as a friend and as a pastor.)

At another point, a trusted acquaintance explained to me what was "really" going on in the lawsuit with CJ and SGC. (Due to the promise of confidentiality, I am not at liberty to share details.) The gist of the explanation was that the accusations were entirely baseless. My understanding was that this was little more than a liberal egalitarian attacking a complementarian pastor. When this lawsuit was settled, the accuser(s) would move on to another target. I believed this explanation. I shared it with friends and pastors to assure them that all was well. I did not investigate for myself. This was sinful. I cannot recall everyone with whom I shared such assurances—but to those that I did, please forgive me.

Throughout this time, the Lord began to shape and break my heart in many ways. In pastoral counseling, I have shepherded countless women who suffered abuse of various stripes. (And, I might add, I sometimes shepherded them poorly.) Listening to them, I began to hear and see how and why they felt voiceless and defenseless. I saw how often their stories were minimalized, brushed aside, and disbelieved. I witnessed how difficult they found it to speak and to be heard. It was too easy for Christians to either condemn them (for where they were, for what they wore, for what they'd done, for what they didn't do) and to apply quick-fixes with spiritual-cliché band-aids.

At the same time, I experienced false-accusations, abuse, betrayal, and other sufferings through church controversy. While this initially made me defensive of pastoral heroes, the Lord used it to help me hear the cry of the poor. When I was mistreated, many expressed sorrow and support for me in private, but not many stepped up to actively stop it. When I was attacked, some minimized it or applied quick fixes. I had "friends" who refused to listen to or follow me as a pastor merely because influential pastors said and believed otherwise. I learned what it was to be the victim. Through this, the Lord stirred in me a desire to see, hear, and respond to those who experienced abuse.

In 2013, I resigned from being a Lead Pastor and spent one year out of pastoral ministry. During that time, I worked for a mission agency that plants churches among the poor. The Lord used the incredible men and women in that ministry to continue to challenge and change my heart. They wrote and spoke boldly about how the evangelical church too often overlooks, stereotypes, and mistreats the poor—and how such prejudices can be engrained in systems and institutions. They included women in ministry in remarkable ways (in a particularly challenging context)—and did so as conservative, Calvinistic, complementarians! They did not take themselves seriously, but took the Gospel very seriously. They did not fear man, but asked hard questions of influential people. The Lord used them to shake my heart and mind and to stir me to think differently. I am so thankful for those men and women. I am so sorry for the ways I've failed so many.

In 2015, I reentered the pastorate as an Associate Pastor—I entered a changing man. There are innumerable things God used to change my heart over the previous decade. Too many to list. But I want to mention a few germane to the SBC issue and the role you played.

At one point, I attended a conference at which several Southern Baptist leaders spoke. One of the men, a man I admire, shared some things about his personal policies regarding interactions with women, admonishing the pastors and seminarians to adopt them. I disagreed with those policies but did not think much of it. After the talk, a sister sitting next to me commented, "I was hurt several times by what he said." I didn't follow-up on that comment immediately, but I tucked it away in my heart for meditation. Why did I disagree but remain unoffended, while this sister was "hurt"? As I mulled over that question, I began to see what his statements (unintentionally) communicated to women about women. I understood why she was hurt. I wondered how often my ignorant, unthoughtful (though well-intentioned) comments and actions hurt the sisters in the churches I pastored. I resolved to listen, ask, listen, ask, listen more than I commented, assumed and acted in regards to women in the church.

As the #MeToo movement rose, I listened. Twenty years earlier, I would have responded to #MeToo as a calloused, knee-jerk (emphasis on jerk), Rush Limbaugh conservative. I would have mocked and minimized the movement. But now I read and listened and wept. I wept. Reading the stories of complete strangers, I recognized the stories of women that I knew, that I loved. I wept. Reading the stories of how these women were treated, I saw the world that my mom grew up in, that my wife lived in, that my daughter would enter. I wept.

I remember the first time I saw your name on Facebook. You were being (rightly) heralded as a hero for your role as the *first woman to speak publicly against Larry Nassar, the former Michigan State University and USA Gymnastics doctor, accusing him of sexual assault.*[4] Christians celebrated you and *your victim impact statement* as a model of Christian boldness and grace—which it was.[5]

As I read your statement—which is worthy of all the praise it received—this sentence floored me: "My advocacy for sexual assault victims, something I cherished, cost me my church and our closest friends three weeks before I filed my police report." I wondered how on earth this could be.

It broke again when I read your interview with *Christianity Today*, particularly these paragraphs:

> Yes. Church is one of the least safe places to acknowledge abuse because the way it is counseled is, more often than not, damaging to the victim. There is an abhorrent lack of knowledge for the damage and devastation that sexual assault brings. It is with deep regret that I say the church is one of the worst places to go for help. That's a hard thing to say, because I am a very conservative evangelical, but that is the truth. There are very, very few who have ever found true help in the church.
>
> The reason I lost my church was not specifically because I spoke up. It was because we were advocating for other victims of sexual assault within the evangelical community, crimes which had been perpetrated by people in the church and whose abuse had been enabled, very clearly, by prominent leaders in the evangelical community. That is not a message that evangelical leaders want to hear, because it would cost to speak out about the community. It would cost to take a stand against these very prominent leaders, despite the fact that the situation we were dealing with is widely recognized as one of the worst, if not the worst, instances of evangelical cover-up of sexual abuse. Because I had taken that position, and because we were not in agreement with our church's support of this organization and these leaders, it cost us dearly.
>
> When I did come forward as an abuse victim, this part of my past was wielded like a weapon by some of the elders to further discredit my concern, essentially saying that I was imposing my own perspective or that my judgment was too clouded. One of them accused me of sitting around reading angry blog posts all day, which is not the way I do research. That's never been the way I do research. But my status as a victim was used against my advocacy.
>
> . . . rather than engaging with the mountains of evidence that I brought, because this situation was one of the most well-documented cases of institutional cover-up I have ever

seen, ever, there was a complete refusal to engage with the evidence.[6]

When I learned that it was a Southern Baptist Church—in particular, a church that networked in the same circles that I did—my surprise vanished. I knew what happened. That had been me. I grieved for you, for victims, for my own callousness. (I am thankful those pastors apologized.[7])

Soon after, I read your "Public Response to Sovereign Grace Churches"[8] (and subsequent post [9]). Your meticulous documentation and important questions rocked my world. This was 180-degrees different than the explanation I'd received (mentioned above). I felt betrayed and deceived by men I trusted and admired. CJ Mahaney had been invited (and agreed) to speak at the 2018 T4G. The public statements of the brothers leading that conference did not address the important issues you raised. So, in protest, I canceled my registration and did not attend T4G for the first time. (I'm thankful that Al Mohler has recently apologized for his support of CJ.[10,11] I'm praying that more men—and some women—across evangelicalism who offered the same public support and justifications will follow his example, publicly repent, and call for a truly impartial, qualified, third-party investigation into the SGC situation.)

Following your example, I resolved to no longer be silent, but to use whatever platform and influence I may have to speak about injustices, mainly to allow my sisters to be heard. I resolved to know and listen to the women in my church. I sought conversations with women in my church and just listened as they helped me understand how to shepherd them better. I've listened as women have shared how I offended them or failed to protect them. I'm repenting and learning.

In speaking publicly, I've been accused of many horrible things. I've watched friends distance and disassociate themselves. That hurts. But it is not a fraction of what you and other brave women have endured. I cannot imagine what you have been through for merely speaking the truth in the national spotlight.

This past year has been a wild ride, but a good one. The Lord continues to show me my errors, my wrong assumptions, my cowardice. He continues to open my eyes to the experiences of abuse survivors, as well as women in the church and culture in general. To do this, the Lord used women like you, Karen Swallow Prior, Beth Moore, Elyse Fitzpatrick, countless valued sisters in the church and on social media, and fifteen years' worth of wise, godly, patient female friends in my local churches.

In my silence and my speech, in my actions and inaction, I sinned against you, against women in my churches, against women in the SBC, and against women in the world. Of you and them, I ask—forgive me.

You asked, "Pastors, where were you? When we were pleading for you to speak up against your peers or the leaders your support props up, where were you?"

This is where I've been, where I am, and (by the grace of God), where I am going.

Thank you, sister, for your part in it. You're valued and valuable in the kingdom of God.

Your brother
Eric

"Worthy—A Song of Praise"

Theology leads to doxology. That is, knowing God leads to worshiping God.

We argued at the start of this book that God's worth is seen, in part, in what he has made. Therefore, as we see the worth of women, created in his image, we see the glory of God. As we see how God loves and uses women in the storyline of the Bible, we see the glory of God. As we see how God redeems women in Christ, we see the glory of God.

This book fails if you walk away from it valuing women but not the God who created, loves, and redeems women.

So this book ends in doxology—praising God for what he has done and what he has shown us of himself in the creation and redemption of women. What follows is an original worship song written for this book and for you, its readers. We pray it is useful in equipping and assisting you to remember and rejoice in the God who gives us worth and who is worthy of all praise.

You will find a recording of the song, along with downloads to use in your personal and church worship, at http://hymni.city /hymns/worthy.

Worthy—A Song of Praise
by Eric Schumacher and David L. Ward

In your likeness and bearing your name
You have made us to rule and to reign
To be fruitful on earth and to image your worth—
Declaring it all "very good."

But we tarnished the worth of your name
And like Eve we were covered in shame
But despite what was done, you have promised a Son—
A King who would rescue and reign.

> Worthy! You are worthy
> Of all glory and honor and power and blessing and
>   fame!
> For you made us. In Christ, you saved us.
> Make us worthy, Lord, to bear your name!

Through the ages, in famine and feast
You have called from the greatest and least
Countless women of faith who found hope in your grace
And spoke of the Kingdom to come.

From the weakness of young Mary's womb
Came a Champion to conquer the tomb
One whose life and whose death would be our
   righteousness
And blessed is the one who believes!

> Worthy! You are worthy
> Of all glory and honor and power and blessing and
>   fame!
> For you made us. In Christ, you saved us.
> Make us worthy, Lord, to bear your name!

Though we have fallen, we have strayed
And clothed ourselves in shame
Though we have made ourselves
Unworthy of your name . . .
Though we are broken and abused,
Mistrusted and misused,
We find our hope, our joy,
Our life, our worth in you.

By the Spirit your work has begun:
You are sending your daughters and sons
To bear children of faith by proclaiming your grace
'Til Christ and his kingdom have come.

On the day when all things are made new
We, the Bride, will be brought to the Groom
And then clothed in his worth, we will rule on the earth
And all of creation will sing:

> "Worthy! You are worthy
> Of all glory and honor and power and blessing and
>   fame!
> For you made us. In Christ, you saved us.
> Made us worthy, Lord, to bear your name!"[1]

ACKNOWLEDGMENTS

(Elyse)

As with any work of this kind, there are many (too many?) people I need to thank. I've been well-taught by many wonderful women and men and I'm thankful for them. I'm thankful for all the women who have bravely stepped out to teach the Bible and minister to one another, and for the way their words and also their lives have emboldened me.

I have been encouraged by many men in ministry—men who didn't have to respect or honor me as graciously as they did, but who did anyway.

I'm thankful for Dr. Dennis E. Johnson and for the course he taught at Westminster Theological Seminary in California on Women in Family, Church, and Society—and I'm thankful that he invited me and other women to teach in it. Dr. Johnson always treated me with respect and care, and I'm thankful; and this class, which I first took over a decade ago, was the seedbed for what is presented here.

I'm thankful for Andy McGuire and Bethany House for seeing the need for a book like this. It's a joy to work with such gracious and conscientious professionals.

I'm thankful for my co-author, Eric. He has encouraged and challenged me and has modeled Christlike love and respect, and I'm better for having known him. He's the real deal, people. He loves the Lord and the church and is not only a great songwriter and pastor, but more importantly is a man of integrity and zeal who loves his family. It's an honor, Eric.

I'm thankful for my dear family: for my mother, Rosemary; my daughter, Jessica; daughters-in-law, Michelle and Ruth; and for my wonderful, respectful, brave, and kind sons, James and Joel, and my brother Richard. I'm especially thankful for my dear Phil: a husband who has loved me for more than four decades and continues to see his purpose as being a blessing to me. Without Phil and his gracious care, I would not have been brave enough to serve the Lord as I have. Thank you.

ACKNOWLEDGMENTS

(Eric)

I'm thankful to God the Father for calling me to be his child. To Jesus, for loving me, redeeming me, and incorporating me into his bride, the church. To the Holy Spirit for challenging me, changing me, and conforming me into the image of Christ. May this book bring you glory.

I'm beyond grateful for you, Elyse. You suggested that a Twitter thread become a book. You took a chance in co-writing a book with an unknown author you'd never met. You've taught, instructed, encouraged, and corrected me through this process. I'm forever thankful you let me ride your coattails, sister.

I owe thanks to Andy McGuire and Bethany House for being enthusiastic supporters of this project. Your patience with a first-time author made this work a real pleasure.

I'm grateful for seminary professors, such as Tom Schreiner and Russell Moore, who encouraged me to be faithful to the text of Scripture and compassionate to my neighbor, and who model what it means to value women.

I'm beyond grateful for my church family. Amanda Philgreen and Emily Jensen were patient conversation partners as I began reexamining how to love, relate to, and pastor women. Dixie Carpenter, my secretary and friend, is a model of faith who teaches me how to follow Jesus. My small group faithfully prayed for and encouraged this project. I'm especially grateful for my pastor and friend, Michael Felkins, who sat me down over barbeque and said, "Eric, you need to enjoy your gifts!"—and told me to write more.

Thanks to Jared von Kamp and Claire Kennedy for reading drafts of some chapters and providing helpful suggestions. Emily Jensen read every word I wrote and offered invaluable suggestions. Emily—your humility, wisdom, and boldness make you a unique blessing to both shepherd and partner with in ministry. It's a better book because of you.

My parents laid a foundation for my ministry, teaching me about Jesus from an early age. Mom, you've modeled in more ways than I can recount what it means to be a strong woman who loves her God.

My children—Josiah, Micah, Elijah, Ella, and Judson—sacrificed too much time with dad so that he could write. I love you all! (I'll finish your adventure novel—I promise!)

Words fail to express my appreciation for Jenny, my wife. For more than two decades and through countless storms, you have been a rock of support, a source of wisdom, and a faithful partner—a fellow heir in the grace of life. There is no person—man or woman—whom I admire, respect, value, and love more than you. You are a woman of whom the world is not worthy.

Notes

Introduction: Worthy: Celebrating the Value of Women in God's Word

1. Martin Luther, *Preface to The Epistle to the Romans* (1532), trans. J. Theodore Mueller (Grand Rapids, MI: Kregel, 1976), xiii.

2. "About Antiques Roadshow," *PBS.org*, September 9, 2016, updated February 11, 2019, http://www.pbs.org/wgbh/roadshow/stories/articles/2016/9/9/about-antiques-roadshow/.

3. "The Hebrew word for *man* (*adam*) is the generic term for mankind." English Standard Version note on Genesis 1:26, https://www.biblegateway.com/passage/?search=Genesis+1%3A26&version=ESV.

In light of the changes in the use of gender-specific language, we're going to look at the original languages and use more gender-inclusive language when the text allows it. In doing so, we are trying to be faithful to the original text and recognize that for some people using the term "man" when the original text allows "mankind" is unnecessarily off-putting or confusing.

4. C.S. Lewis, *The Weight of Glory and Other Addresses*, rev. ed. (New York: HarperCollins, 2001), 45–46.

5. Eric Schumacher, "21 Places Women Emerge Front and Center in Scripture's Storyline," *TheGospelCoalition.org*, June 2, 2018, https://www.thegospelcoalition.org/article/21-places-women-emerge-front-and-center-in-scriptures-storyline/.

Chapter 1: The Worth of Women in Creation

1. The Hebrew word often translated "rib" is always translated "side" when used elsewhere in the English Bible. There is no linguistic warrant for translating it "rib."

2. Peter J. Gentry and Stephen J. Wellum, *Kingdom Through Covenant* (Wheaton, IL: Crossway, 2012), 191. Gentry and Wellum make the helpful distinction between horizontal and vertical relationships in image and likeness that we use here.

3. Victor P. Hamilton, *Genesis* (Grand Rapids, MI: Eerdmans, 1990), 135.

4. The Lord called Israel his "firstborn son" (Exodus 4:22); as such, Israel was another Adam (Luke 3:38).

Israel was to function as a representative ruler—a kingdom of priests (Exodus 19:6)—exercising God's dominion on the earth. It is only when they reject God as their king that he gives them a human king (1 Samuel 8:7). Though Israel rejected the Lord's reign in the Promised Land (as Adam rejected the Lord's reign in the Garden), the Lord does not abandon his purpose to have a royal son ruling in his name. The Lord makes a covenant with King David, promising that one of David's sons will reign forever in God's house (2 Samuel 7:13, 16). That king will be "a son" to God (2 Samuel 7:14). This crystallizes the idea that Israel's king is a "Son" to God. Psalm 2 is an inauguration Psalm, probably used when a new king was installed. In it, God "adopts" the king, declaring him to be his "Son" on that day. When Jesus arrives, his identification as "the Son of God" is rich with kingly allusions—it is a title for the Messiah, God's anointed King! When we are united with Jesus through faith, our sonship (and the reign that goes with it) is restored to us—and that includes women. Women are made "sons" through Christ. While it is popular to choose the term "daughter" (which is accurate in a relational sense), it is good to recognize the scriptural sense of sonship—a category guaranteeing an inheritance and authority in the father's house.

5. This is true of the abuse of men as well. For the purposes of highlighting the value of women (the focus of our book), we are concentrating on women here.

6. See Exodus 18:4; Deuteronomy 33:7, 26, 29; Psalms 33:20; 115:9–11; 124:8; 146:5.

7. A note on "gender roles": In the New Testament, Paul twice appeals to the sequence of Genesis 2 to defend his instruction in the church (see 1 Timothy 2:13; 1 Corinthians 11:8–9). From these, he infers the primacy of male leadership in the local church. He does not base his instruction on subordination or inequality. He points out the sequence of events and stated purpose. It should be noted that any distinctions in role do not serve to diminish the value of women; rather, they highlight it. The "helper" was created due to a deficiency (a need) in the man. Her value is indispensable. Paul emphasizes the interdependence of men and women today (1 Corinthians 11:12).

We should honor any and all distinctions that God places between men and women in any context. Yet, where God has not placed limitations, the church should celebrate freedom. Our aim is not to avoid a "slippery slope" toward wrong applications of conservatism. Faithfulness to Scripture and the glory of God in his creation is our charge. The church should encourage women to serve in any capacity not prohibited by the normative instruction of the New Testament.

8. "Priestly-helpers" is an odd term, isn't it? The word *priest* can bring to mind all sorts of images and outfits that have little to do with the biblical concept of priest. Israel's first priests served in the tabernacle—a special tent in which the Lord dwelled in Israel's midst. The priests would offer sacrifices, representing the people to God and God to the people.

Some might balk at the idea of women as "priestly-helpers" because Israel's Law only allowed men to serve as priests. But let's remember (as discussed in note

4 for this chapter) that *every* Israelite was to be a priest—they were redeemed to be a "kingdom of priests." There are certainly distinctions in the priesthood (there is a high priest), but one being a high priest and another assisting does not reduce the title of priest.

In the end, Jesus Christ is our "great high priest" (Hebrews 4:14). In him, we are all—male and female—made priests to God (Revelation 5:10). In Jesus—the Prophet, Priest, and King—all of his people prophecy (Acts 2:17), offer priestly service (Revelation 5:10), and reign on earth (Revelation 20:6). What glorious good news!

Chapter 2: The Worth of Women in the Fall

1. As quoted by Chad Meister and James Stump, *Christian Thought: A Historical Introduction*, 2nd ed. (New York: Routledge, 2017), 496.

2. The article on the Greek word for "γυνή" (female) in *The Theological Dictionary of the New Testament* edited by Gerhard Kittel and Gerhard Friedrich (Grand Rapids, MI: Eerdmans, 1988), 781, offers this summary of the views of women in first-century Judaism:

> Woman is openly despised. "Happy is he whose children are males, and woe to him whose children are females" (bQid, 82b). The honorable title of "daughter of Abraham" is rare in Rabbinic literature as compared with the corresponding "son of Abraham."[17] Women are greedy, inquisitive, lazy, vain, and frivolous. (Gn. r., 45 on 16:5) "Ten [measures] of empty-headedness have come upon the world, nine having been received by women and one by the rest of the world" (bQid, 49b). "Many women, much witch-craft" (Hillel, *c* 20 B.C. 2, 7). The custom of women preceding corpses in many places finds aetiological explanation in their assumed responsibility for death (Slav. En. 30:17; Vit Ad, 1, 3, etc.; jSanh. 20b, 44).[18] Conversation should not be held with a woman (cf. Jn. 4:9, 27), even though she be one's own (bErub., 53b; Ab., 1,5). "May the words of the Torah be burned, they should not be handed over to women" (jSota, 10a, 8). "The man who teaches his daughter the Torah teaches her extravagance" (Sota 3, 4; cf bSota 21b). The wife should neither bear witness, instruct children, nor pray at table; she is not even bound to keep the whole Torah.[19] In the synagogues women are assigned special places behind a screen. Special chambers are provided for them not only in Palestine but even in Alexandria (Philo Flacc., 89). Hellenistic Judaism generally shows little enlightenment on this question. Philo says (Op. Mund., 165): "In us the attitude of man is informed by reason . . . of woman by sensuality."

3. Later in the chapter we will note examples of both active and passive ways the worth of women can be diminished.

4. It is notable that in Genesis 2:16 and 3:11, "you" is singular in Hebrew. But in Genesis 3:1–4, "you" is plural.

The difference is rarely noted by those who interpret the passage as described above. But that difference highlights the primary responsibility of the man as the receiver and guardian of the commandment.

5. Jesus and the Apostles were infallible interpreters of the Old Testament. But this does not suggest that they were handling the Old Testament in ways that we cannot. The Spirit is not illuminating the New Testament authors to use Scripture in ways that are counter to what it says. The Spirit does not misapply the Word to make a true point. Rather, he illumines and inspires these authors to see and apply the proper meaning of the passage. In that way, they teach us how to read God's Word.

6. In fact, the Bible records instances where the Lord speaks to husbands through their wives. We'll see some of these in later chapters.

7. Victor P. Hamilton, "The Book of Genesis, Chapters 1–17," *The New International Commentary on the Old Testament* (Grand Rapids, MI: Eerdmans, 1990), 171.

Chapter 3: The Worth of Women in the Promise

1. We acknowledge that in answering this question we are presenting the ideal, the "best case scenario," relationships as they ought to be. We recognize that this is easier said than done. Past sexual sin, abuse, wrong teaching, and more combine to produce mindsets, consciences, and involuntary feelings that condition our reactions to male-female relationships. We live in the "already and not yet"—Jesus is already reigning, but the fullness of that reign is not yet being experienced by us. This is where we must look to him with eyes of faith, repenting and believing the Gospel on a daily basis, hoping in his return, and showing grace to fellow sinners and sinner-saints as we await his appearance and our perfection in glory.

Chapter 4: The Worth of Women in Israel's History

1. First Abram tried to fulfill the promise by suggesting that Eliezer of Damascus, his servant, would be his heir (Genesis 15). In all likelihood, once Sarai understood that Abram no longer believed God could provide the promised son through her, she thought up the scheme with her servant, Hagar (Genesis 16). Neither Abram nor Sarai were pillars of faith at this point, but it is important to recognize that they both desired to fulfill God's plan of a promised son.

2. Carolyn Custis James, *Lost Women of the Bible: Finding Strength and Significance through Their Stories* (Grand Rapids, MI: Zondervan, 2005). "Blessed Alliance" is the way that James describes the relationship between the man and his *ezer-helper*. I particularly love it because males and females working together in an alliance to establish God's kingdom beautifully describes how we should fulfill the creation mandate, each bringing our strengths and insights to bear.

3. English Standard Version Study Bible note on Exodus 4:24–26.

Chapter 5: The Worth of Women in Israel's Law

1. In fact, anything that comes out of our body, including feces, is to be deemed as unclean and treated in a certain way (Deuteronomy 23:12).

2. Mark F. Rooker, "Leviticus," vol. 3A, *The New American Commentary* (Nashville: Broadman & Holman, 2000), 206.

3. 9.47 θυγάτηρb, τρός f: (a figurative extension of meaning of θυγάτηρα "daughter," 10.46) a woman for whom there is some affectionate concern (Johannes P. Louw and Eugene Albert Nida, *Greek-English Lexicon of the New Testament: Based on Semantic Domains* (New York: United Bible Societies, 1996), 110.

4. R. A. Torrey, *Studies in the Life and Teachings of Our Lord* (Los Angeles: Bible Institute of Los Angeles, 1907), 98.

5. Walter A. Elwell and Barry J. Beitzel, "Divorce, Certificate Of," *Baker Encyclopedia of the Bible* (Grand Rapids, MI: Baker, 1988), 637.

6. We learn something of what this "indecency" might be from Matthew 1:19, "And her husband Joseph, being a just man and unwilling to put her to shame, resolved to divorce her quietly." In this case, Mary was considered naked or indecent because she was pregnant. Joseph could have insisted that she be stoned for adultery, but because he loved her thought it kind to just give her a certificate of divorce quietly.

7. 88.224 σκληροτράχηλος, ον; σκληροκαρδία, ας f; ἀπερίτμητος καρδία καὶ τοῖς ὠσίν (an idiom, literally "uncircumcised in heart and ears"): pertaining to being obdurate and obstinate—"stubborn, completely unyielding." . . . "Moses gave you permission to divorce your wives because you were so obstinate" . . . the focus of the stubbornness and obstinacy is the unwillingness to be taught or to understand. (Louw and Nida, *Greek-English Lexicon*, 765.)

8. Of course, they weren't really interested in righteousness, they were just trying to find a way to charge him with breaking Moses' Law.

9. While it's true that the Law doesn't have the power to make us holy, it does have the power to restrain some acts of evil.

10. English Standard Version Study Bible note on Colossians 2:17.

Chapter 6: The Worth of Women in Israel's Worship

1. Sandra McCracken and Joshua Moore, "We Will Feast in the House of Zion," from *Psalms*, released April 14, 2015. Drink Your Tea (ASCAP)/Joshmooreownsthis Music (ASCAP). Used by permission.

2. Although there were no outright laws against polygamy, it does violate God's command to Adam to leave and cleave to his wife thereby becoming one flesh (Genesis 2:24). This one-flesh union is broken when he seeks to cleave to another woman or become one with her.

3. Jerram Barrs, *Through His Eyes: God's Perspective on Women in the Bible* (Wheaton, IL: Crossway, 2009), 169.

4. English Standard Version Study Bible note on 1 Samuel 1:20: "*Samuel* sounds like the Hebrew for *heard of God*.

5. ESV Study Bible note on 1 Samuel 2:1–10

6. Barrs, *Through His Eyes*, 167.

7. Barrs, *Through His Eyes*, 167.

8. ESV Study Bible note on Judges 5:1.

9. "Brethren, We Have Met to Worship," George Askins, public domain, 1819.

10. Another birth rite was the naming of the newborn. Done more often by women than men in Genesis (e.g., Genesis 4:25; 30:6, 8, 24; 35:18; 38:3–5), it was likely a woman's practice.

Chapter 7: The Worth of Women in Israel's Wisdom

1. Melissa Noel, "New Book 'Hidden Figures' Reveals Black Women Who Helped the Space Race," *NBCNews.com*, September 6, 2016, https://www.nbc news.com/news/nbcblk/hidden-figures-n643421, retrieved January 26, 2018.

2. See 1 Kings 1:16–17.

3. ESV Study Bible, Introduction to the book of Proverbs.

4. See Al Wolters, *The Song of the Valiant Woman: Studies in the Interpretations of Proverbs 31:10–31* (Waynesboro, GA: Paternoster Press), 2001.

5. Jerram Barrs, *Through His Eyes: God's Perspective on Women in the Bible* (Wheaton, IL: Crossway, 2009), 305.

6. Note Chapter 2 and our discussion of the deception of Eve.

7. Carolyn Custis James, *Lost Women of the Bible: Finding Strength and Significance Through Their Stories* (Grand Rapids, MI: Zondervan, 2005), 110.

8. In case anyone is wondering about God's stance on spousal sexual abuse, the Lord is clear here.

9. Bruce K. Waltke, *Genesis* (Grand Rapids, MI: Zondervan Academic, 2001), 513.

10. Eugene H. Peterson, *The Message: The Bible in Contemporary Language* (Colorado Springs, CO: NavPress, 2005), Genesis 38:26.

11. James, *Lost Women*, 117.

12. John Calvin, *Corpus Reformatorum*, vol. 58, col. 546, quoted in Wolters, *Song of the Valiant Woman*, 112.

13. Wolters, *Song of the Valiant*, 13.

Chapter 8: The Worth of Women in Jesus' Birth

1. Pete McMartin, "Beautiful Blondes, a Boyle and Lingering Ideas about Sexuality," *The Vancouver Sun*, 18 April 2009, https://web.archive.org/web/20090421061343/http://www.vancouversun.com/Life/Beautiful+blondes+Boyle+lingering+ideas+about+sexuality/1509204/story.html. Archived from the original on 21 April 2009.

2. McMartin, "Beautiful Blondes."

3. Boaz was likely still unmarried due to being the son of Rahab. No father would give his daughter in marriage to a man who was excluded from the assembly of the Lord—and whose offspring were perpetually cut off from the assembly. But Boaz saw his father's gracious example in marrying a forbidden woman. In marrying Rahab, Salmon surely understood that she was part of Israel by her faith, not by the flesh. Likewise, in being forbidden from the assembly, Boaz knew that his hope of dwelling with the Lord must come by faith and not on the basis of the Law. From his parents' marriage, he understood being one of God's people by grace through faith, and not of ourselves. Thus, he was willing to show kindness to and marry Ruth, a true Israelite by faith, if not by the flesh. (In a remarkable twist, we note that Boaz is descended from Judah and Tamar—another union whose offspring is forbidden from the assembly to the tenth generation. Their grandson David will be the tenth generation, the restoration of the line and so much more.)

4. Although the shepherds and Simeon spoke of Jesus' arrival, they did so to Joseph and Mary directly. Anna's words are the first portrayed as a public proclamation.

5. Yes, some women hate men and seek to destroy them—just as there are men who hate women and try to destroy them. These are not sisters in Christ. They are wolves in sheep's clothing. When we see them, we attempt to correct them. When they fail to repent, we put them out of the church. Such women (and men) exist. The existence of such women is no more cause for suspicion of our sisters than the existence of promiscuous women calls for suspicion of my wife.

6. Although Christians differ regarding their views of the nature and authority of prophecy in the apostolic church, we believe that prophecy is a spontaneous, Spirit-given utterance to provide edification, exhortation, and comfort at the moment, which may or may not include new special revelation.

Chapter 9: The Worth of Women in Jesus' Life and Ministry

1. Donald Trump, "Statement from Donald J. Trump," October 7, 2016, Trump Pence Make America Great Again! 2016, https://web.archive.org/web/20161007210105/https://www.donaldjtrump.com/press-releases/statement-from-donald-j.-trump, retrieved January 22, 2018.

2. Bill Clinton, "Response to the Lewinsky Allegations," archived February 23, 2009, at the Wayback Machine, Miller Center of Public Affairs, January 26, 1998, https://web.archive.org/web/20090223181444/http://millercenter.org/scripps/archive/speeches/detail/3930, retrieved January 22, 2019.

3. Monica Lewinsky, "Emerging from 'The House of Gaslight' in the Age of #MeToo," *Vanity Fair*, February 25, 2018, https://www.vanityfair.com/news/2018/02/monica-lewinsky-in-the-age-of-metoo, retrieved January 22, 2018.

4. Kathy Ireland, @kathyireland, Twitter.com, November 15, 2018, https://twitter.com/kathyireland/status/1063257310988926976, retrieved January 22, 2018.

5. Ireland, Twitter, November 16, 2018, https://twitter.com/kathyireland/status/1063571578498117632, retrieved January 22, 2018.

6. Beth Moore, "A Letter to My Brothers," *The LPM Blog*, May 3, 2018, https://blog.lproof.org/2018/05/a-letter-to-my-brothers.html, retrieved January 22, 2018.

7. Leon Morris, *The Gospel According to Matthew* (Grand Rapids, MI: William B. Eerdmans Publishing Company, 1992), 726.

8. C.H. Spurgeon, *The Gospel of the Kingdom* (Pasadena, TX: Pasadena Publications, 1996), 252.

9. For more examples, see also John 4; Matthew 9:18–26; Mark 5:21–43; Luke 8:40–56.

10. James Edwards, *The Gospel According to Mark* (Grand Rapids, MI: Eerdmans, 2002), 486.

11. Andreas Köstenberger, *John* (Grand Rapids, MI: Baker Academic, 2004), 148.

12. Köstenberger, *John*, 148.

13. As quoted in Leon Morris, "The Gospel According to John, Revised," *The New International Commentary on the New Testament* (Grand Rapids, MI: Eerdmans, 1995), 242.

14. D.A. Carson, "The Gospel According to John," *The Pillar New Testament Commentary* (Grand Rapids, MI: Eerdmans, 1991), 217–218.

15. F.F. Bruce, *The Gospel of John: Introduction, Exposition, and Notes* (Grand Rapids, MI: Eerdmans, 1994), 112.

16. Carson, *John*, 227.

17. Jerram Barrs, *Through His Eyes: God's Perspective on Women in the Bible* (Wheaton, IL: Crossway, 2009), 284.

18. Barrs, *Through His Eyes*, 282.

19. Barrs, *Through His Eyes*, 283.

20. Edwards, *Mark*, 486.

21. Robert H. Stein, "Luke, Vol. 24," *The New American Commentary* (Nashville, TN: Broadman Press, 1992), 164.

22. Thabiti Anyabwile, *Christ-Centered Exposition Commentary: Exalting Jesus in Luke* (Nashville, TN: B&H Publishing Group, 2018), 184.

23. Craig L. Blomberg, "Matthew," *The New American Commentary* (Nashville, TN: Broadman Press, 1992), 143.

24. Morris, *Matthew*, 197.

25. Leon Morris, "John," *New International Commentary on the New Testament* (Grand Rapids, MI: Eerdmans, 1995), 512.

26. Andreas Köstenberger, *John* (Grand Rapids, MI: Baker Academic, 2004), 362n18.

27. Köstenberger, *John*, 362.

28. Blomberg, *Matthew*, 350.

29. Walter L. Liefeld, "Luke," *The Expositers Bible Commentary* (Grand Rapids, MI: Zondervan, 1995), 150.

30. Stein, *Luke*, 322.

31. Anyabwile, *Exalting Jesus in Luke*, 184.

32. Blomberg, *Matthew*, 143.

33. Dorothy L. Sayers, *Are Women Human?* (Grand Rapids, MI: Eerdmans, 2005), 68–69.

Chapter 10: The Worth of Women in Jesus' Death and Resurrection

1. If you have witnessed a criminal act against a woman (or anyone), you must report it to the civil authorities. Many of these acts are criminal offenses, which fall under the God-appointed jurisdiction of the state. While the church should exercise spiritual discipline in local congregations, it has no right to fail to report crimes against women and children (or anyone else).

2. English Standard Version Study Bible, note on Matthew 26:7.

3. ESV Study Bible note on Matthew 27:26.

4. See ESV Study Bible note on Luke 23:27–31: "If God did not spare his innocent son ('green' wood), how much worse will it be when he allows the Romans to unleash his wrath on a sinful nation ('dry' wood)?"

5. Emily Jensen is co-author of *Risen Motherhood* and co-founder of Risen Motherhood, a ministry devoted to encouraging, equipping, and challenging moms to apply the Gospel to their everyday lives. We highly recommend the book and ministry.

6. ESV Study Bible note on Mark 16:7.

Chapter 11: The Worth of Women in the Church

1. The Apostle Paul proclaimed this change when he wrote to the Corinthians, "To the unmarried and the widows I say that it is good for them to remain single, as I am" (1 Corinthians 7:8). This teaching would have been shocking to both Jewish and Gentile believers, as women had been valued primarily for their ability to produce children.

2. It's not our intent to discuss whether circumcision in the OT and baptism in the NT are completely analogous—i.e., that babies should or should not be baptized (that is another discussion we have opinions about, but won't derail our discussion here). Our point here is only that there was an outward sign of the covenant given only to males in the old covenant, which signified inclusion in the family of God (for men who were circumcised and women who were related to them either through birth or marriage) and that now that sign has been replaced by baptism, given to both women and men and without regard to their family of origin or their marital status.

3. Study Note in the Gospel Transformation Bible on Genesis 17:9–14.

4. Jerram Barrs, *Through His Eyes: God's Perspective on Women in the Bible* (Wheaton, IL: Crossway, 2009), 308.

5. Carolyn Custis James, *Lost Women of the Bible: Finding Strength and Significance through their Stories* (Grand Rapids, MI: Zondervan, 2005), 209–210.

6. If, in fact, men are uninterested in Christianity, perhaps it is because the message they've heard is loaded with impossible laws about being the perfect husband and father. That's not the message that the apostles and church martyrs faced death for. It's hardly motivating to hear, once again, how everything is riding on your piety saving your wife and children.

7. Lydia probably was a widow. It would have been very unusual in that culture for a woman to have attained her level of business success if she had never married, though it isn't impossible. She probably maintained two homes, one in Philippi and one in Thyatira, and used them in her dyed-fabric business. Tradition also teaches that the church in Thyatira met in her home.

8. It should be noted that the only people named as financial supporters of Jesus were women.

9. "The Bible affirms that the early church was situated in predominately an oral culture . . . (1 Thess 5:27; Col 4:16; 1 Tim 4:13). The congregations likely included both slaves and slave owners. . . . Harry Gamble argues that in a time when the ability to read was rare, perhaps Paul's letter carrier would have been required to read the letter's content upon his arrival at the church, not knowing if there would have been a proficient reader present." Daniel S. Diffey, Brian A. Brandt, Justin McClendon, ed., *Journal of Biblical and Theological Studies*, Issue 3.2 (2018).

10. Barrs, *Through His Eyes*, 311–312.

11. ESV Study Bible Note on 1 Corinthians 14:34–35.

12. James, *Lost Women*, 210–211.

13. Barrs, *Through His Eyes*, 311.

14. Ben Witherington, *Women in the Earliest Churches* (Cambridge, UK: Cambridge University Press, 1988), 40.

Chapter 12: The Worth of Women in the Twenty-First Century

1. This is signaled even through the subtitle of the leading book on men's and women's roles: *Recovering Biblical Manhood and Womanhood: A Response to Evangelical Feminism.*

2. John Calvin and William Pringle, *Commentaries on the Epistles to Timothy, Titus, and Philemon* (Bellingham, WA: Logos Bible Software, 2010), 69, 70.

3. Martin Luther, *Luther's Works*, vol. 28: 1 Corinthians 7, 1 Corinthians 15, Lectures on 1 Timothy, ed. Jaroslav Jan Pelikan, Hilton C. Oswald, and Helmut T. Lehmann (St. Louis: Concordia, 1999), 278.

4. Eric Schumacher, "21 Places Women Emerge Front and Center in Scripture's Storyline," *TheGospelCoalition.org*, June 2, 2018, https://www.thegospelcoalition .org/article/21-places-women-emerge-front-and-center-in-scriptures-storyline/.

5. We also suspect that by saying that as we did, there are others we have disappointed. We know that there are astute and godly women and men who believe that ordination should not be limited to one gender, and we respect them, though we respectfully disagree.

6. For a helpful critique of this emphasis, see Michelle Lee-Barnwell, *Neither Complementarian nor Egalitarian* (Grand Rapids, MI: Baker Academic, 2016).

7. "In an attempt to make sure the command proper was never violated, the rabbis created secondary, rigid rules which, if followed, would theoretically prevent a person from ever violating the biblical command itself. This was known as 'putting a fence around the law.' Such nonbiblical rules (e.g., the sabbath day's journey) are prescribed exhaustively in the Talmud, but this burdensome 'tradition' is contrary to the spirit of biblical law (Matt 15:3; 23:4)." https://www.bible studytools.com/dictionaries/bakers-evangelical-dictionary/law.html.

8. Egalitarianism is a belief system that holds to (1) ontological equality of both sexes, i.e., males and females being created in the image of God and (2) there are no economic or role differences between the sexes. In other words, males and females are equally created in the image of God, equally redeemed by Christ, equally gifted by God, and in the home and the church leadership and submission is mutual, so that believing women may function as leaders in the home or pastors in the church.

9. "Just 48 percent of unchurched Millennial women self-identify as Christian. The number of women who identify as atheist or agnostic has risen from 8 percent in 2000 to 15 percent today. Among Millennial women, that number is even higher; more than a quarter now identify as atheists (26%), up from 18% in 2005." *Barna Trends 2017: What's New and What's Next at the Intersection of Faith and Culture* (Grand Rapids, MI: Baker, 2016), 153.

10. Jerram Barrs as quoted in Elyse Fitzpatrick, *Good News for Weary Women: Escaping the Bondage of To-Do Lists, Steps, and Bad Advice* (Carol Stream, IL: Tyndale, 2014), 10.

11. Complementarianism is a belief system that holds to (1) ontological equality of both sexes, i.e., males and females being created in the image of God, and (2) economic or role differences between the sexes. We would call ourselves soft complementarians. In other words, we do believe in equality by creation and creational role distinctions, but find troublesome some of what others have extrapolated these similarities and differences to mean.

12. ESV Study Bible note on Galatians 3:26.

13. ESV Study Bible note on Galatians 3:26.

14. Jared von Kamp, personal correspondence.

15. See "Perpetua: High Society Believer," *ChristianityToday.com*, https://www.christianitytoday.com/history/people/martyrs/perpetua.html.

16. Laura Polk, "20 Christian Women Who Shaped History," *Crosswalk.com*, n.d., https://www.crosswalk.com/slideshows/20-christian-women-who-shaped-history.html.

17. Chelsey Gordon is a pastor's wife, mother, biblical counselor, and assistant to Chris Moles.

18. Rev. Chris Moles (MABC) is a certified biblical counselor (ACBC and IABC) and a certified group facilitator in domestic violence intervention and prevention. He is the author of *The Heart of Domestic Abuse: Gospel Solutions for Men Who Use Violence and Control in the Home* as well as the founder of PeaceWorks. PeaceWorks is a domestic violence prevention and intervention ministry that provides a variety of resources to churches and families including Men of Peace coaching for abusive men and PeaceWorks University, a membership website that exists to train and support people in a variety of ministry contexts to address domestic violence with the gospel of peace. Find out more about PeaceWorks at ChrisMoles.org or at FaceBook.com/RevChrisMoles.

19. Dorothy L. Sayers, *Are Women Human? Penetrating, Sensible, and Witty Essays on the Role of Women in Society* (Grand Rapids, MI: Eerdmans, 2005), 12.

20. Jerram Barrs, *Through His Eyes: God's Perspective on Women in the Bible* (Wheaton, IL: Crossway, 2009), 316.

21. *Barna Trends 2017*, 153.

22. Alyssa Leader, @alittleleader, July 5, 2019, Twitter.com, https://twitter.com/alittleleader/status/1147191691675414528.

23. Carolyn Custis James, *Lost Women of the Bible* (Grand Rapids, MI: Zondervan, 2005), 207.

Conclusion: A Call to Hope-Driven, Courageous, Compassionate Conviction

1. As quoted by Herman Selderhuis in "Luther at the Diet of Worms," *Crossway*, April 18, 2018, https://www.crossway.org/articles/luther-at-the-diet-of-worms/, retrieved February 9, 2019.

2. "Rachael Denhollander: The Voice That Began End of Nassar," *The Detroit News*, January 24, 2018, https://www.detroitnews.com/story/news/local

/michigan/2018/01/24/nassar-denhollander/109787862/, retrieved February 16, 2019.

3. "Read Rachael Denhollander's Full Victim Impact Statement about Larry Nassar," *CNN*, CNN.com, January 30, 2018, https://www.cnn.com/2018/01/24 /us/rachael-denhollander-full-statement/index.html, retrieved February 16, 2019.

4. Morgan Lee, "My Larry Nassar Testimony Went Viral. But There's More to the Gospel Than Forgiveness," *Christianity Today*, January 31, 2018, https:// www.christianitytoday.com/ct/2018/january-web-only/rachael-denhollander -larry-nassar-forgiveness-gospel.html, retrieved February 16, 2019.

5. Fortunately, the pastors of her former church did issue an apology—"Our Pastors' Statement to the Washington Post: We Were Rachael's Church," Immanuel Baptist Church, May 31, 2018, https://immanuelky.org/articles/we-were -rachaels-church/, retrieved February 16, 2019.

6. Robert Downen, Lise Olsen, and John Tedesco, "Abuse of Faith," *Houston Chronicle*, February 10. 2019, https://www.houstonchronicle.com/news/investi gations/article/Southern-Baptist-sexual-abuse-spreads-as-leaders-13588038.php. Retrieved February 16, 2019.

7. For Eric's personal response to this situation, see Appendix 5, "An Open Letter to Rachael Denhollander."

8. We take this phrase from C.S. Lewis's Memorial Lecture at King's College, University of London, in 1944. It is available online at https://www.lewissociet y.org/innerring/. It is a helpful meditation on the futility of pursuing entrance into the "in-crowd."

9. "Law," *Baker's Evangelical Dictionary of Biblical Theology*, ed. Walter A. Elwell (Grand Rapids, MI: Baker, 1996), https://www.biblestudytools.com/dictio naries/bakers-evangelical-dictionary/law.html, retrieved February 9, 2019.

10. The prefix "paedo" (from the Greek for "child") denotes a variety of Christian traditions that baptize the infant children of believers. The prefix "credo" (from the Latin for "I believe") denotes a variety of Christian traditions that reserve baptism for those who personally confess their faith.

11. J.R.R. Tolkien, *The Lord of the Rings* (New York: Houghton Mifflin Harcourt, 2004), 951.

Appendix 2: What Women Wish Their Pastors Knew

1. If you're going to say something like that, be sure to say that sexual abuse will be dealt with as the crime that it is and that women need not fear the men in leadership protecting other men while abandoning them to face being sinned against alone.

2. That means that if you have 200 people in your church at least 40 of them have experienced sexual trauma, including rape (see Boz Tchividjian, "How Safe Is Your Church?" video, GRACE [Godly Response to Abuse in the Christian Environment], https://www.netgrace.org/). That number is very low, especially because only 16 percent of sexual crimes are reported to police.

Appendix 5: An Open Letter to Rachael Denhollander on #SBCtoo

1. Originally published February 15, 2019, at https://www.emschumacher.com /an-open-letter-to-rachael-denhollander-on-sbctoo/.

2. Robert Downen, Lise Olsen, and John Tedesco, "Abuse of Faith," *Houston Chronicle*, February 10, 2019, https://www.houstonchronicle.com/news/investi gations/article/Southern-Baptist-sexual-abuse-spreads-as-leaders-13588038.php, retrieved February 16, 2019.

3. Rachael Denhollander, @R_Denhollander, Twitter.com, https://twitter.com /R_Denhollander/status/1095133698868035584, retrieved February 16, 2019.

4. "Rachael Denhollander," Wikipedia, https://en.wikipedia.org/wiki/Rachael _Denhollander, retrieved February 16, 2019.

5. "Read Rachael Denhollander's full victim impact statement about Larry Nassar," *CNN*, CNN.com, January 30, 2018, https://www.cnn.com/2018/01/24 /us/rachael-denhollander-full-statement/index.html, retrieved February 16, 2019.

6. Morgan Lee, "My Larry Nassar Testimony Went Viral. But There's More to the Gospel Than Forgiveness," *Christianity Today*, January 31, 2018, https:// www.christianitytoday.com/ct/2018/january-web-only/rachael-denhollander-lar ry-nassar-forgiveness-gospel.html, retrieved February 16, 2019.

7. "Our Pastors' Statement to the Washington Post: We Were Rachael's Church," Immanuel Baptist Church, May 31, 2018, https://immanuelky.org/arti cles/we-were-rachaels-church/, retrieved February 16, 2019.

8. Rachael Denhollander, "Public Response to Sovereign Grace Churches," *Facebook.com*, February 5, 2018, https://www.facebook.com/notes/rachael -denhollander/public-response-to-sovereign-grace-churches/1694664773947169, retrieved February 16, 2019.

9. Rachael Denhollander, "Update on Sovereign Grace Churches," *Facebook. com*, February 13, 2019, https://www.facebook.com/OfficialDenhollander/posts /2201216753291966, retrieved February 16, 2019.

10. Robert Downen, "Leading Southern Baptist apologizes for supporting leader, church at center of sex abuse scandal," *Houston Chronicle*, February 14, 2019, https://www.houstonchronicle.com/houston/article/Leading-Southern -Baptist-apologizes-for-13618120.php, retrieved February 16, 2019.

11. R. Albert Mohler Jr., "Statement from R. Albert Mohler Jr. on Sovereign Grace Churches," *Southern News*, The Southern Baptist Theological Seminary, February 15, 2019, http://news.sbts.edu/2019/02/15/statement-r-albert-mohler-jr -sovereign-grace-churches/, retrieved February 16, 2019.

Epilogue: "Worthy—A Song of Praise"

1. © 2019, Hymnicity. Used by permission. All rights reserved.

Elyse Fitzpatrick is a wife, mother, and grandmother and lives in San Diego, California. She earned a BTh from Berean Bible College, an MA in Biblical Counseling from Trinity Theological Seminary, and a Certificate in Biblical Counseling from Christian Counseling & Education Foundation (San Diego). She is the author of two dozen books and speaks extensively on the intersection of the gospel of grace and the Christian life.

Eric Schumacher is a husband, father, author, songwriter, and pastor. He lives with his wife, Jenny, and their five children in his home state of Iowa, where he pastors a church and hunts pheasants. He earned a BA in General Communications from the University of Northern Iowa and an MDiv. in Biblical and Theological Studies from The Southern Baptist Theological Seminary. He has written songs for corporate worship for more than twenty years. Eric would love to connect with you at emschumacher.com and on social media (@emschumacher).

More from Elyse Fitzpatrick

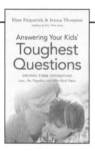